Competitive Strategies
for the Protection
of Intellectual Property

Competitive Strategies

for the Protection

of Intellectual

Property

EDITED BY OWEN LIPPERT

The Fraser Institute

Vancouver   British Columbia   Canada

1999

Canadian Cataloguing in Publication Data

Main entry under title:
Competitive Strategies for the Protection of Intellectual Property

   Includes bibliographical references.
   ISBN 0-88975-200-1

   1. Intellectual property (International law).   2. Intellectual property--Economic aspects.   I. Lippert, Owen.   II. Fraser Institute (Vancouver, B.C.)

K1401.C663 1999   341.7'58   C99-911278-3

Contents

Acknowledgments

Special thanks should be given to Ms. Lorena Baran of The Fraser Institute for her help in organizing the conferences. Thank you as well to the staffs of the Instituto Libertad y Desarollo and the Fundacion Republica.

About the Authors

CARSTEN FINK is an Economist in the Development Research Group of the World Bank. He holds a Bachelor Degree in economics from the University of Heidelberg, Germany, and a Master of Science degree in economics from the University of Oregon, United States. He is also a Ph.D. candidate in economics at the University of Heidelberg. Previously, Mr Fink held positions at the World Bank in the Telecommunications and Informatics Division and has been a consultant for TechNet, a World Bank program on Science and Technology for Development. Mr Fink's research interests include international trade policy (especially intellectual property rights protection and trade in services), international finance, transnational corporations, and the telecommunciations and informatics industries. He has published many papers on the economic implications of protecting intellectual property rights as well as on the institutional aspects of intellectual property rights reforms in developing countries.

OWEN LIPPERT is the Director, Law and Markets Project, The Fraser Institute. Mr Lippert is based in Ottawa, Ontario, Canada. He earned a B.A. from Carleton College, Northfield, Minnesota and an M.A. and a Ph.D. in European History at the University of Notre Dame. The author has held advisory positions to the Premier of British Columbia, the Attorney General of Canada, and the Minister of Science.

WILLIAM MCARTHUR CD, SSM, B.Sc., M.D., D.P.H., is Senior Fellow in Health Policy at The Fraser Institute, Vancouver, British Columbia, Canada. Dr. McArthur served in the Royal Canadian Air Force for 24 years. He was a fighter pilot, a medical researcher, and a policy writer who specialized in the areas of health, transport, and aviation safety. He is widely known for his work in aircraft accident investigation, and was the founding President of the International Society of Air Safety Investigators. He was the first Chief Coroner for the Province of British Columbia and was responsible for the organization of the coroner's service in the province. In 1982, he returned to medical practice and specialized in palliative care, a practice that he maintains to this day. He joined the Fraser Institute in 1995 and has developed a particular interest in the fields of pharmacoeconomics and intellectual property rights.

SYLVIA OSTRY is Distinguished Research Fellow, Centre for International Studies, University of Toronto. She has a Ph.D. in economics from McGill University and Cambridge. After teaching and research at a number of Canadian universities and at the University of Oxford's Institute of Statistics, she joined the Federal Government in 1964. Among the posts she held were Chief Statistician, Deputy Minister of Consumer and Corporate Affairs, Chairman of the Economic Council of Canada, Deputy Minister of International Trade, Ambassador for Multilateral Trade Negotiations, and the Prime Minister's Personal Representative for the Economic Summit. From 1979 to 1983, Mrs Ostry was Head of the Economics and Statistics Department of the OECD in Paris. In 1989, she was Volvo Distinguished Visiting Fellow, Council on Foreign Relations, New York. From 1990 to 1997, she was Chairman, Centre for International Studies, University of Toronto. She has published widely in her field, received 18 honorary degrees from universities in Canada and abroad, and holds positions on several Canadian and international boards. Mrs. Ostry is a member of the Group of Thirty, Washington, and a founding member of the Pacific Council on International Policy.

WALTER PARK is Associate Professor of Economics at the American University. Professor Park's general field of research is economic growth, with a particular focus on international patenting and research and development, and his publications centre around developing measures of patent rights among countries and examining how patent protection affects innovation, technology diffusion, and productivity growth among countries. He has also published articles quantifying the extent to which research and development generate "international knowledge spillovers." Professor Park obtained a B.A. from the University of Toronto, an M.Phil. from the University of Oxford, and a Ph.D. from Yale University and he has been a visiting scholar at the Institute of Industrial Relations at the University of California, Berkeley. He has also conducted research projects for the Organisation for Economic Cooperation and Development (OECD), the World Intellectual Property Office (WIPO), the World Bank, the United States Department of Energy, and the American Intellectual Property Law Association (AIPLA).

MICHAEL P. RYAN, Ph.D., teaches international business and government at the Georgetown University School of Business, where he specializes in the international political economy of intellectual property and trade policy with emphasis upon international and national institutions. His books include *Knowledge Diplomacy: Global Competition and the Politics of Intellectual Property* (Brookings Institution Press, 1998) and *Playing by the Rules: American Trade Power and Diplomacy in the Pacific*

(Georgetown University Press, 1995). Professor Ryan directs the Study on Innovation, Expression, and Development. At the invitation of the United States State Department, the United States Patent Office, and the World Intellectual Property Organization, he is a frequent speaker to government and business audiences in developing countries regarding intellectual property policy and development.

ROBERT M. SHERWOOD, an author and consultant, has devoted 20 years to researching the role of intellectual property in developing countries. He is also advancing research on the relation between the performance of judicial systems and economic development. Building upon experience as an international corporate lawyer, he conducted in-country diagnoses of intellectual-property systems throughout Latin America for the Inter-American Development Bank.

Supported by a private group of American companies, Mr Sherwood has visited Brazil for four separate weeks each year since 1986 to investigate in depth the influence of intellectual property on a broad range of activities there, writing extensively and conferring with government officials and business leaders to present his findings. His first book, *Intellectual Property and Economic Development* (Boulder, CO: Westview), is drawn largely from this experience and comparable experience in Mexico.

Mr Sherwood's commissioned writings include co-authorship with Carlos Primo Braga, a World Bank economist, of a road map for negotiating intellectual property arrangements in the Western Hemisphere. He assessed the implications of the TRIPS Agreement for developing countries for the World Intellectual Property Organization, and wrote an assessment of the Free Trade Agreement (FTA) for The Fraser Institute (Vancouver, Canada). Many of his writings can be found at www.kreative.net/ipbenefits. He is a graduate of Harvard College, Columbia University, and Harvard Law School.

JAYASHREE WATAL is a former director in the Trade Policy Division of the Ministry of Commerce, Government of India. She represented India in the TRIPS negotiations from 1989 to 1991, during which period she dealt with the subject of industrial property in the Ministry of Industry. Ms Watal has published papers on policy options open to developing countries on TRIPS and the impact of product patents on the Indian pharmaceutical sector. She has been a consultant to UNCTAD and the World Bank and is presently a visiting scholar at the Institute for International Economics and at George Washington University Law School in Washington, DC. She is completing a book on IPRs in the WTO, *Intellectual Property Rights in the World Trade Organization: The Way Forward for Developing Countries*, to be published in 2000.

Competitive Strategies for the Protection of Intellectual Property

Introduction

OWEN LIPPERT

In the Middle Ages up to 90 percent of the wealth of Europe came from the owning of land. As a result, the law of the times developed elaborate definitions of and protections for property rights in land. Today, we live in an economy deriving ever more of its income from technological advances based on research and human ingenuity. Modern capitalism's increasing dependence on intellectual property has allowed for *qualitatively* higher levels of efficiency, productivity, and quality of life. Accordingly, the Intellectual Property Rights (IPRs) embedded in patents, trademarks, and copyrights have received increasing attention. The rise of global trade has further broadened the discussion of IPRs from a largely domestic to an international stage.

This century's critical milestone in the improvement and globalization of IPRs came with the conclusion in 1994 of an international treaty on IPRs called TRIPS (Trade Related Aspects of Intellectual Property Rights) as part of the Uruguay Round of trade talks that upgraded the General Agreement on Trade and Tariffs (GATT). The TRIPS signatories acknowledged that a higher standard of international protection for IPRs was not just possible but desirable. While the developed nations had to implement TRIPS immediately, most of the developing nations were given a deadline of January 1, 2000. Canada, the United States, and Mexico committed themselves to even more rigorous standards of protection and enforcement in the 1993 North American Free Trade Agreement (NAFTA).

The passage of TRIPS sparked a vigorous debate on a number of critical questions.

(1) What are the economic, social, and health-care benefits to developing countries of higher levels of protection for IPRs?

(2) How should they re-fashion their domestic patent and trademark legislation to abide not just by the letter but also by the spirit of TRIPS?

(3) How will IPRs continue to evolve in new trade talks such as the proposed hemispheric agreement, the Free Trade Area of the Americas (FTAA) and the "millennium round" of global talks kicked off in Seattle in November 1999?

The Fraser Institute's Law and Markets Project, seeking to further discussion of possible answers to these questions, invited leading scholars in the field to participate in two back-to-back conferences. The first was held in Santiago, Chile on April 19, 1999, co-hosted with the Instituto Libertad y Desarollo. The second was conducted in Buenos Aires, Argentina on April 22, 1999, co-hosted with the Fundacion Republica. This book contains the papers delivered at both conferences.

Professor Michael P. Ryan, Georgetown University, put the TRIPS agreement and current issues surrounding IPRs in the context of the tremendous changes wrought by the development of a knowledge-based economy. Reflecting not only a strong understanding of economic theory but also the historical development of modern capitalism, his work challenges the notion that IPRs are not somehow central to economic growth and technological sophistication.

Professor Walter Park, American University, takes up the questions posed by Professor Ryan and provides empirical evidence of the correlation between patent protection and the diffusion of technology and productivity growth. Using his unique index of international patent rights, he presents a strong econometric case for the interrelatedness of IPRs with economic growth.

Robert M. Sherwood, trade consultant and author based in Washington, DC, examines more closely the connection between strong protection of IPRs and economic growth. He outlines what we know, and do not know, about how they interact. Of considerable interest to developing countries is the theory that he sketches out showing how different levels of protection for IPRs induces varying kinds of new investment.

Dr. William McArthur, Fellow in Health Care Policy with the Fraser Institute, examines the economic impact of incomplete protection of IPRs in the pharmaceutical industry. He outlines the various means through which IPRs are weakened for research-based pharmaceutical drugs and shows some of the losses in investment and income. As well, he shows some of the empirical evidence as to the impact on health outcomes.

Progressing forward from analysis to prescription, Jayashree Watal, a civil servant and scholar who served on India's TRIPS negotiating team, provides a useful and detailed examination of how developing countries may implement TRIPS while remaining sensitive to local conditions. Though Ms. Watal's advice might seem outdated as the deadline of January 1, 2000 is nearly upon us, many developing countries, including Chile and Argentina, have yet to make the necessary legislative changes.

Owen Lippert, Director of the Law and Markets Project with the Fraser Institute, argues that as countries implement their TRIPS obligations, they should actually move beyond that level of protection to the higher one provided in NAFTA. He asserts that the FTAA provides the best vehicle for this upgrade. He would like to see the FTAA intellectual-property section as the basis for discussions in the new round of WTO talks.

Dr. Carsten Fink, trade specialist with the World Bank, gives a fascinating look at one of the most complicated hurdles in achieving an international standard of protection—the exhaustion of IPRs and parallel imports. He discusses the causes and policy implications for trade in goods for which, for instance, patent protection has expired in one country but not another.

Finally, Dr. Sylvia Ostry, University of Toronto, brings her wealth of professional experience and academic research in setting the stage for the new round of intellectual property discussions likely to emerge in the "millennium round" of trade talks launched at the Seattle Ministerial Summit on November 30, 1999. She highlights the upcoming challenges to the "deep integration" of trading economies implicit in a global standard of intellectual property protection.

I hope you, the reader, will find these contributions as useful as did the participants from the private sector and government in Santiago and Buenos Aires.

Markets, Institutions, Intellectual Property Rights, and Development in a Knowledge-Based World Economy

MICHAEL P. RYAN

The phrase "intellectual property" apparently entered our lexicon in the 1950s, but many policy-makers, business people, and citizens are only in recent years learning about the policy institutions and market economics of intellectual property. The institutions of patent, trade secret, and copyright (as well as trademark) have been established by governments for some 500 years as special market interventions to encourage technological innovation and informational and cultural expression for the purpose of spurring activity that markets, left to themselves, tend to under-produce. Intellectual property institutions have been important sources of economic growth and cultural vitality whether the world economy has been based upon the hand-work of craft or upon the machine-work of manufacture. Now that the world economy is based upon the knowledge-work that informs craft, manufacture, and service, the policies of intellectual property are all the more central to economic policy regarding technological innovation, economic growth, and cultural vitality. A knowledge-based world economy

---

Notes will be found on page 36.

depends upon the incentives provided by effective enforcement of intellectual property rights: copyright protection encourages producers of films, music, books, information databases, and computer software to risk expensive creation because they can expect that, though failure in the marketplace is common, success will not be misappropriated through piracy. Patent protection encourages producers of pharmaceuticals, fine chemicals, and the products of information technology to invest in technological innovation because they will be offered a limited period of market exclusivity as reward for their risk-taking. For these reasons, intellectual property has risen near the top of policy agendas around the world in recent years.

Policy-makers in developing countries will, over the coming few years, implement the Agreement on Trade-Related Aspects of Intellectual Property Rights, the "TRIPS Agreement," thereby providing in law, if not in fact, protection for intellectual property rights akin to that established in North America, Europe, and Japan as they were themselves developing into industrialized countries. Policy-makers, business people, and citizens in developing countries agree that the TRIPS Agreement is a condition of World Trade Organization membership but are not certain that enforcing these standards of intellectual property protection will further the cause of their economic, political, and cultural development. Observers frequently lament: "We don't know whether the enactment and enforcement of world-standard intellectual property policies will promote development in poor countries." Perhaps we do not know, for life must be lived forward, but much evidence from experience and scholarship exists to inform policy-makers regarding the complementary roles of markets and institutions and of the special role of the intellectual property institutions in the promotion of economic growth.

Even in our age of the Internet, knowledge is not "out there" someplace. Knowledge is embedded in institutions: know-how institutions are conventionally and rightly thought to be universities, but know-how institutions also are business enterprises. Business enterprises are deeply imbued with knowledge, which possess the organizational capabilities to turn information and know-how into commercially viable products and services. Multinational business enterprises dominate innovation and technology stock in the world economy and, thus, technological innovation and adaptation depend upon cooperation with these enterprises. Business enterprises in developing countries accumulate know-how and build their own organizational capabilities through business strategies that combine cooperation with competition with multinational firms.

This paper reviews scholarship from economics, political science, history, business management, and law for the purpose of summarizing and synthesizing the current state of knowledge regarding intellectual property rights and development. The review proceeds by first examining the relationships among markets, institutions, and economic growth. The special role of the patent institution is studied in relation to technological innovation. The role of the copyright institution is studied in relation to informational and cultural expression. The contemporary international law and organization of intellectual property is discussed. The political economy of development is explained with emphasis upon the shift in economic development strategy that has been simultaneous with, though not caused by, the multilateral TRIPS negotiations. Research regarding intellectual property rights and the global diffusion of knowledge is reviewed. Finally, political, governmental, and judicial institutionalization is examined for its relationship not only with intellectual property rights but also for its general relationship with development.

Markets, institutions, and economic growth

Technological innovations drive long-run economic growth (Grossman and Helpman 1991). It takes new ideas, methods, and inventions to increase productivity, improve industrial processes, and introduce better products in the marketplace. However, "innovation" is only occasionally radical: most innovation is incremental and most research and development aims, most of the time, to achieve nothing more than "innovation through adaptation" (Evenson 1984). Whether incremental or radical, innovative ideas, methods, and products depend upon knowledge and human capital, upon information-rich workers with know-how and learning capacity (Rosenberg, Landau, and Mowery 1992). Innovation depends upon the capacity for the expression of information and, in this way, technologists, software writers, and database compilers are linked in important ways.

Institutions—social organizations and norms, governments and laws—are crucial in making markets function well or poorly (North 1990; Eggertsson 1990). To function properly, markets demand credible, enforceable commitments and, though game theory shows that cooperation can emerge through iterated interaction (Axelrod 1984), property rights and the contract have been institutional constructions to reduce the transaction costs of commercial activity (North 1990). The institutions of government and law influence patterns of scientific advance and technological innovation patterns across history (Cardwell 1995; Huff 1993). When effective, they establish (1) growing demand markets, (2) vigorous producer competition, and (3) risk-taking capital—necessary market conditions for innovation (Rosenberg, Landau, and Mowery 1992; Mowery and Rosenberg 1989). Innovative, globally competitive industry sectors tend to cluster in certain countries and not in others because of characteristics of markets and institutions (Porter 1990) and thus it appears that technological innovation depends upon characteristics of a country's mix of markets and of institutions.

Growing demand in the United States provided incentive to the rising industrialists whose manufacturing management innovations (Chandler 1977) drove economic growth for nearly a century after the end of the Civil War (Nelson 1990). When nineteenth-century Belgian iron producers realized their market was too small for scale economies, their government sought a customs union with France, which was re-buffed. As a result, Belgium instead forged a 50 percent tariff-cut agreement with the German government (Landes 1969: 155). Twentieth century manufacturers such as August Thyssen in Germany and Kiichiro Toyoda in Japan aggressively marketed their products to foreign customers in order to increase sales, profits, and scale economies (McCraw 1997). But, is it "demand-pull" or "discovery-push"? It took both in the chemical industry: discovery in anticipation of demand; actual demand pulled mightily, generating rapid incremental innovation (Walsh 1984).

Does more competition lead to more innovation? Does a monopolist innovate as much as an oligopolist? Can there ever be too much competition? The answers, are (1) yes, to a point; (2) no; (3) yes, but it will not last long. Research regarding product innovation in specific industry sectors shows that market structure greatly influences innovative patterns. While monopolists and hegemonic firms tend not be great innovators, they do tend to respond aggressively when challenged by a competitor and decisively bring to bear all their organizational capabilities to maintain their dominance. For example, after achieving market dominance in razor blades and photographic supplies respectively, neither Gillette nor Kodak introduced innovative products but both leveraged market power furiously to win back the marketplace (Scherer 1992: 48). Oligopoly markets tend to be viciously competitive and can be aggressively innovative, though capabilities beyond innovative capacity tend to determine winners and losers. In colour televisions and videocassette recorders, the American innovators (RCA in TVs and Ampex in VCRs) were unable to match the consumer marketing skills and the manufacturing process innovations deployed by Japanese competitors Matsushita and Sony and exited the market (Scherer 1992: 56). A market structure with lots of young, small firms tends to foment lots of innovative ideas. Yet, capital shortages, production inadequacies, and marketing deficiencies pose challenges that small, inexperienced firms often cannot meet and so they have trouble getting products to market. For example, some 50 American semiconductor producers lost out to deeper-pocketed Japanese integrated electronics manufacturers in the 1980s (Methe 1991).

Financial capital fuels firm innovativeness (Boskin and Lau 1992). The lower cost of capital in Japan and Germany relative to the cost to their competitors, for example, contributed in the 1970s and 1980s to Japanese competitiveness (Bernheim and Shoven 1992; Calder 1993) and to German adaptive capacity (Zysman 1983) in manufacturing but capital market-corporate governance structures produce weaknesses as well as strengths as measured by firm performance (Fukao 1995). Corporatist capital market-corporate governance structures in countries such as Japan and Germany, including oligopolistic competition patterns in many industries including banking, equity-based capitalization that reinforces bank power, networks of firms with interlocking equity and managerial control, and bank-business-ministry-parliament cooperation, discouraged investment into risky information technology and biotechnology by constricting the fuel line (Feigenbaum 1995; Jasonoff 1985) while risk-taking venture markets produced booming new industries despite the busts in the United States (Beltz 1994).

Human capital and mobile labour markets have long been understood to be critical factors in innovation and economic growth. Nevertheless, it is the institutional organization of human capital that turns innovative potential into actuality. Science and technology are valued more by some religions, philosophies, and ideologies than by others and it is the social organization of these ideas that pass on to successive generations the commitment to the values of autonomy, diversity, and experiment characteristic of innovative societies (Skolnikoff 1993). Science progresses or retards depending upon social institutions: teaching and research organizations, publication outlets, societal value of scientists (Huff 1993). A world scientific centre from the eighth to the fourteenth centuries, the Arabic Middle East declined scientifically because education was loosely organized, professional networks of philosopher-scientists were discouraged by Koranic law, and Islamic thought valued interpretation of dogma over human reason and the questioning of authority. "The problem was not internal and scientific, but sociological and cultural. It hinged on the problem of institution-building" (Huff 1993: 212). A global technological leader before the advent of the Ming Dynasty in the fourteenth century, China declined technologically because education was organized for the examination system, organizational structures were strictly hierarchical, and Confucian thought valued social harmony over deliberative debate (Baum 1982).[1]

By contrast, science advanced in Europe because of the establishment of universities, the group and individual autonomy conferred by rivalry between Church and State, and the re-emphasized Aristotelian value placed upon observation and experiment. Science and technology grew together in Western Europe and North America, the product of markets, culture, and political and legal institutions (Cardwell 1995). The German chemical industry eclipsed that of the French in the nineteenth century due, in part, to research in German universities; the American chemical makers matched the German companies in the twentieth century with the intellectual contribution of the establishment of chemical engineering departments at MIT and the universities of Pennsylvania and Michigan (Landau and Rosenberg 1992).

A major study by the National Science Foundation (National Science Board 1996) recently provided considerable empirical data to support the claim that American technological advance in the 1980s and 1990s, which led to renewed productivity growth in the United States while productivity continued to languish in Japan and western Europe (Eaton and Kortum 1997), has been in part the result of its high-quality, broad-based, large higher-education system. American colleges and universities are know-how institutions that contribute skilled, knowledge-rich workers as well as scientific and technological knowledge to business enterprises.

Business enterprises are themselves know-how institutions but they are much more than depositories of discrete facts. Business enterprises are deeply imbued with knowledge, possessing the organizational capabilities to turn information and know-how into commercially viable products and services. Indeed, business enterprises exist because they organize knowledge better than do markets (Kogut and Zander 1992). Measured by technological indicators such as expenditures on research and development and patents, multinational business enterprises dominate innovation and own much of the world stock of technology (Patel and Pavitt 1991). The collective knowledge, know-how, and learning maintained by the enterprise, its so-called "core competency," is difficult for a competing enterprise to replicate (Prahalad and Hamel 1990), yet discrete information and know-how may be of great competitive value and must be protected through intellectual property management in order to preserve the enterprise's competitive advantage in the marketplace.

Know-how and learning capabilities tend to become institutionalized as sector-specific knowledge, organizing principles, and governance structures, and these patterns of sectoral competitiveness tend to establish their own path-dependent trajectories (Kitschelt 1991; Piore and Sable 1989). Technological innovation tends to be patterned along natural trajectories (Nelson and Winter 1982) because technological paradigms prescribe directions for further R&D and incremental innovation, excluding other possible paths (Dosi 1982). Within these trajectories or path dependencies, technological innovations tend to fall into regular life cycles in which radical innovation disrupts and destroys markets until dominant designs and standards emerge so that innovation is again regular and incremental and market structure has evolved from highly competitive to oligopolistic or even monopolistic (Abernathy and Utterback 1978; Abernathy and Clark 1985; Utterback and Suarez 1993).

Technological innovations in transportation and communication in the late nineteenth century revolutionized the management and organization of business activity in the twentieth century.

> Modern mass production and mass distribution depend on the speed, volume, and regularity in the movement of goods and messages made possible by the coming of the railroad, telegraph, and steamship ... As the basic infrastructure came into being between the 1850s and 1880s, modern methods of mass production and distribution and the modern business enterprises that managed them made their appearance ... The modern industrial enterprise—the archetype of today's giant corporation—resulted from the integration of the processes of mass production with those of mass distribution within a single business firm. (Chandler 1977: 207, 285)

Transportation and communication technologies established new possibilities for production and distribution and business enterprises evolved to turn possibilities into market and institution realities, making a manufacturing-based, industrial, world economy in the process.

Late in the twentieth century, new technological innovations are changing the management and organization of business activity yet again. In little more than a generation, information technology has been revolutionized by the microchip (Malone 1995) and digital compression (Negroponte, 1995). The former put extraordinary information processing and storage capacity into offices and homes during the period from 1975 to 1995; the latter took incompatible means of computation and communication—telephony, broadcast television, cable, wireless—and made them speak the same digital language, unfolding a network era from 1995 (Bradley, Hausman, and Nolan 1993). Interactive communication now includes audio, video, and data, and the data may be described as "intelligent communication" because software computing affords speedy manipulation, processing, and analysis before transmittal. In the workplace, these revolutions are erasing whole job classifications while demanding new knowledge-workers and offering the means for Total Quality Management and other self-regulating, de-centralizing organizational reforms (Grochow 1997; Leebaert 1995). In the marketplace, these revolutions are providing new opportunities for electronic commerce and digital distribution of information-based goods and services (Leebaert 1998).

In the world economy, the structure of world production is changing: in 1980, the year after the conclusion of the GATT Tokyo Round, manufacturing represented 23 percent of world production, while services had expanded to 53 percent. By the end of the GATT Uruguay Round in 1994, manufacturing represented 21 percent of world production and services expanded still more to 63 percent (World Bank 1997: 237). Knowledge and intellectual property-intensive products and services increasingly dominate the world economy.

Sector-specific research indicates that high-innovation knowledge-oriented industries tend to cluster in certain geographic spaces (Almeida and Kogut 1996)—the "Silicon Valley" phenomenon. Small, highly innovative firms especially benefit from the local knowledge networks that characterize knowledge-intensive districts (Almeida and Kogut 1997). Foreign multinational firms deliberately seek American "knowledge-intensive districts" as the geographic spaces within which to carry out their direct investment and joint venture strategies (Almeida 1996). Thus, through recruitment of labour and cooperative research, business enterprises and universities compose institutionalized networks of knowledge.

In short, market-shaping government policies regarding demand, competition, and capital spurred industrial innovation and growth in twentieth century Germany (Katzenstein 1989), the United States (Sklar 1988), and Japan (Johnson 1982; Okimoto 1989): modern capitalism evolved the product of corporate organization and government institution (McCraw 1997).

Technological innovation and the patent institution

A patent system provides incentives to innovate inventions and new processes under circumstances when the costs of developing new product and processes are high while the costs of product imitation (or outright theft) are low, a circumstance that economists call the "appropriability problem" (Dam 1994; Kitch 1977; Meinhardt 1946). Invention is expensive and costs must be recouped to provide incentives for the investment. If others can appropriate the innovation, calling it their own without having made the investment of time, energy, and resources, then a potential innovator may determine that the regular incentives of market opportunity are insufficient to tolerate a free-riding competitor. Government intervenes by extending to the inventor rights of patent. Granted through process of investigation for novelty and utility by public administrators, with limitations of duration and of scope or breadth, governments with patent systems confer to inventors rights of exclusive appropriation of their innovation.

According to section 101 of the 1952 U.S. Patent Act, "whoever invents or discovers any new and useful process, machine, manufacture, or composition of matter, or any new and useful improvement thereof, may obtain a patent." In order to earn the patent, inventors must apply to the patent office, where an examiner will determine whether the invention meets the statutory demands of patent law as interpreted in the courts. To receive a patent the invention must be new and the American decision rests upon the test for novelty and nonobviousness. According to American law, "if the differences between the subject matter sought to be patented and the prior art are such that the subject matter as a whole would have been obvious at the time the invention was made to a person having ordinary skill in the art," then the invention is really not new after all and cannot receive a patent. The examiner searches the relevant prior art to determine what a "person having ordinary skill in the art" knows and then makes a decision regarding the claim. Decisions may be appealed when an applicant fails; competitors may challenge the validity of the patent in court if they think the patent was granted by the patent office in error.

The patent right conferred by the government is the granting of the exclusive right to make, manufacture, distribute, and license to distribute the invention. Nevertheless, the patent right is limited in duration to about 20 years in most legal jurisdictions and is further limited by definition of its scope or breadth. Scope involves the actual breadth of the claim of patent. "The scope of the claims of a patent determines the ability of competitors to produce substitutes without fear of infringement suits, and hence the real 'monopoly power' of the patent holder" (Merges and Nelson 1994: 1). With the policy goal of preventing patent systems from becoming anti-competitive and, hence, discouraging innovation rather than encouraging it, legislatures and courts have through the years attempted to balance the incentive of exclusivity against the incentive of competition when setting the proper scope, or breadth, of patent (Merges and Nelson 1990). Conflicts between competitors (so-called "interference suits") are common and are usually settled "out-of-court" by way of cross-license agreements that make collaborative partners out of them (Lerner 1995; Adelman and Baldia 1996).

Since a patent confers exclusive rights in the marketplace over a product or process, albeit with limitations of time and scope, patent law demands full, public disclosure of the know-how of the innovation when the patent is granted. Policy-makers establish that the inventor enters into a contract with the public such that the inventor receives limited exclusivity as a reward for skill and effort applied to innovate some new invention or process and, in return, the innovator teaches others "skilled in the art" how to do it by way of publication in the patent gazette of the patent claim. The stock of publicly available knowledge grows and thus diffusion of technology is institutionalized into the patent system for the encouragement of yet newer innovations (Ordover 1991).

Searches of current patents yield commercially valuable information regarding the state of technology in a given area, the level of R&D activity in a given area, the names of researchers working in a given field, and the technological competencies of, and R&D paths being taken by, competitors. Patent practitioners point out that most of the information disclosed in patent documents is not revealed anywhere else and, in frequent contrast to scientific and technical journal articles, the information in patent documents is commercially valuable. Competitors are encouraged to learn from the information provided in the patent and even to "design around" the patent if they can. The patent offices of the industrialized countries possess vast treasures of technology and much of what is contained is of real commercial value or the inventors would not have invested the time and attorney's fees in the application and maintenance of patent rights. Patent data provide some of the best evidence of innovative activity: large data-sets covering many decades are available for the industrialized countries and increasingly substantial data-sets are available in countries such as Korea, Brazil, and China. The data may be studied for geographic, country, industry-sector, and firm patterns. Citation patterns afford the tracing of innovation networks and these patterns can be related to variables such as R&D spending, science and technology education, and trade and foreign direct investment flows (Griliches 1990).

Information technology firms such as IBM, Canon, NEC, Motorola, and Fujitsu annually earn the world's biggest shares of patents but, according to research based upon patent renewal investments, the industries most vulnerable to the appropriability problem and most dependent on patent protection are pharmaceuticals and speciality chemicals (Pakes and Simpson 1989) and senior management surveys (Mansfield 1986). A drug maker or agricultural chemical company manufactures a chemical compound that can be duplicated with a modest knowledge of chemistry and manufacturing capability; an information technology maker manufactures a system-based product and the system imposes substantial barriers to entry and to piracy. Some policy makers and commentators who are critical of the policy utility of a patent system demonstrate no grasp of the industry sector-specific nature of the appropriability problem in the innovation process. Economic studies similarly rejecting the policy utility of patent systems have been conducted with research designs wholly ignorant of the industry sector-specific nature of the appropriability problem (Kondo 1995; Thurow 1997).

Policy-makers, commentators, and scholars also frequently misunderstand the nature of the market "exclusivity" provided by the patent system. Some economists argue—with models but without evidence of real technology competitions—that "patents reward the winner of a race when teams are engaged in parallel research" and that the patent "monopoly" renders fruitless the parallel research (Dasgupta 1988).[2] These viewpoints frequently demonstrate no understanding of the notion of patent scope and breadth or of interference-suit litigation and cross-licensing agreements in the real-world. Though apparently aware that patents granted in mechanical and information technology product areas rarely provide market-dominating exclusivity, many policy-makers commonly believe that patent exclusivity grants one or another pharmaceutical maker a monopoly within the marketplace of a particular therapeutic category.

The know-how contained in a patent becomes diffused by the publication of the patent claim but the new technologies protected under patent become diffused beyond their owners through licensing contracts. Licensing of technology has been increasing by about 10 percent per year in the United States and by about 18 percent per year internationally (Kotabe 1996: 73). Licenses typically are either vertical or horizontal with respect to the marketplace. An owner licenses vertically when it provides the patented know-how to firms that may then use and market the invention. Thus, vertical licensing generally intends to carry out a product-distribution strategy. An owner licenses horizontally when it provides the patented know-how to firms that will collaborate in the development of products. Thus, horizontal licensing generally intends to carry out a product-development strategy. Technology licensing, once thought by managers to be most fruitful during the mature technology phase of the product life-cycle as a way to free-up production capacity for new, higher value-added uses or as a mode of entry into foreign markets, is, in the present era of technology parity and hyper-competitive market conditions, considered and carried-out at all phases of the product life cycle. Extensive horizontal licensing has changed the world economy (Cowhey and Aronson 1993).

Inventors, nevertheless, need not disclose their know-how to the world through application and granting of patent for they may simply keep the know-how to themselves, protecting the information under the law of trade secrecy. The inventor who decides to protect an innovation through trade secrecy simply does not disclose the know-how associated with the invention and does so for the competitive advantages conferred by exclusivity, information opaqueness, and unlimited duration. The trade secret, which has been specified in the institutions of magic and shaman-priests in pre-literate societies (Suchman 1989), is intellectually rooted in notions of respect for individual liberty, confidentiality of relationships, common morality, and fair competition (Paine 1991). The law of trade secret involves more the notions of contract, trust, and equity than of property, for the relationships at issue are often between employer and employee or between firms, whether collaborators or competitors. Trade secrecy protection, however, confers few rights and offers weak protections since a competitor is only contravened from illicitly obtaining trade secrets. Furthermore, because of the essential nature of trade secret protection—nondisclosure of information—it is poorly suited for collaborative, sharing-through-negotiation licensing strategies, so licensing relationships typically are based upon patent ownership rights.

Informational and cultural expression and the copyright institution

Students of informational and cultural expression explain that the "appropriability problem" familiar to the patent institution is at work as well with the copyright institution (Johnson 1985; Landes and Posner 1989). Writing a book, composing a tune, producing a film, and compiling a database are expensive propositions, yet can be appropriated or pirated quite easily in many cases. Government, motivated by the goal of encouraging the free expression of ideas, provides a period of distribution exclusivity (often 75 to 100 years) to the copyright owner to encourage the effort. The copyright protects the *expression* of ideas but not the ideas themselves, thereby aiming to encourage creativity in arts and letters rather than the monopolization of ideas.

According to section 102 of the U.S. Copyright Act of 1976, expressions may be copyrighted when "original works of authorship fixed in any medium of tangible expression." Being "original" means that an expression product must pass the so-called "originality test" established by court decision: "All that is needed to satisfy both the Constitution and the statute is that the author contributed something more than 'merely trivial' variation, something recognizably his own'" (Joyce *et al.* 1994: 66). Originality, elaborated the court, "means little more than a prohibition of actual copying." The copyright originality test demands a considerably lower standard than the "novelty/nonobviousness tests" of patent law and this is for the reason that mere ways of expression are being protected by copyrights not inventions, as is the purpose of patent institution.

In the United States, to preserve copyrights works may be (though need not be) registered with the Copyright Office, a unit of the Library of Congress. "Registration" is nothing more than the word implies: there is neither search nor examination in the copyright field as there is in the patent field. The owner of a copyright, according to section 106 of the 1976 Act has the exclusive right to (1) reproduce the copyrighted work, (2) prepare derivative works based upon the copyrighted work, (3) distribute it to the public by sale, lease, or lending, (4) perform works publicly, and (5) display works publicly.

Government limits the scope of the copyright through the so-called "idea-expression dichotomy": only the expression of the ideas but not the ideas themselves may be protected by the copyright. That is, no one may copy verbatim a short story and distribute it as the author's own work but a story-writer is free to take plot-lines from another story. Government also limits the scope of the copyright by allowing the public "fair use" of the work—a verbatim copy made for one's own use, quotation rights for criticism and scholarship purposes, and uses similarly in keeping with the policy motivation to encourage public and competitive access to expressions.

Being "fixed in a tangible medium of expression, now known or later developed, from which they can be perceived, reproduced, or otherwise communicated, either directly or with the aid of a machine or device" includes at least the following: (1) literary works, (2) musical works, including any accompanying words, (3) dramatic works, including any accompanying music, (4) pantomimes and choreographic works, (5) pictorial, graphic, and sculptural works, (6) motion pictures and other audiovisual works, (7) sound recordings, (8) architectural works, (9) database compilations, and (10) computer software. A comparative study of international competition in computer software concluded that stronger copyright protections in the United States were important early sources of global competitive advantage for American software makers over their European and Japanese competitors (Mowery 1996: 4–11). Nevertheless, the extension of copyright to computer software had its critics at the time and has them today, including those who oppose copyright protection for software as a matter of principle and those who accept the principle of it but contend that the policy needs some refinement.

A computer software application that has had significant effect upon the information management capabilities of organizations private and public is database software. During the 1980s, a number of database compilation and management products became available and in the 1990s they have become increasingly popular with those who need to manage long lists of numbers (telephone and otherwise), names, addresses, and the like. The proliferation of quality database compilation and management products has expanded the market in recent years for the compilation of data by companies substantially or exclusively in that business (the "information industry") as well as by a wide variety of financial institutions, brokerage houses, credit raters, marketing firms, and other enterprises possessing information of commercial value. These information database proprietors have an "appropriability problem," for the investment when creating a database is often substantial—purchasing database software, gathering the data, organizing the information for users—but pirated copies on paper or computer diskette or CD-ROM can be widely and inexpensively distributed with relative ease. Thus, many possessors of information databases followed the practice that had been long established by publishers of information in the United States since Noah Webster and his dictionary in the early days of the American republic: they registered the compilations as copyrighted works, thereby obtaining the protections conferred by the copyright institution.

The international law and organization of intellectual property

The World Intellectual Property Organization (WIPO) is the international governmental organization that administers the world's key treaties regarding intellectual property, with the exception of the Agreement regarding Trade-Related Aspects of Intellectual Property Rights (TRIPS), which is administered by the World Trade Organization. WIPO administers a number of intellectual property treaties, including the following:

(1) The *Paris Convention for the Protection of Industrial Property* was signed in 1883 and periodically amended in the twentieth century. Each Paris Union member is free to offer any standard of patent protection it wishes. However, the convention does demand that members not discriminate against foreign property owners, an obligation known as national treatment. The convention bears of the marks of a modest agreement among generally like-minded industrial countries. Even if they disagreed on particulars, the Paris Union agreed that the patent institution was important for industrial innovation. The convention also establishes basic obligations regarding the protection of trademarks.

(2) The *Patent Cooperation Treaty* (PCT), signed in Washington in 1970 and later amended, makes it possible to seek patent protection simultaneously in each of a large number of countries by filing an international patent application through the PCT secretariat housed at the

WIPO headquarters in Geneva. The PCT provides innovators an efficient way of applying to multiple national authorities but does not provide an institutional means of obtaining an international patent (for no international patent exists).

(3) The *International Convention for the Protection of New Varieties of Plants* (the UPOV Convention), signed in 1971 and amended in 1991, establishes a union of contracting parties who agree to confer "breeder's rights" on those who discover or develop new varieties of plants, provided that the variety is "new, distinct, uniform, and stable."

(4) The *Berne Convention for the Protection of Literary and Artistic Works* was signed in 1886 and has been amended many times. The convention provides that signatory countries provide national treatment to authors, including exclusive rights to authorize reproduction of their works.

These WIPO-administered treaties are augmented under public international law by TRIPS agreement administered under authority of the World Trade Organization.

Protection of intellectual property varies from being generally effective and enforceable in the industrialized countries to being generally ineffective and unenforceable in developing countries (Gadbaw and Richards 1988). The 1994 GATT Uruguay Round Agreement on Trade-Related Aspects of Intellectual Property Rights (TRIPS) produced international obligations regarding patents, copyrights, trademarks, integrated circuits, industrial designs, plant varieties, and trade secrets. Regarding patents, the agreement offers patents on products and processes in all fields of technology, limits compulsory licensing, provides a 20-year patent term from date of application filing and obligates compliance with other terms of the Paris Convention. Regarding copyright, the text protects computer programs and databases, generally establishes a 50-year term minimum, grants owners of computer software and sound recordings the right to authorize or prohibit rental of their products, and obligates compliance with the Berne Convention. Key provisions regarding trademarks include the enhancement of protection for internationally well-known marks and the prohibition of compulsory licensing of marks. A considerable length of text in the TRIPS agreement is devoted to infringement of intellectual property and enforcement of rights, including obligations regarding transparency, expeditiousness, fairness, and remedies. Since the agreement establishing the new World Trade Organization, GATT's successor organization, requires member states to accept all WTO agreements, most developing countries will be party to the TRIPS agreement.

During the period of these multilateral negotiations from 1986 to 1994 and under continuing bilateral pressure from the American government, some developing countries reformed their intellectual property protection laws. In the late 1980s, five governments reformed their patent laws, two their trademark laws, and nine their copyright laws. In the early 1990s, intellectual property reforms proliferated widely as 29 countries reformed their patent laws, three reformed trade-secret laws, 12 reformed trademark laws, and 33 reformed copyright laws (United States Trade Representative, various years).

Nevertheless, many other developing countries maintain that they agreed to TRIPS reluctantly, especially in the case of pharmaceuticals, and only because it was a "linkage bargain" deal associated with the creation of the new WTO and reformed international trade dispute settlement procedures. One scholar contends that intellectual property laws in developing countries have been changed in response to American pressure but that minds have not been changed.

> In nearly every instance the targeted countries have engaged in foot dragging and chosen not to implement and enforce the new policies. The continued monitoring and repeated threats of renewed Section 301 action in the absence of satisfactory enforcement of the new policies suggest that the trend toward greater protection of intellectual property is not being as ardently embraced as the United States would wish. The targeted states acquiesce on paper and do just enough to free themselves of U.S. pressure—but no more. While these countries have changed their policies, they have not changed their minds about the merits of intellectual property protection. Even when the United States carried out its threats by imposing sanctions on Brazil, India, Mexico, and Thailand, the targeted countries did not comply. Free riding on others' intellectual property and the profits of piracy still outweigh the liberal norm of respect for property rights (Sell 1995: 332).

Indeed, when TRIPS was concluded, 25 developing countries offered no patent protection to pharmaceuticals (13 did not even confer patent protection to chemicals), and 57 did not offer copyrights for computer software (Primo Braga 1995b: 396). However, it is less clear whether opposition to intellectual property laws as a matter of economic development strategy is universal. Some minds in developing countries may be changing as new strategies are being adopted to encourage investment, licensing, and indigenous innovation and expression. "The positive role of intellectual property in national economic development is not yet well appreciated, notwithstanding that many individuals in most countries are frustrated by inadequate protection. This pent-up demand for better protection has not yet found a political voice, the voice of the past, as always, being louder than the voice of future" (Sherwood and Primo Braga 1996).

Policy-makers in developing countries have long tended to think differently about copyrights than they have about patents. The utility of the copyright has been acknowledged by many developing countries, while the utility of the patent has been controversial. Brazil has had copyright law for a generation and India for two generations, although neither has always effectively enforced the laws against pirates. The institutional histories of patent and copyright in the third world are characterized by a philosophical tension between natural property rights and incentives for risky investment in innovation and expression. This tension results in a tendency to confer legitimacy on the copyright because it appears to protect the "moral rights" of (local) authors and to deny the "economic rights" of (foreign) firms. Yet, despite the opposition to intellectual property law reforms, especially of patent policies, the context in which development strategy is formulated in the era of TRIPS implementation is very different from the context in any previous era.

Economic development strategies: from import-substitution industrialization to emerging market

Whether born of revolution (e.g., Mexico in 1917), de-colonization (e.g., India in 1947), or civil war (e.g., China in 1949), developing countries in the twentieth century typically adopted state-led models of development, investing public resources into the organization of production and establishing state-owned enterprises to lead industrialization and energy creation—Mexico by the 1930s, India and China by the 1950s. These new regimes, led by Cardenas, Nehru, and Mao as well as by leaders such as Ataturk and Nasser, mistrusted their own business interests as much as they mistrusted multinational business enterprises, identified high barriers to entry in these industry sectors as compelling rationales for public enterprise, and seem to have genuinely believed that state-owned enterprises would achieve national goals (Waterbury 1993).

The developing countries adopted an import-substitution industrialization (ISI) model of economic development strategy, thereby rejecting the liberal, free-trade ideology that the industrialized countries institutionalized into the GATT regime after World War II. The industrialized countries had entangled them into economic crises (the Great Depression) and political crises (World War II) not of their own making, exploited their natural resources, denied them international sovereignty, and undermined the domestic political independence of their governments (Biersteker 1987; Haggard 1990).

The *dependencia school,* headquartered at the United Nations Economic Commission on Latin America under the leadership of economist Raul Prebisch, charged in the 1950s that the world economy was structured to ensure that developing countries were burdened with over-dependence on exports of raw material exports, which tended toward price volatility; maldistribution of national income, which created elite preferences for imported foreign luxury goods; investments in manufacturing by multinational corporations that destroyed local production. The *dependencia school* also contended that trade with the industrialized countries promoted excessive reliance on foreign capital while facilitating foreign domination of local capital markets, introduced technology inappropriate to local skills, created an international division of labor, prevented indigenous, self-sustaining technological development, and distorted the local labour market because multinational corporations paid higher wages than local firms could afford to pay, and promoted reliance on foreign capital (Gilpin 1987: 263–305). They contended that greater independence would be achieved if domestically produced goods and services were substituted for imported goods and services and if governments in the third world imposed restrictions on imports and foreign direct investment restrictions. Thus, the political leaders imposed high tariffs and demanded license approval for imports, restricted foreign direct investment by demanding joint equity ownership and local managerial control and by rejecting foreign direct investment outright in some cases. Some governments even expropriated assets of foreign multinational enterprises, thereby earning the enmity of multinational managers and their government representatives, who demanded from developing country governments prompt, adequate, and effective compensation under authority of public international law regarding foreign direct investment (Lipson 1985).

Developing countries presented proposals for restructuring the world political economy at the first United Nations Conference on Trade and Development (UNCTAD) in 1964. They requested trade preferences for their manufacturing goods, commodity price stabilization, resource and technology transfers, reductions in freight and service charges, debt rescheduling and reductions, and a new forum to replace the GATT (Cutahar 1984). Creating an economic strategy to mirror the security strategy of the nonaligned movement and inspired by the success of the OPEC oil cartel, in 1974 the Group of 77 developing countries used their numbers in the United Nations (in which one-nation, one-vote decision-making afforded them power they did not have in the weighted-voting International Monetary Fund and World Bank and the rarely voting GATT) to pass a Declaration on the Establishment of the New International Economic Order (NIEO). The NIEO reiterated the UNCTAD demands and asserted the right to nationalize foreign enterprises, create commodity cartels, and regulate multinational corporations (Bhattarcharya 1976). Thus, the G-77 used the UNCTAD forum to establish raw materials and agricultural cartels—the Commodity Common Fund—intended to monitor and manage supply, demand, and therefore prices. The Commodity Common Fund managed supply by amassing stocks of the commodities, much as the OPEC cartel managed the supply of oil (Finlayson and Zacher 1990). It was an era in which third world governments weakened intellectual property policies, as India did with its changes in patent policy in 1972 (Gadbaw and Richards 1988: 200).

The GATT initiatives in the 1960s to help solve the economic problems of the developing countries were feeble except for the tariff-cutting offered by the Generalized System of Preferences, which were trade preferences valuable to exporters in developing countries even if critics charged that importers manipulated the system for their own benefit (Wilson 1992: 44). Neither the Kennedy Round negotiations nor the subsequent Tokyo Round contributed much to development. If anything, they compounded the problems with antidumping and subsidy-countervailing duty agreements and the Multifiber Agreement that worked against the interests of developing countries (Hudec 1987).

Nevertheless, whether the measure is economic growth rates, current account balances, or income distribution, the economic development strategy of import substitution industrialization performed poorly. The Commodity Common Fund achieved some success in stabilizing, then, raising prices but turned out to be fool's gold; oil is the only exception to the rule that commodities are substitutable with alternatives (Krasner 1974). Furthermore, the oil shocks of the 1970s increased the dollar needs of the developing countries that were not oil producers and falsely raised the hopes of the oil-producing developing countries. The banks of the industrialized countries recycled petro-dollars through the developing countries and the outcomes were levels of national debt that contributed to a "debt crisis" in 1982 (Kahler 1986).

The Group of 77 lacked the power in the world political economy to achieve the New International Economic Order and by the end of the 1980s their proposal was dead; UNCTAD mattered little in the world economy; import substitution industrialization had come to be seen as a failed strategy. ISI failed, however, neither because of greedy foreign banks nor because of the structure of world power but because the strategy itself was flawed. It depended on markets that were too small to provide economies of scale, on demand conditions that were too isolated to produce globally competitive industries, and typically resulted in inefficient production and bad products by insulated state-owned and private enterprises. Perhaps only crisis could sufficiently alter political dynamics within Latin American and African developing countries (Nelson 1990) so they would be willing to adopt a new development strategy.

The International Monetary Fund used its power as source of capital and guarantor to other public and private lenders to lend to developing countries on the condition that they adjust their economic policies to follow liberal-tending, market-oriented prescriptions (Kahler 1986; Williamson 1983). Perhaps as important, developing countries had a new economic development model in the strategies of South Korea and Taiwan. Both countries had adopted import substitution policies after the end of Japanese colonialism and during the era of American protection and had been heavily dependent upon American aid until they were met with the demands of the Eisenhower Administration that they wean themselves from that aid. South Korean and Taiwanese government leaders initiated transitions toward export-led economic development strategies in order to achieve balance of payments equilibrium and earn foreign exchange for domestic development (Cheng 1990). The regimes in South Korea and Taiwan faced serious external threats that motivated industrialization of the economy, not predation of it for the benefit of wealthy elites.

South Korea and Taiwan are "late industrializers" and late industrializers are good learners (Amsden 1989). They visit international trade expositions, attend international professional and academic conferences, tour foreign production plants, consult foreign buyers and suppliers, hire foreign experts, and beg, borrow, buy, and occasionally steal foreign product designs and know-how. They imitate innovations in order to learn until their knowledge results in innovations of their own making, as Korean information technology companies have done (Kim 1997). The South Korean and Taiwanese strategies involved a great deal of planning and intervention by government; high levels of investment in key industries, more investment than would have occurred without government intervention; the exposure of industries to international competition in foreign, though typically not in domestic, markets (Wade 1990). The governments intervened in the markets through land redistribution, financial system controls to put industrial production ahead of consumer spending, price controls, undervalued foreign exchange rates, wage controls (and repression of unions), export performance rewards, foreign direct investment controls, foreign technology acquisition, and sector-specific subsidies and export promotion assistance. They did it all with great success, for, by the late 1980s, the Korean foreign ministry was planning admission into the OECD (achieved in late 1996) and Taiwan, though diplomatically isolated, was by then even richer than Korea. Thus, propelled by chronic poverty, dilapidated infrastructure, deadening stagnation, and punishing debt and motivated by the examples of countries doing better, the political leaders of developing countries have been dropping their ISI strategies and articulating strategies that call for fuller engagement in the world economy, including export promotion and (qualified) liberalization of import and direct investment policies. In so doing, they have acquired the label "emerging markets" (Garten 1997).

Until 1978, China's economic development strategy had been an especially autarkic import substitution strategy (Lardy 1992): "self-reliance" was more than mere slogan in Mao's China. Domestic production was state-owned, for the Chinese communists established a centralized, planned economy by the mid-1950s (Riskin 1987). This strategy resulted in chronic poverty, poor infrastructure, a widening technological gap between world standards and Chinese capabilities, and a standard-of-living gap between China and rapidly industrializing East Asian neighbors. Fearing the implications for national security of the growing technology and wealth gap, advocates for change in economic development strategy within China argued that "socialism" must not mean "egalitarianism on the basis of universal poverty" (Pearson 1991) and after a consolidation of power by Deng Xiaoping, the Chinese government announced in December 1978 a new "Open Door" policy to stimulate China's modernization in science and technology, agriculture, and the military (Ho and Huenemann 1984). However, the economic logic of the Open Door policy was not liberalization but the adoption of Western technology and the export of manufactured goods.

Motivated by factors similar to those that confronted Mao's political successors in China, the socialist command strategies of the Soviet Union and its eastern European satellites by the end of the 1980s underwent their own political upheaval and economic strategy shift. Socialist command placed the state in control of resource allocation through planning, with resource deployment favouring heavy manufacturing and energy sectors over light manufacturing sectors, a strategy maintained through establishment of a dyadic, asymmetrical regional economy in isolation from the world political economy (Commisso 1986). The socialist command strategy industrialized the Soviet Union and created a mighty war machine but did so at the expense of consumers. Nevertheless, the strategy and its system might have survived had not the pace of technological advance in the West and the Chernobyl disaster de-legitimized the Soviet state. Russia (Aslund 1995), the former Soviet republics, and the eastern European states have been undergoing radical economic reform. The focus of the transitions has been on macroeconomic stabilization, liberalization, and institutionalization but have generally been unstable save for Hungary (Islam and Mandelbaum 1993).

Challenged by debt crisis, Mexico acceded to the GATT and initiated a free-trade agreement with the United States and Canada, liberalizing its trade and investment policies in the process. Developing countries have been acceding to the GATT and its WTO successor at the pace of one or two each month, so that the membership exceeds 130 countries, though the commitment to liberalization does not yet run deep (Haggard 1995). Brazil and other governments in Latin America overcame domestic political obstacles (Haggard and Kaufman 1995) to begin liberalization of trade and investment policies through free-trade agreements and customs unions (Krueger 1995). India is liberalizing its economy, though at an erratic pace; Indonesia and the other member states of the Association of Southeast Asian Nations (ASEAN) have agreed to phase in a free-trade agreement, while Vietnam has been pursuing *doi moi* marketization and liberalization reforms and has joined ASEAN. The countries of the Middle East (Chaudhry 1997) continue to be driven by the political economy of oil and petrochemicals, though Turkey, Israel, and several other Middle Eastern states lack oil and hence find incentives for other types of trade and investment. The central Asian republics have also recently been drawn into the political economy of oil and petro-chemicals. The African continent offers some encouraging growth prospects, anchored in the sub-Saharan region by South Africa, but many of the governments in Africa continue to be unable to establish credible and effective institutions.

Not only are the economic *strategies* of developing countries changing but so are their economic *structures*. The World Bank (1997: 134–36) reports that, since 1980, manufacturing has been declining and services have been increasing as a percentage of Gross Domestic Product in middle-level developing countries such as Brazil, Mexico, South Korea, and Singapore (see table 1). Even in poorer developing countries, services are increasing as a percentage of Gross Domestic Product in countries such as China, India, Indonesia, Kenya, and Peru (see table 1). Whether services or manufacturing or agriculture, productive capability and competitive advantage in the contemporary world economy increasingly depends upon the capacity to learn and manage knowledge.

Table 1: Change in manufacturing and services as percentage of GDP for selected developing countries

Country	Manufacturing	Services
Brazil	33% > 24%	45% > 49%
Mexico	22% > 19%	59% > 67%
South Korea	29% > 27%	45% > 50%
Singapore	29% > 27%	61% > 64%
China		21% > 31%
India		36% > 41%
Indonesia		34% > 41%
Kenya		47% > 54%
Peru		48% > 55%
Source: The World Bank 1997: 134–36.		

Global knowledge diffusion and intellectual property rights

Trade, foreign direct investment, licensing and collaborative relationships, recent research shows, are important media for the global diffusion of knowledge. A study that matches patent citation data with trade data supports the proposition that trade flows encourage knowledge flows (Sjoholm 1996). Perhaps one-half of American, and even more European, productivity growth derives from foreign technology (Eaton and Kortum 1994) acquired through trade, license, and direct investment (including joint-equity venture and wholly-owned subsidiary). Collaborative business strategies contribute essential new knowledge that cannot be obtained by reading books and journal articles or doing Internet searches. Simple product innovations can often be quickly imitated by producers in developing countries but organizational, managerial-process innovations and other forms of business know-how are substantially more difficult to learn and incorporate into routine activities. "Best practice is more fraught with difficulty than the acquisition of technologies" (Kogut 1991: 39).

A study finds that, comparing the East Asian countries with the countries of Latin America, the Asian countries show larger flows of trade, foreign direct investment, and licensing behavior, thus pointing to possible reasons for its stronger technological growth (Dahlman 1994). A study of 77 developing countries over a period of 20 years finds that "a developing country's total factor productivity is larger the greater is its foreign R&D capital stock, the more open it is to trade with the industrial countries, and the more educated its labour force" (Coe, Helpman, and Hoffmaister 1995). The relative contributions of trade, licensing, and direct investment to knowledge flows, however, are unclear, though may relate to other country and institutional characteristics (Pack and Saggi 1997).

Since the early 1990s, developing countries have generally been encouraging more investment by multinational business enterprises. Governments in developing countries and those making transitions from non-market economies recognize that investment, while not scarce, is limited and they are competing for it. Thus some policymakers have been exploring the usefulness of investment incentives, including tax abatements, investment credits, subsidized loans, and performance requirements. These inducements affect the potential investor's revenues, cost of inputs, factors of production, and profitability (Guisinger 1986). When offering incentives, states that make certain their policies are stable and that their commitments are credible do better (Murtha 1991). Nevertheless, though some of these policies may encourage inward foreign direct investment, policy incentives must be considered in the light of restrictions placed on export subsidies under the GATT. The direction of policy in the world economy has been toward multilateral agreement to restrict investment incentives because they artificially distort comparative advantages and lead states into costly bidding wars (Hufbauer 1984).

Furthermore, incentives generally matter less to multinational business enterprise managers than do political stability, asset control, earnings remittance, predictability in monetary and fiscal policy, transportation and communication infrastructures, business behaviour standards, import barriers, export quotas, and regulatory factors (Wallace 1992). Developing countries with small populations, however, do face special challenges in gaining the attention of decision-makers in multinational corporations and must overcome the perception of "marginality" in the world economy by understanding the goals, interests, and decision-making patterns of multinational managers (Goodman 1987). In general, clever incentives matter less than market and institution fundamentals: human capital, market opportunities, infrastructure, macroeconomic stability and foreign exchange, political and legal predictability.

Weak intellectual-property institutions apparently discourage precisely the kind of knowledge-intensive, knowledge-diffusing, foreign direct investment that is most desired in the countries of the emerging market. In the late 1980s and the early 1990s, while TRIPS negotiations were being conducted, research sponsored by international governmental organizations started to demonstrate with systematically gathered evidence what anecdotal evidence had been suggesting for some years: weak protection of intellectual property discourages foreign direct investment in certain industry sectors, especially pharmaceuticals, fine (including agricultural) chemicals, and information technologies. An UNCTAD study in 1986 found that investment in new technology areas such as computer software, semiconductors, and biotechnology was influenced by intellectual property policies (UNCTAD 1986). A 1987 OECD study found weak intellectual property policies to be significant barriers to international technology licensing (OECD 1987). A study by the United Nations Commission on Transnational Corporations (UNCTC) in 1989 found that weak intellectual property protection reduced computer software investment. Another study by the UNCTC announced in 1990 that weak patent policies reduced pharmaceutical investment (UNCTC 1989, 1990). Survey research sponsored by the International Finance Corporation of the World Bank found that, with variations by sector, country, and technology, at least 25 percent of American, German, and Japanese high-technology firms refused direct investment or joint ventures in industrializing countries with weak intellectual property policies (Mansfield 1995: 2). Given scarce resources, they invested in countries where the intellectual property risks were lower. World Bank research supports the conclusions of the survey research by tracing actual patterns of American foreign direct investment and finding that countries with weak intellectual property policies do indeed have less foreign direct investment than would otherwise be expected (Primo Braga 1995a).

Thus, a growing body of evidence supports theory: weak national intellectual-property systems, it is hypothesized by transaction-cost economics (Williamson 1996), confer appropriability hazards that influence the market-entry strategies of firms (Teece 1987). Given scarce resources, they enter countries where the risk of intellectual-property leakage is lower. International technology and knowledge flows are an important new variable in the political economy of intellectual property policy. Previously, some American economists argued that intellectual property rights ought to depend on levels of development and that the least developed countries should not adopt international standards but that middle-income countries possibly should (Deardorff 1992; Maskus 1990). However, these studies may not have taken sufficient account of trade, investment, capital, and technology flows. Nevertheless, the absorptive capacity of developing countries varies considerably (Keller 1996): it depends upon the capabilities of their knowledge institutions.

Political, governmental, and
judicial institutionalization

The implementation of liberal-tending economic development strategies, however, will take much better governance and public administration than that which developing countries are generally possess.
Samuel Hungtington explains, in words just as true today as when they
were written:

> The most important political distinction among countries con-
> cerns not their form of government but their degree of government
> ... The differences between democracy and dictatorship are less
> than the differences between those countries whose politics em-
> bodies consensus, community, legitimacy, organization, effective-
> ness, stability, and those countries whose politics is deficient in
> these qualities. (Hungtington 1968: 1)

Nevertheless, type of political regime matters to economic performance (Garrett and Lange 1995) and emerging market policy-makers
will have to construct effective political institutions in which either
inter-party or intra-party competition (Haggard and Kaufman 1995)
produce development through rule-based political legislative processes
managed by merit-based, Weberian, bureaucratic administration characterized by continual bargaining over societal goals and means rather
than predation, in which resources are extracted at the expense of society and individual goals (especially those of an elite) take precedence
over collective goals–that is, a developmental rather than a predatory
state (Evans 1995).

Unfortunately, as has been well-known since the politics of post-
colonial developing countries first came under study, in such countries
weakly institutionalized political systems in which a single set of elites
perform all the tasks of government—military, political, administrative, economic, and sometimes even religious—has been the norm
(Riggs 1963, 1964). The bureaucratic elite are also the political elite
and they resist competitive party and legislative institutionalization.
The rules of the game being as they are, i.e., corrupt, "a typical Indian
entrepreneur or trader must pick his way through a plethora of state
and local regulations that are at best confusing and at worst contradic-
tory. Given such conditions of great uncertainty, he is easily tempted to
seek protection by using his connections and/or wealth" (Scott 1972).
A durable legacy of colonialism has been a big gap between "civil servant" and "citizen" in terms of educational attainment, status, and access to information, rendering minimal the citizen's capacity to
demand service from the civil servant.

State-owned enterprises provide political and bureaucratic elites with great opportunity for patronage and corruption, discouraging privatization even though the IMF recommends it in its economic reform and restructuring advice and even though the political logic of state-owned enterprises—too many bosses, too few incentives for innovative products, processes, and services, too little information for managers (Waterbury 1993)—recommends against state-owned production. Public ownership of production through state-owned enterprises and the Ministry of Finance's authority regarding trade and investment empowered the state sectors while economic stagnation rigidified class cleavages (Frieden 1991; Evans 1987).

The states of the developing countries were granted international sovereignty but the peoples of the developing countries exchanged foreign masters for domestic masters, ranging from corporatist elitism to personal despotism: "Sovereignty gave ex-colonial peoples a legitimate voice in world affairs and membership in international organizations ... However, it could not give them domestic political and civil rights because these are not in the gift of international society" (Jackson 1990: 159).

Courts, customs, and police are the agents of enforcement, and in many developing countries they have performed poorly and often been corrupt. Intellectual-property business interests in the United States, motivated by losses to product piracy, have undertaken a deliberate, long-term effort to improve the quality of agents of enforcement in developing countries. The annual "Special 301" recommendations of the International Intellectual Property Alliance (IIPA), the Software Publishers Association, and others detail the inadequacies of enforcement country-by-country. "Mexican criminal procedures," said IIPA in its 1997 report, "are often unfathomable, intricate, ad hoc, and seemingly random." The report also said, "Criminal elements dominate much of urban Brazil." Bulgaria is the biggest source of CD piracy in Europe because of government-owned pirate factories and exports controlled by organized crime. The courts in Pakistan are "hopelessly backlogged." Nintendo offers the assessment that "Venezuela's legal system has not evolved at the same pace as its modern economy ... Until Venezuela addresses some of these serious deficiencies that have given their judicial system the reputation of being 'among the most corrupt in the world,' Nintendo and other U.S. intellectual property owners will continue to suffer irreparable harm and loss" (International Intellectual Property Alliance, various years; Arter & Hadden, 1996).

Competition and trade in intellectual property places on states an enforcement problem qualitatively different from that of financial capital flows and trade in real property. Enforcing policies toward financial assets and trade are essentially problems of central government power and capacity to control its borders. Policies in developing countries regarding financial assets such as capital controls and more general macroeconomic policies have frequently been subject to change at the behest of IMF bankers, and their implementation challenges the power of the central government to act contrary to the demands of domestic interest groups. Trade policy commitments made through international treaty, as illustrated by the Uruguay Round agreements, tend to fall into three categories: customs and border measures, subsidies and "unfair" trade practices, and product regulations and standards testing. As with the IMF's "conditionality-imposed" policy changes, implementing the GATT-imposed trade policy changes challenges the power of the central government to resist the demands of domestic interest groups and to control border flows of traded goods. By contrast, the enforcement of intellectual property rights additionally depends upon the government's capacity to enforce policies at local levels when localized corruption and cronyism are ways of life in many developing countries. For this reason and in large measure due to pressure from business interests in the United States dependent upon intellectual property, the TRIPS agreement imposes extensive obligations upon signatory states regarding enforcement, adjudication, remedy, and appeal under both civil and criminal law.

Legal scholars hypothesize that institutionalization of effective judiciaries depends upon fidelity to legal discourse and democratic accountability (Mattli and Slaughter 1998). The World Bank has undertaken a study of judicial institutionalization in developing countries and its preliminary finding is that judicial independence and competence are the key attributes of effective dispute settlement and enforcement (Dakolias 1995). Judicial independence means detachment from interest groups, the executive and legislature, practising attorneys, and even fellow judges. It means rendering adjudicatory decisions according to law rather than the interests of politics or commerce. Judicial independence is apparently achieved through appointment procedures based upon merit to ensure highly qualified and respected judges; frequent participation by judges in professional development education so they can stay current of legal knowledge; and evaluation procedures that ensure ethical conduct. Governments need to ensure that judges are insulated from political and commercial pressures through secure judicial terms, adequate salaries, and control over case assignment and court scheduling. In order to be effective, courts must have adequate staffing and capable administrators to aid the timely disposition of cases, i.e., administrative capacity. The World Bank study finds that corruption may as often be the product of overburdened courts whose delays cause frustrated litigants to pay bribes to get their cases heard as it is the product of corrupt judges who will swing adjudicatory outcomes in one direction or the other for a price or of powerful litigants who demand preferred outcomes from fearful judges. Thus, it appears that democratic accountability, judicial independence and competence, and administrative capacity may be crucial determinants of effective commercial dispute settlement and judicial institutionalization.

The essence of the state is its capacity to enforce policy as well as to make it. Concomitant with the pursuit of profits and of anti-Communist containment of the Soviet bloc and its supposed revolutionary ideology, American multinational corporations and foreign policy-makers have long been accused of propping up authoritarian regimes in developing countries with little regard for local rule of law (Kwitny 1984; Gaddis 1982; Krasner 1978). American business and government insistence in the TRIPS negotiations that the final agreement impose obligations to reform judiciaries and build enforcement capabilities is generally little recognized and its potential impact under-appreciated by scholarly and policy communities. The TRIPS agreement may ultimately be seen as a seminal act international law and organization for this achievement alone. However, neither the laws of intellectual property protection nor the judicial reforms necessary for their effective enforcement will be easily implemented in developing countries.

Conclusion

The institutionalization and enforcement of world-standard protection of intellectual property rights in developing countries will in the coming years contribute to the transformation of their economies, polities, and societies. Experience from the industrialization era of Western Europe, North America, and Japan suggests that adoption of world-standard intellectual property policies will promote technological innovation and adaptation, economic growth, informational diversity, and cultural vitality in developing countries. When the world political economy was cleaved South and North, East and West, and when the South and the East were pursuing economic development strategies that sought as much as possible to go their own, independent way, opportunities for sustained economic growth in these regions were foregone. The debt crisis in the South and economic failure in the East provide new opportunities for economic development but we can expect that the highest growth rates and most dynamic economies will be achieved in countries where the governments ensure the right mixes of markets and institutions.

Acknowledgments

I gratefully acknowledge comments received from participants at government conferences in Jordan and in Peru and at the InfoDev seminar of the World Bank.

Notes

1 Stated with the precision of the specialist, Chinese cultural traditions possess five distinctive patterns that have discouraged scientific advance: cognitive formalism, narrow empiricism, dogmatic scientism, feudal bureaucratism, and compulsive ritualism (Baum 1982).
2 Partha Dasgupta has frequently written studies with Joseph Stiglitz, presently chief economist at the World Bank.

References

Abernathy, William J., and Kim B. Clark (1985). Innovation: Mapping the Winds of Creative Destruction. *Research Policy* 14:3–22.

Abernathy, William J., and James M. Utterback (1978). Patterns of Innovation in Technology. *Technology Review* 80, 7: 40–47.

Adelman, Martin J., and Sonia Baldia (1996). Prospects and Limits of the Patent Provision in the TRIPS Agreement: The Case of India. *Vanderbilt Journal of Transnational Law* 29: 507–33.

Almeida, Paul (1996). Knowledge Sourcing by Foreign Multinationals: Patent Citation Analysis in the U.S. Semiconductor Industry. *Strategic Management Journal* 17: 155–65.

Almeida, Paul, and Bruce Kogut (1996). Technology and Geography: The Localization of Knowledge and the Mobility of Patent Holders. Working Paper. Philadelphia, PA: The Huntsman Center for Global Competition and Innovation; The Wharton School of the University of Pennsylvania.

Almeida, Paul, and Bruce Kogut (1997). The Exploration of Technological Diversity and the Geographic Localization of Innovation. *Small Business Economics* 9: 21–31.

Amsden, Alice (1989). *Asia's Next Giant: South Korea and Late Industrialization.* New York: Oxford University Press.

Argote, Linda (1999). *Organizational Learning: Creating, Retaining and Transferring Knowledge.* Norwell, MA: Kluwer Academic Publishers.

Arter & Hadden (1996). *Special 301 Comments on Video Game Piracy.* Washington, DC.

Ascher, William (1983). New Development Approaches and the Adaptability of International Agencies: The Case of the World Bank. *International Organization* 37: 415–39.

Aslund, Anders (1995). *How Russia Became a Market Economy.* Washington, DC: Brookings Institution Press.

Ayres, Robert L. (1983). *Banking on the Poor: The World Bank and World Poverty.* Cambridge, MA: MIT Press.

Axelrod, Robert (1984). *The Evolution of Cooperation.* New York: Basic Books.

Baum, Richard (1982). Science and Culture in Contemporary China: The Roots of Retarded Modernization. *Asian Survey* 22: 1166–86.

Beltz, Cynthia A. (1994). *Financing Entrepreneurs.* Washington, DC: American Enterprise Institute.

Bernheim, B. Douglas, and J.B. Shoven (1992). Comparing the Cost of Capital in the United States and Japan. In Nathan Rosenberg, Ralph Landau, and David C. Mowery (eds.), *Technology and the Wealth of Nations* (Stanford, CA: Stanford University Press): 151–74.

Bhattacharya, Anindya K. (1976). The Influence of the International Secretariat: UNCTAD and Generalized Tariff Preferences. *International Organization* 30: 76–90.

Biersteker, Thomas J. (1987). *Multinationals, the State, and Control of the Nigerian Economy.* Princeton, NJ: Princeton University Press.

Boskin, Michael J., and Lawrence J. Lau (1992). Capital, Technology, and Economic Growth. In Nathan Rosenberg, Ralph Landau, and David C. Mowery (eds.), *Technology and the Wealth of Nations* (Stanford, CA: Stanford University Press): 17–56.

Bradley, Stephen P., Jerry A. Hausman, and Richard L. Nolan, eds. (1993). *Globalization, Technology, and Competition: The Fusion of Computers and Telecommunications in the 1990s.* Boston, MA: Harvard Business School.

Burkhart, Ross E., and Michael S. Lewis-Beck (1994). Comparative Democracy: The Economic Development Thesis. *American Political Science Review* 88: 903–10.

Buscaglia, Edgardo, and Maria Dakolias (1999). An Analysis of the Causes of Corruption in the Judiciary. *Law and Policy in International Business* 30: 95–116.

Calder, Kent E. (1993). *Strategic Capitalism: Private Business and Public Purpose in Japanese Industrial Finance.* Princeton, NJ: Princeton University Press.

Cardwell, Donald (1995). *The Norton History of Technology.* New York: Norton.

Chandler, Alfred D. (1977). *The Visible Hand: The Managerial Revolution in American Business.* Cambridge, MA: Harvard University Press.

Chaudhry, Kiren Aziz (1997). *The Price of Wealth: Economies and Institutions in the Middle East.* Ithaca, NY: Cornell University Press.

Cheng, Tun-jen (1990). Political Regimes and Development Strategies: South Korea and Taiwan. In Gary Gereffi and Donald L. Wyman (eds.), *Manufacturing Miracles: Paths of Industrialization in Latin America and East Asia* (Princeton, NJ: Princeton University Press): 138–78.

Coe, David T., Elhanan Helpman, and Alexander W. Hoffmeister (1995). North-South R&D Spillovers. Working Paper. Boston, MA: National Bureau of Economic Research.

Commisso, Ellen (1986). State Structures, Political Processes, and Collective Choice in CMEA States. *International Organization* 40:195–238.

Cooper, Frederick, and Randall Packard, eds. (1997). *International Development and the Social Sciences: Essays on the History and Politics of Knowledge.* Berkeley, CA: University of California Press.

Cowhey, Peter F., and Jonathan D. Aronson (1993). *Managing the World Economy: The Consequences of Corporate Alliances.* New York: Council on Foreign Relations.

Cox, Robert W. (1973). The Executive Head: An Essay on Leadership in International Organization. In Leland M. Goodrich and David A. Kay (eds.), *International Organization: Politics and Processes* (Madison, WI: University of Wisconsin Press): 155–80.

Cox, Robert W., Harold K. Jacobson, *et al.* (1974). *The Anatomy of Influence: Decision Making in International Organization.* New Haven, CT: Yale University Press.

Cutahar, Michael Zammit, ed. (1984). *UNCTAD and the South-North Dialogue: The First Twenty Years.* New York: Pergamon.

Dahlman, Carl J. (1994). Technology Strategy in East Asian Developing Economies. *Journal of Asian Economics* 5: 541–72.

Dakolias, Maria (1995). A Strategy for Judicial Reform: The Experience in Latin America. *Virginia Journal of International Law* 36:167–232.

Dam, Kenneth (1994). The Economic Underpinnings of Patent Law. *Journal of Legal Studies* 23: 247–71.

Dasgupta, Partha (1988). Patents, Priority, and Imitation, or, the Economics of Races and Waiting Games. *The Economic Journal* 98: 66–80.

Deardorff, Alan V. (1992). Should Patent Protection Be Extended to All Developing Countries? *World Economy* 13: 497–08.

Diwan, Ishac, and Dani Rodrik (1991). Patents, Appropriate Technology, and North-South Trade. *Journal of International Economics* 30: 27–47.

Dornbusch, Rudiger, and F. Leslie C.H. Helmers, eds. (1988). *The Open Economy: Tools for Policymakers in Developing Countries.* New York: Oxford University Press.

Dosi, Giovanni (1982). Technological Paradigms and Technological Trajectories. *Research Policy* 11: 147–62.

Eaton, Jonathan, and Samuel Kortum (1994). International Patenting and Technology Diffusion. Working Paper. Boston, MA: National Bureau of Economic Research.

——— (1997). Engines of Growth: Domestic and Foreign Sources of Innovation. *Japan and the World Economy* 9: 235–59.

Escobar, Arturo (1995). *Encountering Development: The Making and Unmaking of the Third World.* Princeton, NJ: Princeton University Press.

Eggertsson, Thrain (1990). *Economic Behavior and Institutions.* New York: Cambridge University Press.

Evans, Peter (1987). Class, State, and Dependence in East Asia: Lessons for Latin Americanists. In Frederic C. Deyo (ed.), *The Political Economy of the New Asian Industrialism* (Ithaca, NY: Cornell University Press): 203–26.

——— (1995). *Embedded Autonomy: States and Industrial Transformation.* Princeton, NJ: Princeton University Press.

Evenson, Robert E. (1984). International Invention: Implications for Technology Market Analysis. In Zvi Griliches, (ed.), *R&D, Patents, and Productivity* (Chicago, IL: University of Chicago Press): 89–123.

—— (1993). Patents, R&D, and Invention Potential : International Evidence. *AEA Papers & Proceedings*: 463–68.

Feigenbaum, Edward A. (1995). Where's the Walkman in Japan's Software Future? In Derek Leebaert (ed.), *The Future of Software* (Cambridge, MA: MIT Press): 215–26.

Finlayson, Jock A., and Mark W. Zacher (1990). *Managing International Markets: Developing Countries and the Commodity Trade Regime*. New York: Columbia University Press.

Firmin-Sellers, Kathryn (1995). The Politics of Property Rights. *American Political Science Review* 89: 867–81.

Frieden, Jeffrey A. (1991). *Debt, Development, and Democracy: Modern Political Economy and Latin America, 1965-1985*. Princeton, NJ: Princeton University Press.

Fukao, Mitsuhiro (1995). *Financial Integration, Corporate Governance, and the Performance of Multinational Companies*. Washington, DC: Brookings Institution Press.

Gadbaw, R. Michael, and Timothy Richards, eds. (1988). *Intellectual Property: Global Consensus, Global Conflict?* Boulder, CO: Westview.

Gaddis, John Lewis (1982). *Strategies of Containment: A Critical Appraisal of Postwar American National Security Policy*. New York: Oxford University Press.

Garrett, Geoffrey, and Peter Lange (1995). Internationalization, Institutions, and Political Change. *International Organization* 49: 627–56.

Garten, Jeffrey E. (1997). *The Big Ten: The Big Emerging Markets and How They Will Change Our Lives*. New York: Basic Books.

Gilpin, Robert (1987). *The Political Economy of International Relations*. Princeton, NJ: Princeton University Press.

Ginsburg, Jane C. (1990). Creation and Commercial Value: Copyright Protection of Works of Information. *Columbia Law Review* 90 :1865–938.

—— (1992). No "Sweat"? Copyright and Other Protection of Works of Information After *Feist v. Rural Telephone*. *Columbia Law Review* 92: 338–88.

Goldstein, Judith, and Robert O. Keohane, eds. (1993). *Ideas and Foreign Policy: Beliefs, Institutions, and Political Change*. Ithaca, NY: Cornell University Press.

Goodman, Louis M. (1987). *Small Nations, Giant Firms*. New York: Holmes & Meier.

Gorman, Robert A. (1992). The Feist Case: Reflections on a Pathbreaking Copyright Decision. *Rutgers Computer and Technology Law Journal* 18: 73–172.

Griliches, Zvi (1990). Patent Statistics as Economic Indicators: A Survey. *Journal of Economic Literature* 28: 1661–707.

Grochow, Jerrold M. (1997). *Information Overload! Creating Value with New Information Systems Technology*. Upper Saddle River, NJ: Prentice Hall.

Grossman, Gene, and Elhanan Helpman (1991). *Innovation and Growth in the Global Economy*. Cambridge, MA: MIT Press.

Guisinger, Stephen (1986). Host-Country Policies to Attract and Control Foreign Investment. In Theodore H. Moran (ed.), *Investing in Development: New Roles of Private Capital* (New Brunswick, NJ: Transaction Books): 157–72.

Haggard, Stephan (1990). *Pathways from the Periphery: The Politics of Growth in the Newly Industrializing Countries.* Ithaca, NY: Cornell University Press.

———— (1995). *Developing Nations and the Politics of Global Integration.* Washington, DC: Brookings Institution Press.

Haggard, Stephan, and Robert Kaufman (1995). *The Political Economy of Democratic Transitions.* Princeton, NJ: Princeton University Press.

Hamel, Gary, and C.K. Prahalad (1989). Collaborate with Your Competitors—and Win. *Harvard Business Review* 63, 4: 149–58.

Hirschman, Albert O. (1958). *Strategy of Economic Development.* New Haven, CT: Yale University Press.

Ho, Samuel P.S., and Ralpy W. Huenemann (1984). *China's Open Door Policy: The Quest for Foreign Technology and Capital. A Study of China's Special Trade.* Vancouver: University of British Columbia Press.

Hudec, Robert E. (1987). *Developing Countries in the GATT Legal System.* Brookfield, VT: Gower Publishing.

Hufbauer, Gary C. (1984). *Subsidies in International Trade.* Washington, DC: Institute for International Economics.

Huff, Toby E. (1993). *The Rise of Early Modern Science: Islam, China, and the West.* New York: Cambridge University Press

Huntington, Samuel P. (1968). *Political Order in Changing Societies.* New Haven, CT: Yale University Press.

International Intellectual Property Alliance (various years). *Special 301 Recommendations.* Washington, DC: IIPA.

Islam, Shafiqul, and Michael Mandelbaum (1993). *Making Markets: Economic Transformation in Eastern Europe and the Post-Soviet States.* New York: Council on Foreign Relations.

Jackson, Robert H. (1990). *Quasi-States: Sovereignty, International Relations, and the Third World.* New York: Cambridge University Press.

Jacobson, Harold K. (1984). *Networks of Interdependence: International Organizations and the Global Political System.* New York: Alfred A. Knopf.

Jasonoff, Sheila. (1985). Technological Innovation in a Corporatist State: The Case of Biotechnology in the Federal Republic of Germany. *Research Policy* 14: 23–38.

Johnson, Chalmers (1982). *MITI and the Japanese Miracle.* Stanford, CA: Stanford University Press.

Johnson, William R. (1985). The Economics of Copying. *Journal of Political Economy* 93: 158–74.

Joyce, Craig, *et al.* (1994). *Copyright Law.* 3rd edition. New York: Matthew Bender.

Kahler, Miles, ed. (1986). *The Politics of International Debt.* Ithaca, NY: Cornell University Press.

Katzenstein, Peter J., ed. (1989). *Industry and Politics in West Germany: Toward the Third Republic.* Ithaca, NY: Cornell University Press.

Keller, Wolfgang. (1996). Absorptive Capacity: On the Creation and Acquisition of Technology in Development. *Journal of Development Economics* 49: 199–227.

Keen, Peter G.W. (1991). *Shaping the Future: Business Design through Information Technology.* Boston, MA: Harvard Business School Press.

Kim, Daniel H. (1993). The Link between Individual and Organizational Learning. *Sloan Management Review* 35: 37–50.

Kim, Linsu (1997). *Imitation to Innovation: The Dynamics of Korea's Technological Learning.* Boston, MA: Harvard Business School Press.

Kitch, Edmund W. (1977). The Nature and Function of the Patent System. *Journal of Law and Economics* 20: 265–90.

Kitschelt, Herbert (1991). Industrial Governance Structures, Innovation Strategies, and the Case of Japan: Sectoral or Cross-National Comparative Analysis? *International Organization* 45: 453–94.

Kogut, Bruce (1991). Country Capabilities and the Permeability of Borders. *Strategic Management Journal* 12: 33–47.

Kogut, Bruce, and Udo Zander (1992). Knowledge of the Firm, Combinative Capabilities, and the Replication of Technology. *Organization Science* 3: 383–97.

Kondo, Edson K. (1995). The Effect of Patent Protection on Foreign Direct Investment. *Journal of World Trade* 29: 97–122.

Kotabe, Massaki. (1996). Emerging Role of Technology Licensing in the Development of Global Product Strategy: Conceptual Framework and Research Propositions. *Journal of Marketing* 60: 73–88.

Kraske, Jochen, et al. (1996). *Bankers with a Mission: The Presidents of the World Bank, 1946–91.* New York: Oxford University Press.

Krasner, Stephen D. (1974). Oil Is the Exception. *Foreign Policy* 14: 64–85.

——— (1978). *Defending the National Interest: Raw Materials Investments and U.S. Foreign Policy.* Princeton, NJ: Princeton University Press.

——— (1981). Power Structures and Regional Development Banks. *International Organization* 35: 303–28.

Krueger, Anne O. (1995). *Trade Policies and Developing Nations.* Washington, DC: Brookings Institution Press.

Kwitny, Jonathan (1984). *Endless Enemies: The Making of an Unfriendly World.* New York: Congdon & Weed.

Landes, David S. (1969). *The Unbound Prometheus: Technological Change and Industrial Development in Western Europe from 1750 to the Present.* New York: Cambridge University Press.

Landes, William M., and Richard A. Posner (1989). An Economic Analysis of Copyright Law. *Journal of Legal Studies* 18: 325–63.

Landau, Ralph, and Nathan Rosenberg (1992). Successful Commercialization in the Chemical Process Industries. In Nathan Rosenberg, Ralph Landau, and David C. Mowery, *Technology and the Wealth of Nations* (Stanford, CA: Stanford University Press): 73–120.

Lardy, Nicholas (1992). *Foreign Trade and Economic Reform in China, 1978–1990.* New York: Cambridge University Press.

Leebaert, Derek, ed. (1991). *Technology 2001: The Future of Computing and Communications.* Cambridge, MA: MIT Press.
——— (1995). *The Future of Software.* Cambridge, MA: MIT Press.
——— (1998. *The Future of the Electronic Marketplace.* Cambridge, MA: MIT Press.
Lerner, Josh (1995). Patenting in the Shadow of Competitors. *Journal of Law and Economics* 38: 463–95.
Levitt, Barbara, and James G. March (1988). Organizational Learning. *Annual Review of Sociology* 14: 319–40.
Lipson, Charles (1985). *Standing Guard: Protecting Foreign Capital in the Nineteenth and Twentieth Centuries.* Berkeley, CA: University of California Press.
Malone, Michael S. (1995). *The Microprocessor: A Biography.* New York: Springer-Verlag.
Mansfield, Edwin (1986). Patents and Innovation: An Empirical Study. *Management Science* 32: 173–81.
——— (1995). Intellectual Property Protection, Direct Investment, and Technology Transfer: Germany, Japan, and the United States. Discussion Paper 27. Washington, DC: International Finance Corporation, World Bank. First circulated in 1992 as Unauthorized Use of Intellectual Property: Effects on Investment, Technology Transfer and Innovation. Unpublished paper. University of Pennsylvania, Philadelphia.
Maskus, Keith (1990). Normative Concerns in the International Protection of Intellectual Property Rights. *World Economy* 13: 387–410.
Mattli, Walter, and Anne-Marie Slaughter (1998). Revisiting the ECJ. *International Organization* 52: 177–210.
Meinhardt, Peter (1946). *Inventions, Patents, and Monopoly.* London: Stevens & Sons.
Merges, Robert P. (1988). Commercial Success and Patent Standards: Economic Perspectives on Innovation. *California Law Review* 76: 805–76.
Merges, Robert P. and Richard R. Nelson (1990). On the Complicated Economics of Patent Scope. *Columbia Law Review* 90: 839–916.
——— (1994). On Limiting or Encouraging Rivalry in Technical Progress: The Effect of Patent Scope Decisions. *Journal of Economic Behavior and Organizations* 25: 1–24.
Methe, David T. (1991). *Technological Competition in Global Industries: Marketing and Planning Strategies for American Industry.* Westport, CT: Qurum Books.
Miller, Arthur (1993). Copyright Protection for Computer Programs, Databases, and Computer-Generated Works: Is Anything New since CONTU? *Harvard Law Review* 106:978–1073.
Moran, Theodore H. (1998). *Foreign Direct Investment and Development: The New Policy Agenda for Developing Countries and Economies in Transition.* Washington, DC: Institute for International Economics.
Mowery, David C., ed. (1996). *The International Computer Software Industry: A Comparative Study of Industry Evolution and Structure.* New York: Oxford University Press.
Mowery, David C., and Nathan Rosenberg, eds. (1989). *Technology and the Pursuit of Economic Growth.* New York: Cambridge University Press.

McCraw, Thomas K., ed. (1997). *Creating Modern Capitalism: How Entrepreneurs, Companies, and Countries Triumphed in Three Industrial Revolutions.* Cambridge, MA: Harvard University Press.

Murtha, Thomas P. (1991). Surviving Industrial Targeting: State Credibility and Public Policy Contingencies in Multinational Subcontracting. *Journal of Law, Economics, and Organization* 7: 117–43.

National Research Council and the World Bank (1995). *Marshaling Technology for Development.* Washington, DC: National Academy Press.

National Science Board (1996). *Science and Engineering Indicators 1996.* Washington, DC: National Science Foundation.

Negroponte, Nicholas (1995). *Being Digital.* New York: Alfred A. Knopf.

Nelson, Joan M., ed. (1990). *Economic Crisis and Policy Choice: The Politics of Adjustment in the Third World.* Princeton, NJ: Princeton University Press.

Nelson, Richard R., and Sidney G. Winter. (1982). *The Evolutionary Theory of Economic Change.* Cambridge, MA: Harvard University Press.

North, Douglass C. (1989). Institutions and Economic Growth: An Historical Introduction. *World Development* 17: 1319–32.

——— (1990). *Institutions, Institutional Change, and Economic Performance.* New York: Cambridge University Press.

Okimoto, Daniel I. (1989). *Between MITI and the Market: Japanese Industrial Policy for High Technology.* Stanford, CA: Stanford University Press.

Ordover, Janus A. (1991). A Patent System for Both Diffusion and Exclusion. *Journal of Economic Perspectives* 5: 43–60.

Organisation for Economic Cooperation and Development [OECD] (1987). *International Technology Licensing: Survey Results.* Paris: OECD.

Ostrom, Elinor (1995). New Horizons in Institutional Analysis. *American Political Science Review* 89: 174–78.

Paine, Lynn Sharpe (1991). Trade Secrets and the Justification of Intellectual Property: A Comment on Hettinger. *Philosophy and Public Affairs* 20: 247–63.

Pack, Howard, and Kamal Saggi (1997). Inflows of Foreign Technology and Indigenous Technological Development. *Review of Development Economics* 1: 81–98.

Pakes, Ariel, and Margaret Simpson (1989). Patent Renewal Data. *Brookings Papers: Microeconomics:* 331–73. Washington, DC: Brookings Institution Press.

Patel, Pari, and Keith Pavitt (1991). Large Firms in the Production of the World's Technology: An Important Case of "Non-Globalization." *Journal of International Business Studies* 22: 1–21.

Pearson, Margaret M. (1991). *Joint Ventures in the People's Republic of China.* Princeton, NJ: Princeton University Press.

Piore, Michael J., and Charles F. Sable. (1984). *The Second Industrial Divide: Possibilities for Prosperity.* New York: Basic Books.

Porter, Michael E. (1990). *The Competitive Advantage of Nations.* New York: Free Press.

Prahalad, C.K., and Gary Hamel (1990). The Core Competence of the Corporation. *Harvard Business Review* 68, 6: 79–91.

Primo Braga, Carlos A. (1995a). The Economic Justification for the Grant of Intellectual Property Rights: Patterns of Convergence and Conflict. Paper presented at the Public Policy and Global Technological Integration Symposium, Kent College of Law, Illinois Institute of Technology, Chicago, IL (October 1995).

———— (1995b). Trade-Related Intellectual Property Issues: The Uruguay Round Agreement and Its Economic Implications. In Will Martin and L. Alan Winters (eds.), *The Uruguay Round and the Developing Economies* (Washington, DC: World Bank): 381–411.

Pucik, Vladimir, Noel M. Tichy, and Carole K. Barnett, eds. (1992). *Globalizing Management: Creating and Leading the Competitive Organization*. New York: John Wiley & Sons.

Riggs, Fred W. (1963). Bureaucrats and Political Development. In Joseph LaPalombara (ed.), *Bureaucracy and Political Development* (Princeton, NJ: Princeton University Press): 120–67.

———— (1964). *Administration in Developing Countries: The Theory of Prismatic Society*. Boston: Houghton Mifflin.

Riskin, Carl (1987). *China's Political Economy: The Quest for Development since 1949*. New York: Oxford University Press.

Rodwin, Lloyd, and Donald A. Schon, eds. (1994). *Rethinking the Development Experience: Essays Provoked by the Work of Albert O. Hirschman*. Washington, DC: Brookings Institution Press and Cambridge, MA: Lincoln Institute.

Rosenberg, Nathan, Ralph Landau, and David C. Mowery, eds. (1992). *Technology and the Wealth of Nations*. Stanford, CA: Stanford University Press.

Rosenberg, Nathan, and Richard R. Nelson (1994). American Universities and Technical Advance in Industry. *Research Policy* 23: 323–48.

Samuelson, Pamela, *et al.* (1994). A Manifesto Concerning the Legal Protection of Computer Programs. *Columbia Law Review* 94: 2308–431.

Scherer, F.M. (1992). *International High-Technology Competition*. Cambridge, MA: Harvard University Press.

Scott, James C. (1972). *Comparative Political Corruption*. Englewood Cliffs, NJ: Prentice–Hall.

Sell, Susan K. (1995). Intellectual Property Protection and Antitrust in the Developing World: Crisis, Coercion, and Choice. *International Organization* 49: 315–50.

Shapiro, Carl, and Hal R. Varian (1999). *Information Rules: A Strategic Guide to the Network Economy*. Boston, MA: Harvard Business School Press.

Sherwood, Robert M., and Carlos A. Primo Braga. (1996). Intellectual Property, Trade and Economic Development: A Road Map for the FTAA Negotiations. North-South Agenda Papers 21. University of Miami, Florida.

Sjoholm, Fredrik (1996). *International Transfer of Knowledge: The Role of International Trade and Geographic Proximity*. Weltwirtschaftliches Archiv 132: 97–115.

Sklar, Martin J. (1988). *The Corporate Reconstruction of American Capitalism, 1890–1916: The Market, the Law, and Politics*. New York: Cambridge University Press.

———— (1992). *The United States as a Developing Country: Studies in U.S. History in the Progressive Era and the 1920s*. New York: Cambridge University Press.

Skolnikoff, Eugene B. (1993). *The Elusive Transformation: Science, Technology, and the Evolution of International Politics*. Princeton, NJ: Princeton University Press.

Shihata, Ibrahim F.I. (1991). *The World Bank in a Changing World: Selected Essays*. Boston, MA: Martinus Nijhoff.

Smith, W. Rand (1993). International Economy and State Strategies: Recent Work in Comparative Political Economy. *Comparative Politics* 25: 351–72.

Stewart, Thomas A. (1997). *Intellectual Capital: The New Wealth of Organizations*. New York: Doubleday.

Stern, Nicholas (1989). The Economics of Development: A Survey. *Economic Journal* 99: 597–685.

Stiglitz, Joseph E. (1974). Incentives and Risk Sharing in Sharecropping. *Review of Economic Studies* 41: 219–55.

——— (1989). Markets, Market Failures, and Development. *American Economic Review* 79: 197–203.

Stiglitz, Joseph E., and Lyn Squire (1998). International Development: Is It Possible? *Foreign Policy* 38: 138–51.

Stiglitz, Joseph E., and Andrew Weiss (1981). Credit Rationing in Markets with Imperfect Information. *American Economic Review* 71: 393–410.

Suchman, Marc C. (1989). Invention and Ritual: Notes on the Interrelation of Magic and Intellectual Property in Preliterate Societies. *Columbia Law Review* 89: 1264–94.

Teece, David J. (1987). Profiting from Technological Innovation: Implications for Integration, Collaboration, Licensing, and Public Policy. In David J. Teece (ed.), *The Competitive Challenge: Strategies for Industrial Innovation and Revival*: 185–219.

Thurow, Lester C. (1997). Needed: A New System of Intellectual Property Rights. *Harvard Business Review* 75, 5: 94–107.

United Nations Commission on Transnational Corporations [UNCTC] (1989). *New Issues in the Uruguay Round of Multilateral Trade Negotiations*. E.90.II.A.15. New York.

——— (1990. *The Determinants of Foreign Direct Investment: A Survey of Evidence*. E.92.II.A.2. New York.

United Nations Conference on Trade and Development [UNCTAD] (1986). Period Report 1986: Policies, Laws, and Regulations on Transfer, Application, and Development of Technology. TD/B/C.6/133. Geneva.

United States Trade Representative (various dates). "Special 301" on Intellectual Property. Annual press releases. Washington, DC. (Note: "Special 301" is the annual review of country-by-country intellectual property policies announced by the Office of the United States Trade Representative under authority of the Section 301 trade policy. Under Special 301, the United States administration announces its bilateral and multilateral negotiation agenda for the year to follow.)

Utterback, James M., and Fernando F. Suarez (1993). Innovation, Competition, and Industry Structure. *Research Policy* 22: 1–21.

Valenzuela, J. Samuel, and Arturo Valenzuela (1978). Modernization and Dependency: Alternative Perspectives in the Study of Latin American Underdevelopment. *Comparative Politics* 10: 535–57.

Valor, Josep, W. Earl Sasser, and Cate Reavis (1997). Information at the World Bank: In Search of a Technology Solution. *Harvard Business School Cases.* Boston, MA.

von Hippel, Eric (1987). Cooperation between Rivals: Informal Know-How Trading. *Research Policy* 16: 291–302.

Wade, Robert (1990). *Governing the Market: Economic Theory and the Role of Government in East Asian Industrialization.* Princeton, NJ: Princeton University Press.

Wallace, Cynthia Day (1992). Foreign Direct Investment in the Third World. In Cynthia Day Wallace (ed.), *Foreign Direct Investment in the 1990s* (Washington, DC: Center for Strategic and International Studies).

Walsh, Vivien (1984). Invention and Innovation in the Chemical Industry: Demand Pull or Discovery Push? *Research Policy* 13: 211–34.

Waterbury, John (1993). *Exposed to Innumerable Delusions: Public Enterprise and State Power in Egypt, India, Mexico, and Turkey.* New York: Cambridge University Press.

Weingast, Barry R. (1997). The Political Foundations of Democracy and the Rule of Law. *American Political Science Review* 91: 245–63.

Williamson, John, ed. (1983). *IMF Conditionality.* Washington, DC: Institute for International Economics.

Williamson, Oliver (1996). *The Mechanisms of Governance.* New York: Oxford University Press.

Wilson, Dick (1992). Benefits and Beggars: The GSP Is Complicated, Unpredictable, and Controlled Essentially by Importers. *Far Eastern Economic Review* (March 19): 44.

World Bank (1993). *The East Asian Miracle: Economic Growth and Public Policy.* New York: Oxford University Press.

—— (1997). *World Development Report 1997: The State in a Changing World.* New York: Oxford University Press.

—— (1998). *World Development Report 1998: Knowledge for Development.* New York: Oxford University Press.

Ziegler, J. Nicholas (1995). Institutions, Elites, and Technological Change in France and Germany. *World Politics* 47: 341–72.

Zysman, John (1983). *Governments, Markets, and Growth: Financial Systems and the Politics of Industrial Change.* Ithaca, NY: Cornell University Press.

Impact of the International Patent System on Productivity and Technology Diffusion

WALTER PARK

Why should developing nations provide stronger patent protection? What is in it for them? The purpose of this paper is to gauge some of the economic benefits of increased patent protection. Does increased patent protection, for instance, stimulate international diffusion of technology and productivity growth? This paper provides *empirical evidence* that suggests that it does. Until now, most studies investigating the economic effects of patent protection have been largely theoretical in nature or have assumed channels by which patent protection affects economic performance (See, for example, Diwan and Rodrik 1991; Helpman 1993; Taylor 1994).

The empirical analysis of this chapter determines the extent to which patent protection matters to research and development (R&D) and to international patenting and, thus, to productivity growth. International patenting activity is an important source of the international diffusion of technology: it involves not only the diffusion of new products and processes but also "knowledge spillovers" from the information *disclosed* by inventors in exchange for the patent protection they receive.

There has been much international policy debate about the costs and benefits of strengthening patent régimes in developing economies

Notes will be found on page 64.

47

(the "South"). Strengthening, on the one hand, reduces the ability of the South to imitate foreign technologies important to their development. On the other hand, it should better enable the South to attract new technologies from the developed economies (the "North") and to foster a domestic (i.e. innovative rather than imitative) research sector.

There exist few studies on the impact of patent protection on international patenting. Two previous studies that investigate this issue are Bosworth 1984 and Eaton and Kortum 1996. Bosworth studies patent applications to and from the United Kingdom using a cross-sectional sample for 1974 and finds that patent law differences across countries do not in any significant fashion explain patenting to and from the United Kingdom. Eaton and Kortum study the determinants of patenting and productivity for a cross-section of OECD countries for 1990 and find that strong patent protection does significantly stimulate patenting. This study differs from these previous studies in the following respects. First, this paper has a larger sample of countries, including both developed and developing nations. This helps capture any bias derived from the sample in studying the economic effects of patent protection. Second, this paper uses a different measure of patent protection, which has both a time-series and a cross-sectional dimension. The time-series part helps to capture changes in patent law over time (particularly since standards have changed for a number of countries). Previous measures of patent protection have constrained research to cross-sectional analyses. For example, Eaton and Kortum (1996) use the Rapp and Rozek (1990) index, which describes the state of patent laws in 1984.

There also exist few studies on the effects of patent protection on economic growth. One study that investigates this issue is Gould and Gruben (1996), from which this study differs in two respects. First, Gould and Gruben also uses the Rapp and Rozek index. Second, Gould and Gruben attempt to estimate the "direct" effect of patent rights on long-run productivity. This study focuses on the "indirect" effects of patent rights on growth via their effects on factor accumulation. Gould and Gruben (1996) essentially find that, once other growth variables are controlled for, patent laws are not directly statistically significant determinants of growth but that they interact with the "openness" variable in contributing to growth. That is, countries that trade more and have strong patent laws tend (in general) to grow faster. From this result, it is not clear by what channel stronger patent laws promote economic growth. Do they, for instance, encourage economies to be more open?

This chapter is organized as follows: section 1 describes how the measure of the strength of patent protection is constructed; section 2 describes some sample statistics of patenting, research intensity, and patent protection in Latin America; section 3 presents the empirical findings on the effects of patent protection on the international diffusion of technology (using international patenting data); section 4 presents the empirical findings on the effects of patent protection on economic growth; and section 5 concludes.

1 Measurement of patent rights

This section describes how patent-rights protection is measured. Information was obtained directly from national patent laws. The index of patent rights (PR) takes on values between 0 and 5, higher numbers reflecting stronger levels of protection.

The index consists of five categories: (i) coverage, (ii) membership in international patent agreements, (iii) provisions for loss of protection, (iv) enforcement mechanisms, and (v) duration. Each category takes on a value between 0 and 1 and the sum of these five values gives the overall value of the PR for a particular country.

Except for category (v) duration (which is elaborated below), each category consists of *several conditions*, which, if they exist in a country, indicate a strong level of protection in that category. The "scoring technique" is as follows. If there are three conditions in a category and given that each condition is of a binary character (yes, it exists or no, it does not), the value assigned to this category is the fraction of conditions met. As an example, if the value of enforcement is two-thirds, this indicates that the country satisfies two of the three conditions needed for strong enforcement.

(i) Coverage

There are seven conditions referring to whether the following are patentable: (1) utility models (i.e. improved utilization of objects, typically minor inventions such as tools); (2) pharmaceutical products; (3) chemical products; (4) food; (5) plant and animal varieties; (6) surgical products; and (7) microorganisms. A country that provides patent protection for all seven kinds of inventions receives a value of one, those that provide for two receive a value of two-sevenths.

(ii) Membership in international agreements

The three major agreements are: (1) the Paris Convention of 1883 (and subsequent revisions), (2) Patent Cooperation Treaty of 1970 (PCT), and (3) the International Convention for the Protection of New Varieties of Plants of 1961 (UPOV). Countries that are signatories to all three receive a value of 1 in this category; those that are signatories to just one receive a value of one-third.

The Paris Convention provides for national treatment to foreign nationals in the provision of patent rights—that is, it provides for non-discriminatory treatment. The main objective of the Patent Cooperation Treaty is to facilitate administrative procedures in applications for patents. It allows the filing of a single patent application that can be made effective in patent offices in any of the member countries. The UPOV confers plant breeder's rights, a form of protection similar to a patent. This treaty obliges its signatories to adopt common standards and scope of protection as national law, helping to make application procedures and laws much more clear and non-discriminatory.

(iii) Loss of Protection

This category measures protection against losses arising from three sources: (1) "working" requirements, (2) compulsory licensing, and (3) revocation of patents. A country that protects against all three receive a value of 1 in this category.

Working requirements refer to the exploitation of inventions (or utilization of patents). The authorities may, for example, require that a good based on the patent be manufactured or, if the patent is granted to a foreigner, that a good be imported into the country. Some countries impose conditions that inventions must be working by a certain period of time. Compulsory licensing requires patentees to share exploitation of the invention with third-parties, and usually works to limit the capacity of patent holders to appropriate the returns from their inventions (particularly if compulsory licensing is imposed within a short time after a patent is granted). Finally there are countries that may revoke patents entirely, usually if they are not working.

(iv) Enforcement

Laws are not effective without adequate mechanisms for their enforcement. In this category, the pertinent conditions are the availability of (1) preliminary injunctions, (2) contributory infringement pleadings, and (3) burden-of-proof reversals. A country that provides all three receives a value of 1 for this category.

Preliminary injunctions are pre-trial actions that require individuals to cease an alleged infringement. Preliminary injunctions are a means of protecting the patentee from infringement until a final decision is made in a trial. Contributory infringement refers to actions that do not in themselves infringe a patent right but cause or otherwise result in infringement by others. In short, contributory infringement makes third-party participants liable as infringers. Burden-of-proof reversals are procedures that shift the burden of proof in process patent infringement cases from the patentee to the alleged infringer. In light of the difficulty that patentees have in proving that others are infringing on their patented processes (because there are often several means of producing the same product), the shift in burden can be a powerful enforcement mechanism.

(v) Duration

The length of the patent term is important for ensuring adequate returns to innovative activity. Here, a country receives a 1 if it provides the minimum duration recommended by the United States Chamber of Commerce (USCC). The minimum duration is 17 years from the date of patent grant or 20 years from the date of patent application. Countries that give less than this minimum duration receive a value equal to the fraction of the minimum standard provided, and countries that give more than the minimum duration are assigned a value of 1.

2   Sample statistics with emphasis on Latin America

Table 1 (page 65–66) presents sample statistics for some Latin American economies. In particular, the table shows real GDP per capita in this region, the PR levels, patent filing costs, R&D intensities, and patenting activities within this region. In general, the level of patent rights here is low (relative to that of the industrialized world, which typically scores above 3.5).Since the signing of the TRIPS agreement, however, several countries have significantly strengthened their patent régimes (in particular, Brazil, Colombia, Mexico, Peru, and Venezuela). In general also, the R&D intensities are low in this region, where typically less than 1 percent of GDP is devoted to research and development. However, there has been a significant rise in the share of GDP going to R&D in countries like Chile, Mexico, and Peru. In addition, patenting costs are quite high in this region (the next section describes in detail how the patent filing costs were derived). This is likely due to the cost of translating patent documents into Spanish or Portuguese.

The major patenting nations in this region are Brazil and Mexico. In 1995, Brazil filed almost 3,000 domestic patents, which is comparable to the number filed domestically by countries like Austria and Denmark. Brazil and Mexico are also the favoured patent destinations in this region. Mexico, for instance, in 1995 attracted nearly 5,000 patent applications from abroad, and an additional 18,431 PCT applications from abroad (i.e. international applications filed through the World Intellectual Property Bureau). Mexico in turn filed 99 of its inventions in the United States for patent protection in that same period, and an additional seven via the PCT. Brazil filed 115 applications in the United States in 1995 and an additional 62 via the PCT. Brazil's use of the PCT to gain foreign patent protection has increased since the mid-1980s.

Chile has experienced an increase in the inflow of foreign patent applications from abroad; e.g. foreign filings in Chile in 1995 are more than double those in 1990.

These data show low but *rising* levels of patenting and research activities in Latin America, as well as a gradual strengthening of patent rights. The next two sections empirically investigate the effects of this strengthening on international patenting, research, and productivity growth.

3   Patent protection and international diffusion of technology

The purpose of this section is to estimate the effects of patent protection on the international diffusion of technology, using international patenting data to measure the diffusion of inventive knowledge internationally. The empirical results show that the index of patent rights (PR) is a significant determinant of international patenting, even after controlling for other important determinants of patenting (e.g. market size, patent filing costs).

A panel data set of 16 source countries and 40 destination countries was assembled for four time periods: 1975, 1980, 1985, and 1990. "Source" countries refer to the countries from which patent applications emanate and "destination" countries to the countries in which patent applications are filed. Before presenting the empirical results, a few words on the equation to be estimated and the data to be used.

The estimation equation relates the patenting propensity of the source country to various destination factors, like the strength of patent protection. Each source country has a certain number of patentable inventions, and has a choice of 40 foreign markets (or "destinations") in which to file patent applications. In any one destination, the source country may file applications for all of its inventions, for some of them, or none of them. In general, the higher the quality of inventions and the more attractive the destination is in terms of market size, levels of patent protection, and other factors, the greater the fraction of inventions that will be patented in that destination. Thus, the estimation equation in this section relates the fraction of source country inventions that are patented in a destination to the legal and economic characteristics of the destination country.

The reasoning is as follows: assume that a particular source country has $q = 1, \ldots, Q$ inventions, and assume that those inventions are sorted in increasing order of quality; that is, invention 2 is of higher quality than invention 1 and so on. An invention is patented if the value of patenting in a destination (in terms of an increase in the discounted present value of profits) exceeds the patent filing costs. Let q^* be the quality level of that source country invention that breaks even—i.e. the benefit of patenting that invention just equals the cost of patenting it. Then, all inventions whose quality level exceeds q^* will be patented, and those whose quality levels follow below q^* will not be. More precisely, $F = 1 - (q^*/Q)$ is the fraction of Q inventions that will be patented in a destination. Now, holding the quality of inventions constant, this fraction will be higher the more attractive a destination is in terms of market size, patent filing costs, patent protection levels, and so forth because the more attractive a destination is, the lower the threshold q^*—that is, inventions of even lower quality will become profitable to patent.

Thus the basic equation to estimate is:

$$\log(F_{jnt}) = \log(x_{nt})'b_j + e_{jnt}, \qquad\qquad (Equation\ 1)$$

where F denotes the fraction of inventions from source country j (where $j = 1, \ldots, 16$) that are patented in destination n (where $n = 1, \ldots, 40$), $t = 1, \ldots, 4$ denotes the four time periods (i.e. 1975, 1980, 1985, and 1990), and x denotes the vector of destination factors (or explanatory variables). The error term e is motivated by the fact that some profitable inventions fail to be patented, while some unprofitable ones are patented. This is the case either if inventors file (or fail to file) unprofitable (profitable) patent applications or if substantive law differences across destinations result in differences in examination standards.

The error term could also be influenced by specific *destination* and *source* country effects; that is, $e_{jnt} = a_n + l_j + u_{jnt}$, where the u_{jnt}'s are orthogonal and spherical disturbances. The destination effects may be either fixed or stochastic. The source country effects may be reflected in the intercept, error term, or in the slopes. Hence, in what follows, two types of samples are considered. The first is a pooled sample (where all 16 sources countries are pooled) in which the source country heterogeneities are reflected in "intercept" dummies. The second type splits the sample by individual source countries in which source country heterogeneities can be reflected in the coefficient estimates ("slopes"). Moreover, as will be explained later, the individual source country sample allows for an interdependent (cross-source country) error structure.

The explanatory variables (i.e. the x's in equation (1)) are the destination's market size (as proxied by GDP per capita (GDPC) measured in real 1992 PPP adjusted US dollars),[1] the index of patent rights (PR), share of scientists and engineers in the workforce (S&E), and cost of filing patents (PCOST). The number of scientists and engineers per 10,000 workers is used as a crude measure of the capacity of a country to imitate.[2] A European Patent Office (EPO) dummy is also included, which will equal 1 if the destination country belongs to the EPO. An EPO destination is attractive to the extent that it is easier, by design, to add an extra designation to a European patent application than to make a separate application to another state. There may also be time effects (due to technological progress or globalization) that influence trends in foreign patenting. Hence, a time trend (TIME) is also included as a regressor.

International patenting data are from the World Intellectual Property Office's (WIPO) *Industrial Property Statistics*, 1975 to 1990.[3] The PR measure used is the one constructed earlier. The patent cost variable must also be constructed since international patent filing cost data are not widely available. Patenting costs include official filing fees, translation fees, and agent fees. Helfgott (1993) provides estimates of patent filing costs for 28 countries in 1992; the measured filing costs refer to a particular type of invention (e.g. one that allows ten claims, 20 pages of specification, two sheets of drawing, is drafted in English, and has a corporate assignee). Most importantly, the filing costs are from an American applicant's point of view. The estimated filing cost of $690 (in real 1992 US dollars) in Canada need not be the filing cost faced by German or Chilean applicants in Canada.

To generate patent costs for more than the sample covered in Helfgott (1993), and for applicants from countries other than the United States, an equation is first estimated that best fits the patent filing costs data in Helfgott 1993. The fitted equation is then used to predict patent filing costs for all of the required bilateral country pairs. As determinants of filing costs, geographic distance from the United States (and its square) and linguistic similarity with the United States were used. The reason is that the bulk of filing costs is due to translation. Thus, the more similar the languages between two countries, the less expensive it would be to apply for patents in each other's markets. Filing in a foreign market is also likely to be affected by geographic distance, reflecting transportation costs and perhaps differences in economic structure (regulations, customs, and practices), which may make patenting in foreign jurisdictions costly.

Based on Helfgott's original sample of 28 countries, the following regression results were obtained (equation 2):

(*Equation 2*)

$$\log (Patent\ Costs) = -22.17 + 7.57 \log Dist - 0.47^* (\log Dist)^2 - 0.032 \log Ling,$$

(7.5)   (1.81)   (0.11)   (0.015)

(Adj. R^2 = 0.51, Standard Error of the Regression = 0.51)

where standard errors are in parentheses. The two variables (Distance and the Index of Linguistic Similarity) have the expected effects on patent costs, where *Dist* denotes "distance" and *Ling*, "Linguistic Similarity." Distance, however, affects filing costs up to a point. Beyond that (at longer distances), inventors are likely to find ways to reduce global filing costs, such as multiple patent filings (to spread the costs of filing among several destinations) or (if a transnational corporation) establish a corporate patenting branch in a foreign office.

With the above fitted equation, patent costs between any pair of source and destination countries can be generated, as distance and linguistic similarity data are widely available.[4] The data thereby generated are the measure of patent filing costs. The generated costs are in real 1992 US dollars. To obtain time-series estimates of patent filing costs for 1975, 1980, 1985, and 1990, the GDP deflator (where 1992 = 100) was used for each country to infer the filing costs for those years in real 1992 US dollars.[5] For example, if the 1975 deflator = 50, the 1975 filing cost figure was considered to be half the 1992 estimate. This approach, however, assumes no "real" changes in filing costs. To allow for them, the cost figures were adjusted upward by the real GDP per capita growth rates (that is, each cost figure was multiplied by one plus the destination's real GDP per capita growth rate in that period). The working assumption here is that the growth in demand for patenting resources (and consequent rise in real filing costs) parallels the growth in market size.

The empirical results are in tables 2 and 3. Table 2 presents estimates of equation (1) for the aggregate (pooled) sample and table 3 for the disaggregated sample, source-country by source-country.

Pooled sample

Table 2 (page 67) presents the panel-data estimates for the aggregate sample. In this case, the bj's are assumed to be the same for all j source countries. The regressors (i.e. x_n's) all have the expected signs and are statistically significant at conventional levels, except for the ratio of scientists and engineers to the workforce (which has a significance level exceeding 5 percent). The results also show the advantage of applying in European Patent Office (EPO) destinations. Controlling for EPO destinations causes the coefficient estimates of the index of patent rights (PR) to be lower. The coefficient estimate of logPR in all cases is greater than 1, indicating a highly elastic response; that is, a 1 percent increase in the level of patent rights, holding everything else constant, raises the rate of foreign patenting by more than 1 percent. However, it would not be proper to interpret this as a type of increasing return since in order to determine the "return," information is needed on what it costs to strengthen patent rights by 1 percent and on the benefits from foreign patents.

An F-test rejects the null of no individual effects and a c^2-test finds the random effects estimates (RE) not to be consistent (the individual effects indeed are correlated with the RHS variables). There are likely to be a number of omitted destination factors that are important to the foreign patenting decision and that correlate with the market size and level of development of nations (factors such as political rights, property rights in general, and level of institutional development, particularly of their patent offices and administration). There is also a high degree of serial correlation in the residuals, which is consistent with the omission of important variables. Thus the rest of this paper focuses on the fixed effects (FE) estimates.

Country-by-country sample

Equation (1) is now estimated separately for individual source countries, so as to see how reactions of source countries to destination factors can vary. However, the individual source-country equations are estimated as a *system of equations* because the disturbances in the foreign patenting equations (e.g. between e_{int} and e_{jnt}, for source countries i and j) are correlated due to "shocks" that are common to source countries—shocks such as international political and economic events, government policies, and increases in knowledge capital.

To incorporate these correlated disturbances, the following system is estimated, with each equation corresponding to a source country; that is, disaggregating equation (1):

$$(Equation 1')$$

$$\log F_{AUS,\,nt} = a_{AUS,\,n} + \log (x_{nt})'\, b_{AUS} + e_{AUS,\,nt}\,, n = 1, \ldots, 40, t = 1, \ldots, 4$$
$$\log F_{CAN,\,nt} = a_{CAN,\,n} + \log (x_{nt})'\, b_{CAN} + e_{CAN,\,nt}\,, n = 1, \ldots, 40, t = 1, \ldots, 4$$
$$\vdots$$
$$\text{v}\log F_{USA,\,nt} = a_{USA,\,n} + \log (x_{nt})'\, b_{USA} + e_{USA,\,nt}\,, n = 1, \ldots, 40, t = 1, \ldots, 4$$

where, as before, the x's are the vector of destination factors, b's their corresponding parameter vector, a's the fixed effects, and e's the error term. Stacking the above equations gives a 16 by 16 system of equations. Each equation has 160 observations (where $N = 40$ and $T = 4$). While quite large, the system can be readily estimated by a conventional seemingly unrelated regression (SUR).

As there does exist significant individual (or destination) effects, as shown earlier, the SUR is combined with a fixed effects estimation (FE). In practical terms, this means that all the variables (F's and x's) were demeaned by destination unit; that is, a variable, say z_{jnt}, is replaced by $(z_{jnt} - \bar{z}_{jnt})$, where j denotes source country, n destination country, and t time. The bar above $\bar{z}$ refers to the mean of z taken over only the $T = 4$

observations for each destination unit n. The transformed dependent variable and regressors were substituted into the system of equations above, and the system then estimated by SUR (without constant terms).

The results in table 3 (pages 68–69) show how source countries vary in their sensitivity to destination factors. Foreign patenting by the United States, Germany, Japan, and Canada is highly elastic with respect to the destination's level of patent rights (the coefficients of logPR exceed 3), while that of Spain and Sweden is less elastic. Patent rights matter greatly to all but one source country, namely India.

One explanation for India's being an exception is that, since it applies for so few patents abroad, there is not much variation being captured in the data. A second explanation has to do with the fact that different sectors exhibit different sensitivities to patent protection: the pharmaceutical sector is quite sensitive (as discussed in Mansfield 1994) and Indian patents abroad were non-pharmaceutical, the domestic Indian pharmaceutical sector being largely imitative. A third explanation may be that the quality of Indian inventions was not high enough to warrant patent protection. If so, rivals are not likely to target Indian inventions for imitation. This is consistent with the finding that the only statistically significant factor here is the proxy for the capacity to imitate (log S&E). India appears to target regions (for patenting) for their ability to imitate Indian inventions, and not for the strength of their patent regimes.

As for the other regressors, GDP per capita has a significantly positive influence, except to India and New Zealand, and only moderately to Switzerland. The proxy for imitative capacity is not an important determinant of foreign patenting by France, Germany, Japan, Netherlands, New Zealand, Spain, Sweden, Switzerland, the United Kingdom, and the United States.[6] The coefficients for patent-filing costs are significantly negative for *all* the source countries. The EPO dummy is not especially significant at this country level; the variable exhibits little variability within source country samples. The EPO factor matters primarily in explaining patenting behaviour among source countries in the pooled sample.

To summarize, patent rights, patent filing costs, and market size have in general the *expected* effect on international patenting, except that of India. The serial correlation has been eliminated for all source countries but a significant degree of unexplained variance exists. Just 20 percent to 40 percent of the variation in the data is explained by the model; the remainder is due to unobserved destination fixed effects. The model is not capturing all of the other (relevant) motives for international patenting, say for corporate strategic reasons (e.g. obtaining early "priority" or blocking rival patents).

4   Patent protection and productivity growth

The key finding here is that the strength of patent rights affects economic growth by stimulating the accumulation of factor inputs like research and development capital and physical capital. The PR rating does not *directly* explain international variations in growth. What this means is that strong patent laws affect productivity growth indirectly by stimulating the accumulation of those factors (like physical capital and R&D capital) that do directly affect production. The intuition behind this result is that laws *per se* do not directly affect the technical efficiency of production but rather the environment in which research, innovation, and investment can take place.

An implication of the result that the strength of the patent system affects productivity growth through its effect on research and development is that countries that do not have an innovation sector, or have one that is limited, would be less likely to enjoy the "growth" benefits of patent laws (since the main conduit by which the index of patent rights variable (PR) affects economic growth is absent). Countries without an innovative R&D sector are likely, therefore, to attach a low priority to developing the infrastructure for providing patent rights. On the other hand, the development of an intellectual property system has the potential to attract foreign research resources and knowledge capital (via patent filings, for instance, as shown in the previous section), which should help to stimulate the creation of a *domestic* research sector. Policy authorities would then be more inclined to provide and enforce patent laws as there would be something of interest to protect. For policy-making purposes, it is useful to take into account this interdependence (i.e. endogeneity) between the intensity of domestic R&D and the level of the domestic PR rating.

The effect of property rights in general on economic growth have been studied elsewhere (see for example, Torstensson 1994 and Svennson 1994). In these studies, however, property rights are broadly defined while here the focus specifically is on the protection of intellectual property. To ensure that the PR variable is not picking up the effects of property rights in general, the empirical analysis controls for a market freedom variable that captures characteristics of a nation's overall level of property rights.

The empirical results are based on the following structural model of growth:[7]

(*Equation 3*)

(*3a*) GROWTH = G (INITIAL, INVEST, SCHOOL, R&D, NGD, PATRIGHT, MARKET)

(*3b*) INVEST = I (INITIAL, PATRIGHT, MARKET, REVOL, GOVT, EDUC)

(*3c*) SCHOOL = S (INITIAL, PATRIGHT, MARKET, REVOL, GOVT, EDUC)

(*3d*) R&D = R (INITIAL, PATRIGHT, MARKET, REVOL, GOVT, EDUC) where INITIAL denotes the log of GDP per adult worker in 1960, IN-VEST the fraction of GDP invested in physical capital, SCHOOL the fraction of GDP invested in human capital, R&D the fraction of GDP invested in research capital, and NGD the sum of the depreciation rate, population growth rate, and exogenous technical efficiency growth rate. Moreover, PATRIGHT denotes the log of the patent rights index, MARKET the log of the market freedom index, REVOL the log of 1 plus the number of revolutions, GOVT the log of the ratio of government consumption to GDP, and EDUC the log of initial secondary school attainment (in years). Data on INITIAL, GROWTH, NGD, INVEST, and GOVT are from Summers *et al.* 1995. Data on R&D are from UNESCO, MARKET from Gwartney *et al.* (1995), and REVOL and EDUC are from Barro and Lee 1994. GROWTH is the growth rate of GDP per adult worker between 1960 and 1990.

The model shows that productivity GROWTH is a function of standard explanatory factors, plus the PR variable. The explanatory factors in turn are functions of environmental factors like the PR ratings, general market freedom, political events, and the stock of human capital attainment. A few remarks on expected signs. INITIAL should have a negative effect on the rate of growth if conditional convergence occurs, and INVEST, SCHOOL, and R&D should have a positive effect to the extent that they are important factors of production. A higher rate of population growth, depreciation rate, or rate of growth in labour efficiency has a negative effect because the available stocks of capital must be spread more thinly over the population. Since few studies exist on the role of institutions in economic growth, it is difficult to sign the market freedom and patent rights variables. On the one hand, more liberalized markets and protection of legal rights should provide a positive environment for economic activity and thus be conducive to growth. On the other hand, command economies (with less free markets and rights) have also achieved (at times) high growth rates.

Regarding the accumulation equations (3b to 3d), there are two opposing effects of initial development on investment rates. On the one hand, less developed countries have smaller amounts of reproducible assets, and hence higher marginal productivities of those assets. This should make less developed countries have a higher rate of investment than the more developed. On the other hand, the market size is smaller, and hence the less developed should have a lower rate of investment than the developed. The net effect is therefore ambiguous. Higher PR ratings are expected to contribute positively to investment to the extent that they raise the incentive to invest, but may discourage investment in new plants and equipment (and new products and processes) to the extent that they grant excessive market power. Again, market freedom is difficult to sign given the present lack of empirical evidence about the role institutions play. The empirical analysis should shed light on how important "liberal" markets are to investment behaviour. Political revolutions should have a negative effect on investment to the extent that they render investments riskier. The GOVT variable captures the size of government. Larger government sizes might capture the effects of distortionary taxation or financial and resource crowding out. Finally, EDUC proxies for the initial level of education. By raising the marginal productivities of factors, a higher level of EDUC should exert a positive influence on investments.

The system 3a to 3d is also estimated by Seemingly Unrelated Regressions (SUR) in order to exploit the interrelationships among the equations. The combined results are in tables 4 and 5: table 4 (page 70) reports the growth rate equation results and table 5 (page 71) the investment equation results. In each table, there are four columns, each of which corresponds to one set of SUR estimation results. Set (1) considers a full sample of 60 countries (for which data were available) but considers only the patent rights variable as the measure of institutions. Set (2) includes other institutional and related factors (such as market freedom, political instability, government size, and initial education). It is possible that PR ratings are proxies for the effects of property rights in general and thus it is important to control for the broader measure (like MARKET). Finally, in sets (3) and (4) the full sample is split into half, and separate SUR estimates are obtained for countries whose sample average GDP per worker is, respectively, above or below the median level. This allows for an examination of whether PR ratings matter differently for developed and developing regions.

While the estimation of the growth and investment equations was done jointly, the discussion will proceed first with the growth regression results and then the accumulation regression results. Column (1) of table 4 presents the first set of results. Patent rights have no statistically significant influence on growth. Thus the model essentially reduces to a standard growth regression model, driven by reproducible factors of production. Yet this does not preclude PR ratings having an indirect effect on GROWTH through their effect on some of these reproducible factors that do contribute to growth, like R&D.

The purpose of column (2) is to introduce another measure of institutions, namely market freedom. The MARKET index includes the strength of property rights more generally (over land, wealth, and earnings). As the results show, the broader measure does contribute positively to economic growth but the narrower measure (patent protection) does not. The interpretation is that PR ratings do not augment the technical efficiency of factors of production in the act of production.

Column (3) contains estimates for the top 30 countries (in terms of the average level of GDP per worker) and column (4) contains estimates for the bottom 30. The variable PR remains insignificant while MARKET continues to be an important determinant of growth. A key difference is that R&D has a larger measured impact on growth among the richer half. Another difference is that the market freedom measure has a larger impact for the poorer half. These economies, in other words, could benefit more from a given "liberalization" of markets. This could also suggest a type of diminishing returns to improving market freedom. Once quite liberalized, further liberalization does not yield as large a return (in terms of the impact on growth).

Table 5 presents the estimates of the investment equations. The underlying theme is that patent protection is a significant determinant of physical and R&D capital accumulation, even after controlling for market freedom. Indeed, market freedom here does not help to explain investment behaviour. This suggests that the broader measure of property-rights protection does not capture the importance of the ability of investors to appropriate the returns to their investments, as does the patent rights variable. However, neither the narrower nor broader measure of property-rights protection helps explain investments in education. The reason might be that investments in basic, general education are hard to appropriate in the first place, and thus the ability to establish proprietary rights to knowledge is not a factor determining human capital accumulation.

In column (1), table 5, the other control variables are not considered. The results show that patent rights do indirectly affect growth by stimulating the accumulation of physical and research capital. The positive influence of initial GDP per worker indicates that richer countries invest more in reproducible assets, and this certainly is a factor behind cross-country divergence. Since all the variables are in logs, the coefficients can be interpreted in percentage units. For example, a 1 percent increase in the PR (making laws stronger) raises the tangible capital investment rate by 0.26 percent and the research investment rate by 0.77 percent.

In column (2), table 5, the other control factors affecting the rates of return to investment are introduced, including market freedom. The measured impact of PR changes only slightly. A 1 percent increase in the index raises the R&D investment rate by 0.8 percent and the physical capital investment rate by 0.21 percent. Here, MARKET does not contribute to factor accumulation. This suggests that the effects of market freedom work through the "organization" of markets, exchange, and production, to affect directly the technical efficiency of production, but market freedom as a whole is likely to be too broad a measure to influence the relevant rates of return to investments.

The REVOL and GOVT variables have the right sign but are not statistically significant. A higher initial stock of education capital is important to the accumulation of physical and human capital but not of R&D capital. One reason might be that R&D requires much more specialized knowledge (as embodied in, say, the stock of science and engineering education) and thus is insensitive to the initial level of basic education.

Columns (3) and (4) report estimates of the split sample. Even within groups, market freedom does not affect investment (at conventional levels of significance). Patent rights, however, explain only the physical and research capital investment behaviour of the top 30 economies. The PR variable is significant at only the 24 percent significance level for the less-developed countries' R&D investment rates. There are two possible reasons for this: (1) the PR values tend to be low in this (less developed) region and thus R&D, when it does occur, responds to different incentives; (2) much of the R&D here may be adaptive or imitative R&D (for example, in Singapore and South Korea). Patent protection is likely to matter more for R&D activities targeted towards producing new innovations. Note that the result indicates that the less-developed countries' R&D is only weakly positively influenced by patent rights. It does not indicate that it is strongly negatively influenced by PR ratings, which would be the case if all or most of their R&D were imitative for, in this case, stronger patent protection would discourage their kind of R&D.

As for the other variables, INITIAL is not important to determining physical or human capital accumulation. This is attributable to there being less variability within groups in INITIAL than between groups. The initial stock of education also exhibits low variability among the top 30 but high variability within the bottom 30 group, and is thus an important factor determining the latter's rates of return to investment in physical and human capital. Government size has a negative effect on the less-developed countries' research but a positive effect on the developed countries' research. This suggests that, in the former, a larger government size reduces R&D investment through the distortionary effects of taxation but that, in the latter, a larger government size tends to be associated with more subsidies for company and institutional research (including research in higher education). Finally, revolutions have a significantly negative effect on human capital investment only for the top 30. This is due mostly to the presence of Latin American economies in this sample, which experienced coups and assassinations. The results indicate that political instability manifested itself more in disrupting education investments than in discouraging tangible investments.

In conclusion, the split samples show that it is important to distinguish between developed and developing economies when examining the role of patent protection on growth and investment.

5 Conclusion

According to the evidence presented, stronger patent protection has the potential to improve economic growth. Stronger patent rights will not on their own contribute to growth merely by being codified into laws. Rather, they will do so by making it possible for more investment activities to occur, particularly research and development activities. The investments in tangible and intangible capital in turn stimulate long-term growth. Productivity growth is also likely to be enhanced by attracting foreign investment and technologies. The evidence on international patenting shows that stronger patent rights attract foreign patent filings. Foreign patents in turn would be a source of much technological information (through the disclosure function of patents). Moreover, possessing patent rights makes foreign firms more secure in entering into joint ventures or cooperative R&D undertakings with local firms. Access to foreign knowledge, resources, and technology is an important means for technological catch-up and source of economic growth.

Thus, the results suggest that it would very much be in the interest of developing countries to provide stronger patent rights. Stronger patent rights are instrumental in attracting foreign technology and encouraging domestic innovation. Of course, the key barriers are: (1) that some depend (or thrive) on imitation for their livelihood, and are threatened by stronger patent laws; (2) that it is costly to develop an "infrastructure" for protecting and enforcing patent laws (and providing supporting institutions for patent searching and examination, trials, and training of examiners and judges). There is also an *incentive* problem: developing countries with a weak domestic research sector (or lack of one) do not have strong incentives to incur the costs of creating a stronger patent regime and of phasing out their "imitation" sectors. Some innovative activity needs to be present—to give authorities something of interest to protect. However, a sufficiently developed domestic research (or innovation) sector, may take a long time to evolve and may not develop at all. What is perhaps more efficient is for developing nations to take advantage of the stock of technology and knowledge that already exists in the more developed, industrialized world. By linking into foreign research sectors, domestic research sectors (in developing economies) have a greater chance of evolving. But a key *incentive* in turn for the developed world to share its knowledge and resources is the protection and enforcement of patent rights. Thus, once a credible commitment to providing and enforcing patent laws is established, domestic research activities and patent protection levels could co-evolve (endogenously). It need not be the case that the process be *sequential*; that is, a country need not develop a domestic research sector first, and a strong patent regime next.

Future research should ask not whether developing countries should have strong patent protection but how patent protection can be provided in developing countries. A patent system requires resources and training (for searching and examination, administration and enforcement); it also requires a *choice* of patent laws and procedures: should a developing nation join the Patent Cooperation Treaty? Should a developing nation determine invention "priority" based on first-to-file or first-to-invent, allow pre-grant disclosure, or permit pre-trial discovery?

Another issue that all patent systems alike have to face is that of patent filing *costs*, which have increased significantly during the past decade. One component of patent filing costs is translation, and this component will continue to be important as more nations join the international patenting community. Many national offices regard their translation requirement as a matter of sovereignty. From a practical point of view, it is also the case that unless patent documents are translated, no new knowledge is "disclosed" to the local economy (in exchange for patent protection). However, from the point of view of inventors and applicants, translation is a major financial burden, and may even discourage them from seeking protection. This is, therefore, an issue for less developed countries to deal with; it may be necessary to trade off a certain amount of sovereignty (and accept imperfect knowledge disclosure) in order to encourage more patent filings from abroad.

Notes

1 GDP, population, and exchange rate data are taken from Summers, Heston, Aten, and Nuxoll 1995.
2 Data on scientists and engineers are from the UNESCO *Statistical Yearbook*, various years.
3 For 1980, patents filed through the European Patent Office (EPO) were added to the WIPO figures. Subsequent WIPO figures (after 1980) included EPO patents.
4 Data on distance and linguistic similarity are from Boisso and Ferrantino 1996.
5 Deflator data are from Summers, Heston, Aten, and Nuxoll 1995.
6 This could mean either that the capacity to imitate is not a significant determinant of foreign patenting or that log S&E is a poor proxy for the capacity to imitate for these countries.
7 Detailed derivations are in Park and Ginarte 1997.

Tables

Table 1: Patent destination characteristics, Latin America

	Patent Filing Costs	Real GDP per capita	PR Level	R&D as % of GDP	Domestic Patenting	Foreign Patenting Inflows via		Foreign Patenting Outflows to US via	
						National Route	PCT	National Route	PCT
Argentina									
1985	1,088	5,324	2.26	0.482				39	
1990	2,079	4,706	2.26	0.499				56	
1995			3.20	0.400				65	
Bolivia									
1985	2,393	1,754	1.98	0.033	5	41			
1990		1,658	1.98	0.033					
1995	4,271	2,514	1.98		17	106			
Brazil									
1985	1,397	4,017	1.85	0.600	1,954	4,565	1,858	78	10
1990	2,946	4,042	1.85	0.663	2,427	4,148	5,856	88	24
1995	7,796	4,748	3.05	0.600	2,737	3,237	19,803	115	62
Chile									
1985	1,148	3,467	2.41	0.437	122	550			
1990	2,125	4,338	2.41	0.450	169	642			
1995	4,116	9,382	2.74	0.700	171	1,535			
Colombia									
1985	2,908	2,968	1.12	0.150	72	441			
1990		3,300	1.12	0.150					
1995	6,252	5,990	3.24		141	1,093			

Table 1 continued: Patent destination characteristics, Latin America

	Patent Filing Costs	Real GDP per capita	PR Level	R&D as % of GDP	Domestic Patenting	Foreign Patenting Inflows via		Foreign Patenting Outflows to US via	
						National Route	PCT	National Route	PCT
Mexico									
1985	2,101	5,621	1.40	0.180	590	3,091	311	81	
1990	2,776	5,827	1.63	0.180	661	4,400	139	76	
1995	4,204	6,302	2.52	0.400	432	4,802	18431	99	7
Peru									
1985	852	2,565	1.02	0.282	41	211			
1990	1,707	2,188	1.02	0.283	49	219			
1995		3,549	2.37	0.600	52	565			
Uruguay									
1985	987	3,969	2.26	0.100	63	105			
1990		4,602	2.26	0.100					
1995	4,099	6,281	2.26		35	221			
Venezuela									
1985	3,572	6,225	1.35	0.393	227	1,303			
1990	3,184	6,055	1.35	0.420	262	1,090			
1995		7,608	2.75	0.500	182	1,822			

Notes: Domestic Patents are Applications by Residents; Foreign Patent Inflows (Outflows) are Patent Applications into the region (to the U.S. from this region). GDP per capita and Patent Filing Costs are in real 1992 U.S. PPP dollars; PR is the index of patent rights (Source: Ginarte and Park 1997); PCT = Patent Cooperation Treaty

Table 2: Pooled estimates of the international patenting model

Sample Size = 2560 (T=4, N=640 bilateral pairs [16 source countries x 40 destination countries])

	No EPO Effect			With EPO Effect		
	OLS	FE	RE	OLS	FE	RE
Constant	-10.3	—	-11.7	-8.77	—	-10.9
	(0.67)		(0.73)	(0.66)		(0.73)
log GDPC	0.718	1.262	0.909	0.543	1.277	0.862
	(0.068)	(0.145)	(0.075)	(0.066)	(0.144)	(0.074)
log S&E	0.252	0.149	0.150	0.312	0.144	0.169
	(0.049)	(0.077)	(0.052)	(0.046)	(0.076)	(0.051)
log PR	2.161	2.478	2.289	1.679	2.058	1.928
	(0.099)	(0.209)	(0.132)	(0.105)	(0.229)	(0.139)
log PCOST	-0.427	-0.477	-0.442	-0.398	-0.494	-0.469
	(0.049)	(0.078)	(0.056)	(0.047)	(0.077)	(0.055)
Time	0.049	0.026	0.048	-0.024	0.014	0.029
	(0.028)	(0.025)	(0.017)	(0.029)	(0.026)	(0.017)
EPO	—	—	—	1.151	0.304	0.465
				(0.072)	(0.073)	(0.069)
Adj R2	0.64	0.92	0.63	0.66	0.92	0.65
F-test	14.16			13.11		
c2-test			15.6			23.9
DW	0.223	1.298	0.222	0.270	1.305	0.235

Notes: Dependent variable is log(F). Heteroskedastic-consistent standard errors are in parentheses. DW is the Durbin-Watson statistic, F-test the statistic for testing the null of common intercepts (or of no individual effects), and c2-test the statistic for testing the null of no correlation between the individual effects and other regressors. The EPO Effect refers to advantages of filing in European Patent Office destinations. EPO = 1 (for 1980, 85, 90) if the destination is an EPO member (i.e. Austria, Den, Fra, Ger, Ita, Neth, Spain, Swe, Swit, and UK).

Table 3: System of individual countries—seemingly unrelated regression (SUR) and fixed effects (FE) estimation

	log GDPC	log S&E	log PR	log PCost	Time	EPO	DW	Adj R-sq
Australia	0.854	0.425	2.785	-1.122	0.789	0.098	1.82	0.33
	(0.447)	(0.238)	(0.888)	(0.224)	(0.169)	(0.105)		
Canada	1.517	0.545	3.668	-1.057	0.023	0.055	2.004	0.28
	(0.358)	(0.181)	(0.485)	(0.213)	(0.169)	(0.098)		
Denmark	0.806	0.573	2.439	-1.234	0.275	0.007	1.89	0.21
	(0.379)	(0.222)	(0.703)	(0.179)	(0.157)	(0.073)		
France	1.038	0.202	2.358	-1.014	0.204	0.068	2.37	0.25
	(0.355)	(0.184)	(0.501)	(0.191)	(0.149)	(0.07)		
Germany	1.433	-0.128	3.466	-1.073	-0.201	0.044	2.03	0.34
	(0.459)	(0.271)	(0.639)	(0.196)	(0.161)	(0.079)		
India	-0.262	0.482	-0.196	-0.465	0.177	0.023	2.15	0.04
	(0.227)	(0.147)	(0.341)	(0.203)	(0.102)	(0.129)		
Israel	0.868	0.629	2.739	-1.123	0.074	0.134	1.8	0.27
	(0.382)	(0.212)	(0.633)	(0.172)	(0.132)	(0.07)		
Japan	1.579	-0.106	3.774	-0.982	-0.209	0.142	2.13	0.25
	(0.488)	(0.272)	(0.695)	(0.196)	(0.165)	(0.107)		
Netherlands	1.020	-0.243	2.106	-1.217	0.019	0.078	2.16	0.22
	(0.452)	(0.298)	(0.598)	(0.174)	(0.145)	(0.085)		

Table 3continued: System of individual countries—SUR and FE estimation

	log GDPC	log S&E	log PR	log PCost	Time	EPO	DW	Adj R-sq
New Zealand	0.094	-0.307	2.774	-0.977	0.977	0.225	2.27	0.4
	(0.317)	(0.220)	(0.674)	(0.196)	(0.137)	(0.088)		
Norway	0.848	0.470	2.587	-0.749	0.285	0.061	2.06	0.24
	(0.344)	(0.211)	(0.573)	(0.204)	(0.149)	(0.091)		
Spain	0.991	0.073	1.816	-0.790	0.167	0.041	2.07	0.18
	(0.400)	(0.258)	(0.534)	(0.179)	(0.136)	(0.081)		
Sweden	0.919	0.062	1.582	-0.999	0.801	0.009	2.005	0.32
	(0.349)	(0.244)	(0.641)	(0.202)	(0.163)	(0.071)		
Switzerland	0.700	-0.237	2.799	-1.012	0.516	0.021	2.38	0.22
	(0.443)	(0.284)	(0.553)	(0.189)	(0.129)	(0.063)		
United Kingdom	1.343	0.046	2.722	-0.665	0.205	0.111	2.07	0.26
	(0.330)	(0.243)	(0.572)	(0.176)	(0.119)	(0.080)		
United States	1.531	-0.189	3.126	-1.205	0.416	0.106	1.77	0.29
	(0.441)	(0.269)	(0.623)	(0.217)	(0.132)	(0.084)		

Notes: Heteroskedastic-consistent standard errors in parentheses. Number of Equations = 16 (each corresponding to a Source Country). Number of Observations per Equation = 160 (where T = 4 and N = 40 destinations) Fixed Effects Controlled for by demeaning each variable (by destination unit) prior to SUR

Table 4: Effect of patent rights on growth

	Dependent Variable: GROWTH RATE, Average 1960–1990			
	(1)	(2)	(3)	(4)
CONSTANT	3.528	3.714	8.60	6.16
	(1.20)	(1.15)	(1.28)	(2.82)
INITIAL	-0.483	-0.485	-0.841	-0.592
	(0.073)	(0.069)	(0.093)	(0.14)
INVEST	0.537	0.657	0.26	0.71
	(0.137)	(0.134)	(0.149)	(0.197)
SCHOOL	0.196	0.125	0.422	0.097
	(0.086)	(0.087)	(0.129)	(0.119)
R&D	0.121	0.117	0.180	0.133
	(0.042)	(0.041)	(0.066)	(0.053)
NGD	-1.144	-0.861	-0.402	-0.167
	(0.352)	(0.356)	(0.275)	(0.918)
PATRIGHT	-0.045	-0.049	-0.042	-0.06
	(0.098)	(0.094)	(0.132)	(0.114)
MARKET		0.343	0.334	0.47
		(0.141)	(0.131)	(0.208)
Adj R2	0.592	0.628	0.866	0.543
No. Obs.	60	60	30	30

Notes: Standard errors are in parentheses. Estimation is by Seemingly Unrelated Regression (equation in Column x is jointly estimated with equations corresponding to column x's of Table 2, where x = 1, 2, 3, 4). Column (3) represents the above-median income sample, and column (4) the below-median income sample.

Table 5: Effect of patent rights on the dependent variables: INVESTMENT, SCHOOL and R&D (accumulation regressions) 1960–1990

	INVEST				SCHOOL				R&D			
	(1)	(2)	(3)	(4)	(1)	(2)	(3)	(4)	(1)	(2)	(3)	(4)
CONSTANT	-3.32	-2.6	-0.64	-2.53	-6.65	-6.02	-2.46	-8.01	-11.6	-12.1	-12.5	-8.5
	(0.42)	(0.5)	(0.87)	(1.2)	(0.68)	(0.79)	(0.72)	(2.15)	(1.22)	(1.5)	(1.92)	(3.6)
INITIAL	0.19	0.064	-0.19	0.11	0.49	0.29	0.011	0.47	0.7	0.68	0.75	0.12
	(0.06)	(0.07)	(0.098)	(0.17)	(0.09)	(0.11)	(0.08)	(0.29)	(0.16)	(0.21)	(0.22)	(0.49)
PATRIGHT	0.26	0.21	0.43	0.043	-0.04	-0.12	0.036	-0.15	0.77	0.8	1.5	0.47
	(0.09)	(0.096)	(0.14)	(0.13)	(0.15)	(0.15)	(0.11)	(0.23)	(0.26)	(0.29)	(0.3)	(0.39)
MARKET		-0.2	-0.04	-0.33		0.245	-0.03	0.45		0.51	0.62	-0.16
		(0.16)	(0.21)	(0.22)		(0.25)	(0.17)	(0.4)		(0.48)	(0.47)	(0.67)
REVOL		-0.29	0.04	-0.31		-0.25	-0.91	-0.16		-0.75	0.51	-0.03
		(0.98)	(0.36)	(0.44)		(0.46)	(0.29)	(0.79)		(0.88)	(0.78)	(1.32)
GOVT		-0.17	-0.13	-0.02		-0.099	0.11	-0.17		-0.09	0.65	-1.06
		(0.13)	(0.15)	(0.19)		(0.202)	(0.13)	(0.34)		(0.38)	(0.34)	(0.56)
EDUC		0.15	0.092	0.22		0.203	0.083	0.303		-0.15	0.022	-0.27
		(0.06)	(0.066)	(0.095)		(0.093)	(0.054)	(0.17)		(0.18)	(0.14)	(0.29)
Adj R2	0.36	0.43	0.39	0.34	0.37	0.47	0.46	0.43	0.45	0.47	0.75	0.14
No. Obs	60	60	30	30	60	60	30	30	60	60	30	30

Notes: Standard errors in parenthesis. Estimation is by SUR, jointly with Growth Equation. Column (3) represents the above-median income countries, and column (4) the below-median income countries.

71

References

Barro, Robert J., and Lee Jong-Wha (1994). Sources of Economic Growth. *Carnegie-Rochester Conference Series on Public Policy* 40 (June): 1–46.

Boisso, Dale and Michael J. Ferrantino (1996). Economic and Cultural Distance in International Trade: An Empirical Puzzle. Working paper. Washington, DC: U.S. International Trade Commission.

Bosworth, Derek L. (1984). Foreign Patent Flows to and from the United Kingdom. *Research Policy* 13: 115–24.

Diwan, Ishac, and Dani Rodrik (1991). Patents, Appropriate Technology, and North-South Trade. *Journal of Development Economics* 30: 27–48.

Eaton, Jonathan, and Samuel Kortum (1996). Trade in Ideas: Patenting and Productivity in the OECD. *Journal of International Economics* 40: 251–78.

Ginarte, Juan Carlos, and Walter G. Park (1997). Determinants of Patent Rights: A Cross-National Study. *Research Policy* 26, 3: 283–301.

Gould, David M., and William C. Gruben (1996). The Role of Intellectual Property Rights in Economic Growth. *Journal of Development Economics* 48: 323–50.

Gwartney, James, Robert Lawson, and Walter Block (1995). *Economic Freedom of the World: 1975–1995*. Washington and London: Cato Institute and Institute of Economic Affairs.

Helfgott, Samson (1993). Patent Filing Costs around the World. *Journal of the Patent and Trademark Office Society* (July): 567–80.

Helpman, Elhanan (1993). Innovation, Imitation, and Intellectual Property Rights. *Econometrica* 61, 6: 1247–80.

Mansfield, Edwin (1994). Intellectual Property Protection, Foreign Direct Investment, and Technology Transfer. Discussion paper no. 19. Washington, DC: International Finance Corporation of the World Bank Group.

Park, Walter G., and Juan Ginarte (1997). Intellectual Property Rights and Economic Growth. *Contemporary Economic Policy* 15 (July): 51–61.

Rapp, Richard T., and Richard P. Rozek (1990). Benefits and Costs of Intellectual Property Protection in Developing Countries. *Journal of World Trade* 24, 5: 75–102.

Summers, Robert, Alan Heston, Bettina Aten, and Daniel Nuxoll (1995). *Penn World Tables, Version 5.6*. Cambridge, MA: National Bureau of Economic Research.

Svensson, Jakob (1994). Investment, Property Rights and Political Instability: Theory and Evidence. Seminar paper no. 574. Stockholm: Institute for International Economic Studies.

Taylor, M. Scott (1994). Trips, Trade, and Growth. *International Economic Review* 35, 2: 361–81.

Torstensson, Johan (1994). Property Rights and Economic Growth: An Empirical Study. *Kyklos* 47, 2: 231–47.

UNESCO *Statistical Yearbook* (various dates). Paris: UNESCO.

World Intellectual Property Office (various dates). *Industrial Property Statistics*. Geneva: WIPO.

Intellectual Property:
A Chip Withheld in Error

ROBERT M. SHERWOOD

"We well understand the benefits that improved intellectual property protection will probably bring us, but we must resist making those improvements so we will have a bargaining chip for our trade negotiations." Public remarks made early in 1999 to this effect by an Argentine foreign ministry official responsible for his country's trade negotiations sharply etch a dilemma faced by many developing countries. Historically, the chief function of intellectual property (IP) has not been to facilitate trade. IP evolved as an investment stimulant: that is, it emerged over centuries as a means to encourage a nation's inventive people to contribute to national growth and development. Intellectual property standards were grafted onto the world's trading arrangements at the end of the Uruguay Round in 1995. This somewhat artificial linkage has tended to confuse analysis of the role of intellectual property in developing economies.

The withholding of higher levels of intellectual property protection as a bargaining chip in trade negotiations is being done, of course, in the expectation that in future international-trade negotiations, developing countries can gain advantages by withholding and bargaining with this chip. There may be some truth in this supposition, particularly to the extent that it is among a limited number of bargaining chips available to many developing countries.

However, this consideration deserves to be weighed against gains that would result from using, rather than withholding, this chip. To conduct a dynamic analysis, three observations appear relevant.

(1) While there has been a great deal of speculation and theoretical discussion, there is only limited empirical indication of what robust protection for intellectual property will produce in the economies of developing countries. At the same time, there is little solid evidence to support the alleged benefits of weak protection.

(2) Every country on earth has gifted individuals capable of inventive and creative activity at world-class levels, yet they are typically a wasted resource in countries with weak IP systems. The loss may be significant.

(3) Different levels of IP protection are possible and different things happen in an economy at different levels of protection. To make their contribution, the inventive and creative individuals may require a level of protection higher than the TRIPS Agreement, the trade-fostered IP arrangements being adopted currently by most countries.

This paper elaborates these three observations.

What we know and what we do not know

While there has been a great deal of speculation and theoretical discussion, there has been only limited empirical study of what robust protection for intellectual property might produce in the economies of developing countries. Indeed, until more of these countries shift their IP systems to high levels of protection, it will continue to be difficult to appraise the potential effect. The main candidates for such research thus far are Mexico and South Korea. They are almost alone among the developing countries in having made adjustments to their IP systems that are significant enough to merit study in depth.[1]

The seminal empirical work is that done by Edwin Mansfield for the World Bank (Mansfield 1994, 1995). His studies of the influence of IP on investor behavior in 14 developing countries found that "in relatively high-technology industries ... a country's system of intellectual property protection often has a significant effect on the amount and kinds of technology transfer and direct investment" (1995: 1). Beyond this finding, it appears valid to transport to the context of the developing countries other findings from broader economic research on the American economy begun by Robert Solow and carried forward by Mansfield.

Solow showed the importance of newly introduced technology for national economic growth. In his famous study (1957), he attributed one-half of economic growth in the United States between 1909 and 1949 to a "residual" factor later identified as largely the technology injected into the nation's industrial base over that period. Mansfield, in a series of studies (see Mansfield 1988 for overview), then showed the significant social-welfare benefit gained from the introduction of new technology. The work of these two men invites the suggestion that comparable or even greater benefits can be anticipated as higher levels of IP lead to higher private rates of return on research in developing countries. This, in turn, would lead to enhanced social-welfare rates of return there.

A specific observation is in order. Argentina is blessed with vast natural resources in agriculture. Nature has produced great wealth for the country. In an increasingly competitive global-trade setting, however, nature alone is proving less competitive. In countries with high-level IP protection, higher science is being applied to agriculture more and more, largely by private sector actors and less so by the state. The Argentine Ministry of Agriculture has not received funds sufficient to compete in the global application of biotechnology to a wide range of agricultural activities, from more advanced sheep breeding to improving the protein content of crops like soya. The issue is whether Argentina will be able to compete internationally as other countries develop improved versions of what until now have been commodity crops.

It should also be noted that there is little solid evidence to support the alleged benefits of weak protection. A review of some of the major claims for weak protection, together with suggestions for their probable lack of veracity as derived from micro-studies, is available (see Sherwood 1990). In brief, it has been claimed that weak protection saves a country money, promotes local industry, helps acquire technology, and lessens dependency. Various assumptions on which these claims rest deserve to be tested against the empirical evidence provided by a wide range of cases. It appears that these assumptions falter under this examination. It further appears that these claims were articulated after the fact to justify weakened protection.

In countries with weak protection, the political economy of intellectual-property reform deserves comment. In such countries, those interests that benefit from weak protection tend to become well organized and articulate in public discourse. In contrast, precisely because the protection is weak, few interests that typically rely on strong protection will be present. The inventive and creative local individuals are not actively contributing to national wealth; local companies do not conduct in-house research; university research results are not effectively available to increase market activity; start-up firms are not able to attract private risk capital. As a consequence, public discourse is lopsided, with only the voices that favour weak protection being heard. India may be a good current example, although the Indian film-making industry has long sought better protection for its output.

Inventive minds: a national resource

Every country on earth has gifted individuals capable of inventive and creative activity at world-class levels, yet they are typically a wasted resource in countries with weak IP systems. The "brain drain" from developing countries has long been noted but weak IP protection has seldom been highlighted as causative.

The World Development Report for 1998/99 produced by the World Bank under the title *Knowledge for Development* stressed an increasing awareness of the intrinsic economic value of knowledge. While many factors converge to support the creation, transfer, adaptation, and use of knowledge, it seems clear that intellectual property protection provides encouragement to the process which, as Mansfield found (see Mansfield 1994, 1995), is significant in developing countries.

There are abundant examples of gifted individuals in developing countries who have made inventions only to fail in their efforts to bring them to commercial usefulness because of the weak intellectual property system of their country. One telling example involves an invention by a Brazilian professor and two Americans academics. Working at the University of Florida at Gainesville, they invented a genetically altered microbe that digests the bio-waste of sugar production to produce ethanol. For this invention of potentially great significance for energy generation in sugar producing countries, the United States Patent Office awarded them United States Patent 5,000,000.

Patents were eventually obtained in five other large sugar producing countries but not in Brazil, where such inventions were not patentable at that time. Commercial development of the invention is progressing in the United States and elsewhere but not in Brazil, where this new technology could bring substantial benefits. The Brazilian co-inventor returned to Brazil and attempted to generate commercial interest among local companies in development of the process but, in the absence of local patent protection, he was unable to find any interest.

In another example from Ecuador, a small firm had been exporting cut flowers to markets in North America and Europe. The firm owners saw an opportunity to produce a new type of exportable flower through genetic modification of an existing plant that grew well in Ecuador. Just as the first field-grown test crop of the new plants was ready for harvesting, 70 plants were stolen. Without any effective means under the then-existing Ecuadorean IP system to go after the thieves and stop their infringement of the invention, the firm had to consider abandoning Ecuador. The potential to increase Ecuador's export earnings suffered an unnecessary blow.

In Costa Rica several years ago, a young computer engineer had written a spell-checking program for Spanish. It began to enjoy acceptance and commercial success locally, and in Colombia, Panama, and the Spanish-speaking communities in Miami, New York, and elsewhere. However, he could not halt rampant piracy of the program in Costa Rica because of the weakness of protection for IP at the time. His firm survived and began to grow, particularly after an upgrade of the country's IP protection, thereby adding to Costa Rica's foreign exchange earnings and providing his firm with a base from which to develop other software of commercial value to the local economy.

In Nicaragua, a local inventor hit upon the concept of a "melon saver," a simple plastic stand placed under melons as they ripen in the fields. Its function is to increase production by reducing spoilage, eliminating the need to apply pesticides to control rot. He obtained a patent in Nicaragua and also in the United States. Armed with this protection, he was able to attract the capital needed to produce the plastic stands and offer them to melon growers.

This handful of anecdotes points toward a widespread loss for developing countries that fail to encourage their own inventive people. The range of these examples and many more gathered by the author indicate dysfunctions caused in many segments of a developing country's industrial and agricultural base. The cumulative opportunity loss has not yet been measured but is likely to be found substantial.

Different things happen

Many different levels of protection are possible within the concepts of intellectual property and different things happen in an economy at different levels of protection. The implications of this observation for research conceptualization are considerable.

Between 1992 and 1996, the author made diagnoses of the intellectual property systems of 11 Latin American countries for the Inter-American Development Bank. The diagnoses were conducted from the perspective of investment facilitation. This lead to development of a numerical rating system for comparing and assessing intellectual property systems. Analyses of other countries were added to the study, for a total of 18. The countries studied to date are Argentina, Barbados, Bermuda, Brazil, Chile, Costa Rica, Ecuador, El Salvador, Guatemala, India, Mexico, Nicaragua, Panama, Pakistan, Paraguay, Peru, South Korea, and Uruguay. The study has been reported in a law review article (Sherwood 1997a) and in Spanish translation in a book (Sherwood 1997b).

The methodology involved detailed interviews with intellectual property lawyers, government officials, and users of the intellectual property systems in each country. A point system was utilized to evaluate components of each IP system: enforcement, administration, treaties and the statutory treatment of copyright, patents, trademarks, and trade secrets. An eighth component, called "life forms," was introduced to spotlight the relevance of IP to the agricultural sectors of these countries. Sub-categories were developed for each component. For example, under enforcement, an assessment was made as to whether the courts suffered from lack of judicial independence, corruption, poor formation of judges, lack of authority to effectively enforce IP rights, and so forth. A range of points was assigned to each of these categories. A total of 25 points was allocated to enforcement, 15 points to trade secret protection, and so on.

A score was derived for each country. For example, Brazil was assigned 49 of 100 points while South Korea was given 74 points. Guatemala was rated at 13 points and Chile at 62, Peru at 61, Mexico at 69, Uruguay at 48, Argentina at 39 and Panama at 36. With some caveats, the rating system was also applied to the TRIPS Agreement and a rating of 55 points was assigned. While these comparative scores are of interest, their significance in terms of economic development was derived from a cross-reference to the findings of Edwin Mansfield discussed above.

Mansfield had found that investors became concerned about their best and latest technology in relation to five levels of activity: sales and distribution, assembly of parts, manufacture of components, complete manufacture of sophisticated products, and research and development. By comparing his findings with the findings of the numerical rating system study, it was seen that when countries have IP systems that rate in the lower portion of the scale, say below a rating of 45 to 50, the economy will be characterized by sales and distribution, assembly and component manufacture. Only as a country's IP system rises above that level will more sophisticated manufacturing flourish, and only as an IP system rises to a rating of, say, 65 to 75 will local inventors be encouraged to conduct research and development.

Several observations can be made from this cross-reference to the Mansfield findings. One is that at the lower levels of IP protection, the investments a country will attract come swiftly and can leave as swiftly. Only as the IP system moves to robust levels of protection does investment in technology-producing activity become more durable. This is because the types of activity characteristic of the lower ranges of IP protection utilize facilities that can be easily abandoned and sold. At the higher levels of protection, the facilities built for sophisticated manufacturing and for research and development tend to have low salvage value—that is, they are hard to sell at a price that recovers their original cost. Thus, investors assess their risks more carefully before investing.

Another observation is that at the lower levels of intellectual property, employers are reluctant to train their employees in more than rudimentary tasks. At higher levels of protection, companies are willing, even eager, to train their people by exposing them to the cutting edge of their technology. This enriches the human-resource base of the country, essentially without public expense.

Innovation occurs at all levels of IP protection. At the lower levels of protection, however, innovation tends to be random and sporadic. At the middle levels of protection, innovation begins to occur more frequently in some fields. At the higher levels, innovation is planned and constant. Ceramics companies in Cuenca, Ecuador, for example, have reported that they do make innovations in their products and processes from time to time, but almost exclusively in response to a specific problem. These owner-managers indicated that if they believed that innovation could be protected by an effective intellectual-property system, they would gladly devote their time and their company resources to research and development of new processes and products.

Under lower levels of protection, acquisition of proprietary technology is extremely limited. In Ecuador, a textile manufacturer had licensed rudimentary process technology for thread making from firms in Scotland. After some losses of this proprietary technology through infringement without recourse to IP protection, both the licensor and licensee agreed to abandon plans for transfer of more advanced technology. Both recognized that the Ecuadorean firm would be placed at a competitive disadvantage if the newer technology were stolen and used by another Ecuadorean firm that would not pay for the advanced technology. Both firms agreed they would renew their technological cooperation after the IP system of Ecuador improved.

Protection of intellectual property facilitates numerous linkages that operate in the background of technology development. For example, if a firm wishes to collaborate with another firm in some way, it is common to enter into a preliminary agreement that permits both firms to "peek" at the technological assets of the other before entering into an agreement. One of the firms may seek inputs from the other or they may desire a joint venture to achieve some specific objective. These pre-negotiation agreements typically involve confidentiality clauses (trade-secret protection) and will commonly use patents or patent applications as a means of defining the technology that is to be brought to the negotiating table. At the lower levels of IP protection, such agreements are not viable. Consequently, technology development is stunted in a way that the public does not see. At the middle levels of IP protection, there will be some attempts to use these pre-negotiation agreements but usually only in restricted ways. At the higher levels of IP protection, firms feel relatively comfortable in relying on pre-negotiation agreements to facilitate their deal-making.

Under low levels of IP protection there is scant private investment in any kind of technology. At middle levels of protection, private investment can be found for rudimentary technology, whereas at high levels of protection, private investments in high technology become common. Private risk capital is famous for its role in generating new firms, spawning new technology, and even new industries. Many developing countries have attempted to attract this risk capital without realizing the profound relevance of IP protection for venture capital. When venture-capital firms receive applications for funding, they examine first the proposal to ascertain whether there will be adequate protection for the intellectual property involved. If not, the balance of the application will not be considered. It is not by accident that venture capital firms are all but extinct in countries with low levels of IP protection.

Artists, composers, writers, and others who generate the cultural expressions of a country cannot live on praise alone. They must eat. If their works are not protected from piracy, they starve, or they turn to other pursuits, or quite often they leave the country. As a consequence, the country loses the contribution of its potential artists. The evolution of the country's cultural expression is stunted. In subtle ways, this turns the country to reactionary attitudes, making it more difficult to embrace the flow of historical developments in all fields, including the economic and social, as well as the cultural, aspects of life. Low levels of IP protection defeat sustainable cultural expression. However, middle levels of IP protection are sufficient to stimulate cultural advancement. At the higher levels of IP protection, cultural expression is fully encouraged.

In most countries, the universities tend to concentrate some of the best minds in the country. Under low levels of IP protection, the attention given to technology in university settings tends to be theoretical and unused. At the middle levels of IP protection, a more practical orientation emerges alongside theoretical pursuits, and university generated technology begins to find application in the technical base of the country. At high levels of IP protection, university research in science and technology more frequently finds practical application in the local economy, often as graduating engineers join or create local firms that appropriate the inventions based upon university research.

At low levels of protection, the agricultural sector continues chiefly to utilize older science. At the middle levels of IP protection, the agricultural base receives some newer science but it is the higher levels of protection that appear to encourage application of the latest and best new science to the fields and farms of the country. In many developing countries, the agricultural sector remains dominant in the economy, providing employment to large elements of the population. In these countries, applying even small increments of new science to agriculture can have a significant impact on overall economic performance.

At low protection levels, the industrial base is typified by sales and distribution of imported products and by assembly operations. In the middle levels of IP protection, countries experience the manufacturing of components and simple products. Only at higher levels of IP protection is the industrial base characterized by complete manufacturing of more sophisticated products. Most important, it appears that this is the level that fosters research and development of new and improved products and processes. This is the level of IP protection required to tap the natural resource of the country's brightest minds, thereby helping to generate and introduce the new technology that, as Solow and Mansfield found, contributes significantly to economic growth and social welfare.

If nothing more, this brief survey of some of the arenas in which IP plays an influential role in economic development will perhaps serve to suggest a landscape for deeper research (for a fuller treatment, see Sherwood 1997c). The observation that different things happen at different levels of IP protection may contribute to the design of studies that seek to calibrate the influence of IP on a broad range of activities.[2]

Chips withheld: the error

On the eve of new global trade negotiations, many developing countries may feel concern because during the Uruguay Round of the GATT negotiations, they committed themselves to a package of trade arrangements that, among other things, established minimum standards for protecting intellectual property embodied in the TRIPS Agreement. They did so in the expectation that, among other things, they would gain expanded access for their agricultural products to the markets of developed countries. Because that expectation has not been entirely fulfilled, there will be a tendency toward skepticism regarding implementation of TRIPS commitments, to say nothing of hesitation regarding possible demands for new and higher standards.

Companies that operate at the global level, improve and find new products through research they conduct in countries of their choice.

They then sell those products to other countries under cover of the IP protection being established under the TRIPS Agreement. Firms and individuals in developing countries normally do not have that option. They must conduct their research and develop their products in their home country under cover of whatever protection their own IP system affords. Although such countries are moving to the TRIPS level of protection, this middle level of protection will probably not be sufficiently robust to support research and development activities there.

This raises the question whether it is sound policy for developing countries to withhold adoption of high levels of IP protection in the hope of eventual gains in their trade accounts. These would be gains largely for the export of commodity products to which there is limited value-added content. In order to add more value, it will be expedient to improve the quality of the nation's technological base, including the application of new and higher science to agriculture.

A strong argument can be made that through enhanced IP protection many developing countries will improve their ability to export. Commodity crops with improved characteristics give a greater competitive trade advantage. Trade is also expanded, of course, by more advanced products of higher quality. On balance, robust IP protection could eventually do more for export enhancement than any gains obtained from withholding this bargaining chip until the end of a prolonged trade negotiation.

Looking beyond trade enhancement, the upgrading of intellectual property protection to fairly high levels could be expected to attract more domestic and foreign private investment, facilitate the transfer and adaptation of new technology, and contribute to improved social welfare in many developing countries. Thus, it may well be a serious error to withhold higher levels of protection for intellectual property today in expectation of trade gains through international negotiation tomorrow, particularly should the upcoming round prove less productive than earlier rounds.

Notes

1 Ecuador made sweepii g improvements in its system in early 1998 but they have not been implemented.
2 Keith Maskus (forthcoming), under commission by the Institute for International Economics, will identify an exceptionally broad range of linkages between IP and patterns of activity, many of them not considered previously in studies of intellectual property. The working title of the manuscript is Intellectual Property Rights in the Global Economy.

References

Mansfield, Edwin (1988). Technical Change and Economic Growth. In Charls E. Walker, and Mark A. Bloomfield (eds.), *Intellectual Property Rights and Capital Formation in the Next Decade* (Lanham, MD: University Press of America): 3–26.

——— (1994). Intellectual Property Protection, Foreign Direct Investment, and Technology Transfer. Discussion Paper 19. Washington, DC: International Finance Corporation of the World Bank Group.

——— (1995). Intellectual Property Protection, Direct Investment, and Technology Transfer: Germany, Japan, and the United States. Discussion Paper 27. Washington, DC: International Finance Corporation of the World Bank Group.

Maskus, Keith (forthcoming). *Intellectual Property Rights in the Global Economy.*

Solow, Robert (1957). Technical Change and Aggregate Production Function. *Review of Economics and Statistics* 39: 312–20.

Sherwood, Robert M. (1990). Intellectual Property and Economic Development. Boulder, CO: Westview. Out of print but available at www.kreative. net/ipbenefits.

——— (1997a). Intellectual Property Systems and Investment Stimulation: The Rating of Systems in Eighteen Developing Countries. *37 IDEA: The Journal of Law and Technology* 2: 261–370.

——— (1997b). *Los Sistemas de Propiedad intelectual y el Estimulo a la Inversion: Evaluacion y comparacion de 18 sistemas en paises en vias de desarrollo.* Buenos Aires: Editorial Heliasta.

——— (1997c). The TRIPS Agreement: Implications for Developing Countries. *37 IDEA: The Journal of Law and Technology* 3: 491–544.

Intellectual Property Rights and the Pharmaceutical Industry

The Consequence of Incomplete Protection

WILLIAM MCARTHUR MD

Intellectual property rights (IPRs) are described as "the rights given to persons over the creations of their minds" (WTO 1999). The rights conferred give creators an exclusive right over the use of their creations for a specified period of time. These rights are administered and controlled by national legislation, within a framework of international law.

In December 1993, the Uruguay Round of negotiations on the General Agreement on Tariffs and Trade (GATT) completed an Agreement establishing the World Trade Organization (WTO). This included a subsidiary Agreement on Trade-Related Aspects of Intellectual Property Rights, Including Trade in Counterfeit Goods (TRIPS). This built on the existing multi-lateral treaties such as the Paris Convention for the Protection of Industrial Property (1883), the Berne Convention for the Protection of Literary and Artistic Works (1886), and the Treaty on Intellectual Property in Respect of Integrated Circuits (Washington, 1989), and the Patent Cooperation Treaty. Another important body in this context is the World Intellectual Property Organization (WIPO) and since the formation of the WTO there has been collaboration between these two bodies; e.g. in July 1998, in a joint press release, the

---

Note will be found on page 104.

WTO and WIPO announced a joint plan to help developing nations meet their year-2000 commitments on intellectual property.

Patent rights and data exclusivity are two separate and distinct parts of the intellectual property rights required to protect inventions such as a new chemical entity (NCE). The patent protects the inventor from others who might wish to create, use, or sell the patent during the patent period. However, the patent does not prevent another manufacturer from conducting the necessary laboratory, animal, and human tests and then applying for a license to market the product. If the second manufacturer gains access to the originator's data this creates an unfair situation because much of the original experimentation can be bypassed, thereby saving the second manufacturer a large investment. TRIPS provides for the maintenance of the originator's exclusive access to this research data.

A third right, which is not covered under TRIPS but is nevertheless important, is the right to market a product in a competitive environment without undue government regulation or control. From time to time, governments perceive the need to control prices. Various types of price control are sometimes attractive to politicians and bureaucrats because they appear to provide a simple and easy fix for prices that appear to be escalating at a rate perceived to be excessive and potentially injurious to the economy.

This paper examines these issues of intellectual property rights and the manufacturer's right to sell goods in a free competitive market. The benefits of ensuring free and fair competition will be outlined as well as some of the penalties incurred when these conditions are not adhered to.

The nature of intellectual property rights

For over a hundred years, there has been a general recognition that there must be a balance between the interests of inventors who create products or techniques and the interests of society at large: the inventors are entitled to be rewarded for their genius and creativity while society, by creating an environment within which the inventor is rewarded is also, in due course, entitled to benefit from the invention. This concept of balancing the interests of inventors with the interests of society at large has permeated the civilized world since the mid-nineteenth century. Without this arrangement, many, if not most, of the advances observed since the industrial revolution could not have occurred. Sensible manufacturers would not develop and market a product if they knew that a competitor could immediately steal the product design and begin to market it, thereby eliminating any realistic hope of reasonable reward.

These simple concepts of rewarding both inventive genius and society at large remain as valid today as they were a hundred years ago. They are the cornerstones of technological advancement throughout the world and they have become important factors in the economic development of nations.

Traditionally, Intellectual Property Rights (IPRs) have referred to copyright, design right, trademarks, and patents. All of these have an impact upon the pharmaceutical industry but most of the disputes arising around IPRs are focused on patents and patent protection. In recent years, another aspect of IPRs is beginning to assume significant proportions. This is the matter of the protection of research data accumulated during the process of obtaining regulatory approval for the marketing of a new chemical entity (NCE). This "data exclusivity" has become a matter of international concern and it appears that it may become the substance of international trade disputes within the near future.

Patent protection

Articles 27 to 34 of TRIPS set out the basic requirements for patent protection in member countries. Article 33 specifies that the basic term of patent protection is 20 years from the date of filing. This was a change for some countries, which had previously recognized the first to invent as the legitimate patent holder.

Other important aspects of the patent regulations of the TRIPS agreement include the prohibition of discrimination against foreigners and the option for countries to exclude from patent protection diagnostic and therapeutic methods for the treatment of humans, plants, or animals. In addition, member countries may require compliance with reasonable procedures but patents must be issued within a "reasonable time" so as to prevent unwarranted shortening of the period of patent protection.

Article 31 specifies certain circumstances under which a country has the right to issue compulsory licenses and make other exceptions, provided that these do not unreasonably conflict with a normal exploitation of the patent and do not unreasonably prejudice the legitimate interests of third parties. These exceptions cannot be invoked on a trivial basis and the conditions under which they can be introduced are carefully spelled out in the details of article 31. Despite the limitations, nations do have reasonable leeway, within the constraints of TRIPS, to adapt their legislation to local circumstances.

There are now 134 signatories to the WTO but not all are fulfilling the requirements of TRIPS. The European Union, Japan, the United States, and Canada are included amongst those that recognize the 20-year term of patent protection but not all these countries are free from controversy about the way in which they have implemented TRIPS. For example, Canada is presently the subject of an appeal to the WTO because of a practice known as "early working." This arrangement permits a generic manufacturer to obtain regulatory approval to produce and stockpile a patent-protected drug while the patent is still in place. This places the generic company in a position to flood the market with its product as soon as the patent expires. The European Union, the United States, and Japan do not permit "early working" and they do not permit the generic manufacturers to stockpile product prior to the expiry of the original patent. Countries opposed to this procedure claim that permitting the generic manufacturer to apply for regulatory approval during the patent period and to manufacture the product prior to expiry of the patent is a breach of patent. This matter is currently (autumn 1999) before an active panel of the WTO and the decision will provide a new and useful guideline for Canadian legislators.

Recently Japan has been the focus of interest regarding some aspects of patent rights. Prior to 1997, the Japanese courts had held that any experiment or research by a generic manufacturer to test the commercial viability of a patented invention during the term of the patent constituted a violation of the inventor's patent rights. Beginning in 1997, this interpretation of Japanese law was reversed: five decisions of the Osaka and Tokyo courts interpreted the law so as to protect the generic manufacturers rather than the original patent holders (Otsuka Pharmaceutical Co. v. Towa Yakuhin K.K., Heisei 9 [ne] 3498 [Tokyo High Ct. March 31, 1998]; Kyorin Pharmaceutical K.K., v. Sawai Pharmaceutical K.K., Heisei 9 [wa] 138 [Osaka High Ct., April 15 1997]). Japan has a $41 billion pharmaceutical market and because of this the brand-name industry has a strong interest in maintaining the patent rights of innovative companies. The industry can be expected to continue to litigate these issues until the Supreme Court of Japan conclusively resolves the permissible scope of generic manufacturers to make experimental use of information during the period of patent protection.

Patent Term Restoration (PTR) is another contentious topic. This is a procedure whereby a manufacturer is compensated with an extension in patent protection for the time taken to obtain regulatory approval. The argument is that the manufacturer has little or no control over the government's bureaucratic process and should not be penalized for the time taken by that process. The European Union, the United States, Japan, and Australia all provide for patent extension through PTR; Canada and many other countries do not. Failure to provide PTR is perceived as unjust by those countries that make this provision. Consequently, there is growing pressure for non-compliant countries to harmonize their laws with those that do.

Disputes related to patent protection are an ongoing source of litigation in many countries and at the WTO. Many of the disputes arise because national legislation is not sufficiently harmonized with the internationally agreed standards. This is an area that requires more work at the national level because it is in the interest of each country to modify and adapt their laws so that these national and international disputes are minimized.

Data exclusivity

In the process of preparing a new chemical entity (NCE) for regulatory approval, a pharmaceutical company conducts a massive array of laboratory, animal, and human trials. The data so obtained are the property of the company developing them but the patent rights that protect the NCE do not protect the data. In the normal course of events, the licensing process requires that much of these data be turned over to the regulatory body that provides the final approval to market the drug.

If these data, in whole or in part, are turned over to generic competitors who are seeking approval to manufacture a generic version of the original drug, an unfair situation is created. The cost of producing an NCE and taking it to market is approximately US$600 million (1997 dollars) (Kettler 1998: 1) but the cost of setting up a copycat generic production of a product is estimated to be about $1 million. If a regulatory body fails to protect data exclusivity, the consequences are far reaching. First, theft of the proprietary data has been legalized. Second, only about 30 percent of the drugs brought to market actually recover the R&D costs needed to get them there, and release of the research data further reduces the opportunity for the original inventor to make a fair profit. Third, such circumstances create a considerable disincentive for a manufacturer to operate in this type of environment.

The basic requirements for patent protection are set out in Articles 27 to 34 of TRIPS. However, the Trade Secrets portion of the agreement covers data exclusivity and this is included in Article 39. It is significant that TRIPS separates patent protection from trade secrets and in Article 39 requires the members of regulatory bodies to protect data against disclosure.

The 134 signatories to the WTO are required to comply with the TRIPS agreement by January 1, 2000. Some specified countries are permitted, under the agreement, to delay implementing of full patent protection until January 1, 2005. This delay does not apply to the protection of proprietary data. Failure to legislate and implement data protection required under TRIPS will leave countries open to complaint and resolution in accordance with the dispute mechanism.

At this time—autumn 1999—the European Union, the United States and Switzerland have implemented legislated protection of proprietary research data and New Zealand has indicated its intention of doing so. The Europeans have introduced a ten-year period of exclusivity and the United States a period of five years. That is, no application using the inventor's data can be approved for a period of ten (or five) years after the approval of the originators application.

Many other countries have not yet met the standards required by TRIPS and there is a wide degree of non-conformity. For example, Japan has a legal requirement that the originator's test data be published in a medical article or journal. Canada's early working system enables generic manufacturers to file an abbreviated drug submission with the Health Protection Branch. This shortened submission relies heavily upon the innovators R&D and the innovating manufacturers claim that this contravenes the provisions of TRIPS. The magnitude of the deficiencies in the Canadian protection of patents and data exclusivity were illustrated recently by a case in which a generic manufacturer was given regulatory approval to manufacture and market generic *Enalapril* in spite of a Federal Court injunction prohibiting such licensing until 2007. This is now the subject of litigation.

Some other countries have not yet given legislated protection for the 20-year patent rights prescribed under TRIPS and, in the worst circumstances, some jurisdictions have failed to provide any patent protection for pharmaceutical products.

Access to free market competition

In recent years many nations have noted an increase in the total expenditure on state-purchased pharmaceuticals. All too often, politicians and bureaucrats have attributed these cost increases to escalating drug prices and, in reaction, have introduced a policy of "pharmaceutical cost containment," more accurately described as price controls.

Various arguments are made for the introduction of price controls. These include (Butler 1993: 4):

(1) *Inflation control.* The rationale for this stems from the belief that there are "cost-push" factors that cause inflation. The concept is that inflation stems from an increase in a rise in general costs, and these are then passed on to the consumer in the form of higher retail costs.

This theory is no longer accepted by many economists who believe that the root cause of inflation is more often increased demand associated with an expansion in the money supply. While this latter postulate holds more credence, the possibility of stopping inflation through the use of legislative and regulatory controls on prices remains attractive to politicians and bureaucrats.

(2) *Ensuring fair prices.* This postulate holds that the greater social good requires that a just or fair price should be applied to goods and

services. Those who hold to this view often point to various aspects of health care as an example of how all should be deemed equal in their ability to obtain medical care. As Butler points out, this is a view that stems from medieval times (Butler 1993: 4) and is entirely rejected in market economics, which form the basis of the western economies. Nevertheless, the concept that all citizens should have equal access to a particular service is both beguilingly simple and politically attractive.

(3) *Unstable market conditions.* This concept holds that when unusual and unstable circumstances occur, these can be counterbalanced by price controls. War and widespread natural disasters may provide a backdrop for enthusiasm for this attempt to control the economy. There are numerous examples that illustrate that artificial measures such as price controls have been largely unsuccessful in controlling inflation, even in wartime (Schuettinger 1976: 91; Rockoff 1984: 186; Stein 1976: 68.). However, those who promote such measures bolster them with the argument that, "Extreme times require extreme measures."

There are two fundamentally different ways of approaching pharmaceutical price controls. First, an attempt can be made to influence the demand for drugs. These measures usually focus on encouraging physicians and other prescribers to use the lowest-cost drugs as well as discouraging patient's demand for drugs. Second, cost containment can focus on programs that influence the supply of pharmaceuticals to the consumer. Such programs tend to focus on the behaviour and performance of manufacturers, pharmacists, physicians, and other prescribers. Ideally, it is claimed, they have no impact on the consumer, who still receives high-quality products at the lowest cost available. The following classification of pharmaceutical price controls has been developed and explained elsewhere (McArthur 1997).

(1) Demand Side Measures
- Managed Care
- Education
- Cost sharing
- Mandatory budgets

(2) Supply Side Measures
- Assessed value criteria
- Profit limitations

- Legislated price controls
  - Price reductions
  - Maximum entry price control
- State formularies
- Prescription volume controls
- Professional fee controls
- Parallel importing
- Reference based pricing

Short or long term goals

In countries that are producers of pharmaceuticals but are striving to achieve front-line status, there is always a dilemma as to whether short term or long term goals should be pursued. The pharmaceutical industry presents an opportunity for substantial short-term gain. About $1 million and a handful of reliable technicians can quickly put together a generic production plant. By picking widely popular drugs and marketing them on the gray market at home and abroad, a producer can turn a tidy profit in a short time. Such activity requires a government that has little or no protection for intellectual property rights or, at least, is prepared to turn a blind eye to such activities.

The benefits of this type of production accrue to the investor only. The employees are soon out of work as markets dry up when the nature and source of the drug is identified by regulatory authorities in responsible countries. The country that permits this type of activity is damaged as it becomes recognized as a rogue nation in the international community. There are no long-term benefits, no gradual development of production and marketing skills, and no internal investment in R&D. The opportunity to create high-technology employment is lost and neither the country nor its citizens benefit.

Long ago, the leaders of the European Union, the United States, and Switzerland recognized these realities. They responded by developing just and enforceable rules to govern the protection of intellectual property rights. Others are following, and as they take each step forward, they begin to reap the industrial benefits. Vigorous protection of intellectual property rights brings substantial economic advantages but there is no successful short-term route to gaining these benefits.

The economic impact of incomplete protection for intellectual property rights

In the technologically advanced countries, and in those that are progressing toward higher levels of technological development, the pharmaceutical industry is an important part of the economy. Table 1 reveals the pharmaceutical production per capita in some OECD countries.

It is apparent that some of the European countries have the most productive economies with respect to pharmaceutical production. The United States, Japan, and Korea join them in this desirable position. The immediate question arises as to why this group of nations surpasses other technologically advanced countries such as Canada, Australia, and New Zealand which are also low end employers in pharmaceutical manufacturing.[1]

There may be several factors involved in the ascendancy of the more successful nations but it is not by chance that they have the most stringent laws protecting intellectual property rights. The pharmaceutical industry in Germany provides an illustration of the benefits that can accrue from this sector of the economy. Figures 1 through 6 provide an overview of some of these factors. Figure 1 shows capital spending on pharmaceutical production; note that this is 30 percent higher than in both the motor-vehicle industry and overall manufacturing and 73 percent higher than in the mechanical engineering industries.

Table 1: Pharmaceutical production per capita for selected OECD countries (US$ adjusted by purchasing power parity)

	1975	1992	1994
Australia	26	101	
Austria	34	218	235
Belgium	34	255	287
Canada	25	116	133
Denmark	31	238	290
France	58	251	257
Germany	47	190	195
Greece	15	59	
Japan	52	208	215
Korea	19	185	211
Mexico (1980)	25	64	72
Portugal	23	90	93
Spain	59	198	202
Sweden	25	189	289
Switzerland			600
United Kingdom	49	241	
United States	51	261	283

Source: OECD Data, CD-ROM (May 1998).

Figure 2 shows demand from within Germany and from abroad. This demonstrates how the existence of a high-quality product produced in a country with strong protection for intellectual property rights can result in an increasing export demand. Figure 3 also shows the impact of high-quality products and strong protection for intellectual property rights upon the economy of Germany, which is the world's leading exporter of pharmaceuticals. Also of interest in figure 3 is tiny Switzerland, a country with a highly educated and trained population, a very high standard of living, and a high standard of protection for intellectual property rights: it is the world's second-largest exporter of pharmaceuticals. Switzerland's position as an exporter of pharmaceutical products ahead of the United States, the United Kingdom, France, and Japan carries a powerful message for those interested in increasing national wealth through the export of high-technology products. At the same time, the Japanese legislation requiring the public disclosure of research data from patent research may be one of the factors contributing to the relatively lower export performance of the pharmaceutical industry in that country.

The level of skilled to unskilled employment as shown in figure 4 (using percentages of salaried employees and wage labourers as a proxy)

Figure 1: Comparison of capital spending in various german industries (percent of turnover, 1995)

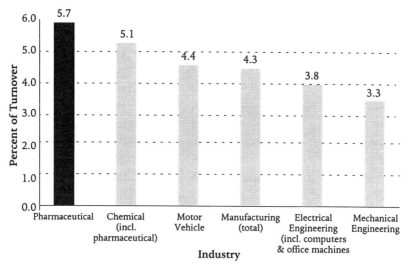

Source: German Statistics Bureau; Verband Forschender Arzneimittelhersteller e.V. (VFA) (www.vfa.de/extern/index_c.html).

Figure 2: Domestic and foreign orders for German pharmaceutical products (1991= 100)

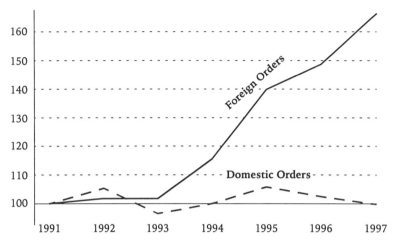

Source: Verband der Chemischen Industrie; after Verband Forschender Arzneimittel-hersteller e.V. (VFA) (www.vfa.de/extern/index_c.html).

Figure 3: Exports (1996) of pharmaceutical products (less primary pharmaceuticals) from Europe, Japan, and the United States

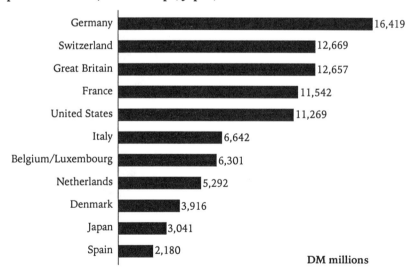

Source: Verband der Chemischen Industrie; Verband Forschender Arzneimittelher-steller e.V. (VFA) (www.vfa.de/extern/index_c.html).

is higher in the pharmaceutical industry than engineering, general manufacturing, or construction. This complements the high added value per
employee and net value-added numbers shown in figures 5 and 6.

The experience in Canada also illustrates some of the benefits of
implementing vigorous protection of intellectual property rights. Prior
to 1987, Canada had poor patent protection for pharmaceuticals and in
that year pharmaceutical R&D spending totaled $106 million. In 1987,
the Canadian parliament enacted Bill C-22, which improved patent
protection, and by 1993 R&D spending had increased to $504 million.
Bill C-91 was passed in 1993, bringing Canadian patent protection
closer to accepted world standards. Over the next 4 years, spending on
R&D increased to approximately $825 million. This increase in spend-
ing on research when intellectual property rights are strengthened is a
pattern that has been seen many times, in many countries, and once
again illustrates the economic benefits that flow from improving the
protection of intellectual property rights.

Canada presents another side of the coin as well. Why would this
nation of some 30 million people, a democratic country with a long established and impartial judiciary, with an enviable record in world trade,

---

**Figure 4: Comparison of percentage salaried employees and
wage labourers in various German industries (1995)**

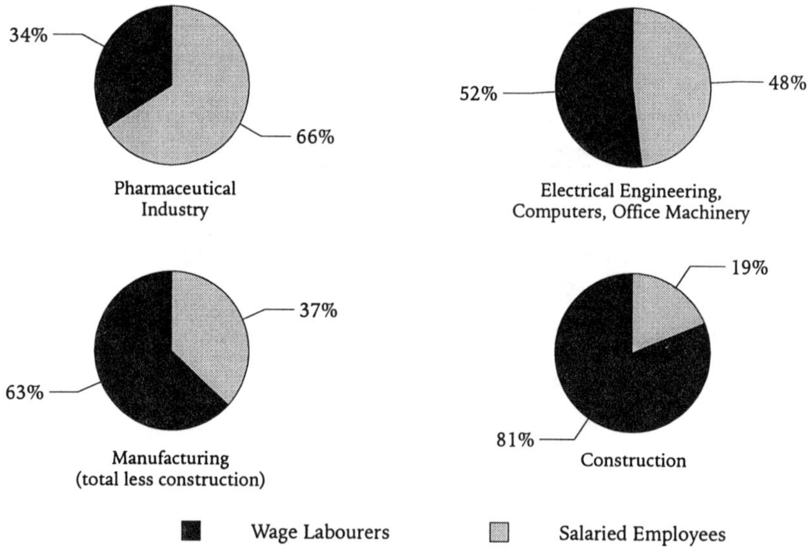

34% / 66%
Pharmaceutical
Industry

52% / 48%
Electrical Engineering,
Computers, Office Machinery

63% / 37%
Manufacturing
(total less construction)

81% / 19%
Construction

■ Wage Labourers   ▨ Salaried Employees

Source: German Statistics Bureau; Verband Forschender Arzneimittelhersteller e.V.
(VFA) (www.vfa.de/extern/index_c.html).

Figure 5: Output and added value per employee in the pharmaceutical and in all manufacturing industries of Germany (DM. 1995)

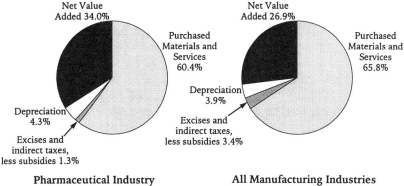

Pharmaceutical Industry
Gross Output = DM 340,000

All Manufacturing Industries
Gross Output = DM 315,000

Source: German Statistics Bureau; Verband Forschender Arzneimittelhersteller e.V. (VFA) (www.vfa.de/extern/index_c.html).

Figure 6: Comparison of added value per employee in various German industries (DM1000s, 1995)

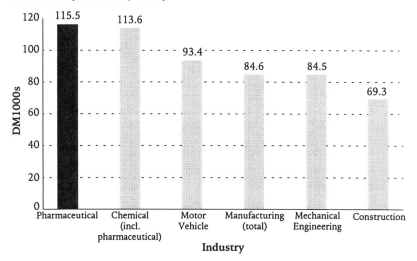

Source: German Statistics Bureau; Verband Forschender Arzneimittelhersteller e.V. (VFA) (www.vfa.de/extern/index_c.html).

perform so poorly in pharmaceutical production compared with its southern neighbour? The weaker protection of intellectual property rights may be a factor. As noted above, Canada permits "early working," and generic stockpiling and does not provide for patent-term restoration. Countries that surpass Canada in pharmaceutical production do not permit protection of intellectual property rights to be weakened in these ways, a factor that probably contributes to their superior performance.

Japan presents an interesting scenario. In 1975, it was second only to France and Spain as a per-capita producer of pharmaceuticals. By 1998, it had fallen to ninth position, far behind Switzerland and significantly behind several countries from the European Union. While impossible to prove, it seems that this fall in ranking may be related to the countries poor protection of data exclusivity.

Viewed from another perspective, the response of the innovative pharmaceutical industry to a jurisdiction that does not protect and enforce intellectual property rights is fairly predictable. Development of each new chemical entity requires a huge financial investment and, on average, less than one in every thousand new drugs discovered will finally get to market. These factors make it imperative for manufacturers to focus their energies and investment in jurisdictions that create the best opportunity for success. Conversely, jurisdictions that fail to provide solid and reliable protection of intellectual property rights are regarded as poor locations for investment and manufacturing of pharmaceuticals and the pharmaceutical industry will respond accordingly. These responses include the following:

(1) *Failure to invest* The large manufacturers of innovative drugs are constantly on the lookout for places to construct new plants for R&D and manufacturing. They seek, among other things, locations where there are solid, long-term assurances of protection of their intellectual property rights. Unless these exist, a company will not invest there and the economy will not have the benefit of the investment and job creation that goes with such a program.

(2) *Relocation* If a plant is located in an environment where there is a perceived economic or social instability, the prudent manufacturer will avoid entering into the production of new drugs there and will instead assign such production to another plant in a location perceived to be more stable.

(3) *Reassignment* If the regulatory environment deteriorates, making production of brand-name pharmaceuticals unprofitable, the manufacturer may choose to reassign plant production to another phar-

maceutical product such as an over-the-counter medication or a veterinary medication that is subject to little regulation; alternatively, the manufacturer may begin making an entirely different product. The result is the loss of pharmaceutical R&D, the probable loss of employment for highly skilled technical workers and researchers combined with a decrease in investment. The jurisdiction so affected will also lose the capability to compete in the lucrative international pharmaceutical trade, thus resulting in a weakening of the nation's export capability.

The industrial response to price controls can be equally devastating. Examples are provided by New Zealand, which some years ago introduced a price control mechanism known as Reference Based Pricing, a scheme that substitutes older and less expensive drugs for the newer and often more effective products. The result of this program has been to have pharmaceutical manufacturing move out of New Zealand to less hostile jurisdictions. Again, in the Canadian province of British Columbia a similar program of Reference Based Pricing was introduced in 1995. The results have been devastating. The provincial government claims to be saving about 40 million dollars per year. However, more than that amount is being withheld in medical research funding from the province by the pharmaceutical industry, which takes the position that it will not supply research funding in jurisdictions where they are impeded in marketing their products fairly and freely. In addition to the loss of research funding, independent analysts have calculated that this venture designed to save money is actually costing the province as much as $300 million per annum. This amounts to an annual loss of nearly $100 for every person in the British Columbia.

The counter-productive economic nature of price controls, in many jurisdictions, for many products forms the basis of a substantial literature and one is hard pressed to find an example where price controls have not, in the long term, created a substantial increase in prices. The pharmaceutical industry is no exception to this experience.

The pharmaceutical industry is a significant net contributor to the economy of many of the technologically advanced countries. Looked at from another perspective, the countries with high levels of production of pharmaceutical products also tend to have high standards of living and generally lower levels of unemployment. This suggests that countries aspiring to achieve front-line status in terms of economic stability and productivity should consider the steps that must be taken to improve industrial performance to these levels.

Overall, it appears that there is a clear correlation between national prosperity, high standards of living, and the strict protection of intellectual property rights. It would be erroneous to conclude that focusing solely on development of the pharmaceutical industry will, in itself, bring prosperity. Rather, the creation of an environment where the pharmaceutical industry prospers will provide opportunity for high technology, intellectually based, general industrial development.

Impact of incomplete protection for intellectual property rights upon health

There are human consequences to weak protection for the intellectual property rights of pharmaceutical manufacturers. There is an erroneous belief that the vigorous protection of IPR somehow inhibits the development of new and better drugs at a rapid rate; often, the reverse is true.

While patent laws prevent imitators from making and marketing copies of a newly identified product, they do not create a monopoly. Indeed the creation of a successful new drug with potent action to benefit a large number of people often stimulates considerable inventive effort to achieve the same means through a different process, using a different chemical compound. A case in point are the drugs for combatting peptic ulcers. Prior to 1975, the recognized treatment for serious peptic-ulcer disease was an operation known as a vagotomy and pyloroplasty (V&P). This major intra-abdominal surgery takes 2 to 3 hours to perform, the patient is hospitalized for a week or more, and the procedure has uncertain results. In 1975, a new drug called *Cimetidine* came to market and reduced the need for V&Ps considerably. In 1983, another new drug with a different mode of action called *Ranitidine* became available and further improved the treatment of peptic-ulcer disease. Then in 1989, *Omeprazole*, a drug with a previously unknown mode of action became available and the result was that V&Ps became an unneeded procedure.

Patents, as in this example, provide an umbrella under which innovative companies can compete and conduct research and development to create and produce new and different drugs that benefit society and, in the process, create profit for those who choose to invest in the producing company. Discovery of the initial drug did not create a monopoly but rather vigorous competition aimed at achieving the same result through different means. The beneficiaries were those patients who gained relief from the newer and more effective drugs, the governments and other insurers who were saved the cost of paying for the previously required surgery, and the investors in the producing companies, who made a profit from these efforts.

This type of competitive research is likely to become more common as the industry moves into the development of vaccines with the potential to cure or even prevent diseases that are presently untreatable. Debilitating and expensive disorders such as diabetes, osteoporosis, and arthritis may be curable within the next ten to 15 years. In fact, within the foreseeable future, we may be able to prevent or cure many of the diseases that now afflict mankind. It is certain, however, that this will only occur if the research and development is permitted to advance without the interference of excessive regulation.

Failure to protect intellectual property rights and the imposition of price controls can have a serious adverse impact upon the care of the ill. R.A. Levy and D. Cocks (1996) present one of the most comprehensive analyses of this topic. Part V of their report describes:

- a Louisiana study that showed markedly increased patient hospitalization in response to increased formulary restriction

- a West Virginia study by Bloomb and Jacobs that revealed increased surgical rates for peptic ulcer patients when access to newer peptic ulcer drugs was restricted

- a report from Smith and Simmons that showed that, when minor tranquilizers were restricted, there was a substantial increase in the prescribing of more potent, more expensive, and potentially more dangerous drugs such as barbiturates

- a study by DeTorres and White that showed restrictions on newer antibiotics for patients resulted in increased renal damage in the patients affected

- a report by Richton-Hewett *et al.* that revealed an example of how substituting a cheaper generic, *Warfarin*, in Boston City Hospital produced a significant increase in morbidity and health costs

- several authors who point out that the people most adversely affected by formularies and other restrictive practices are those with low income and complex illnesses, truly the most vulnerable and frail in society.

In November 1998, P. Authier and J. Robinson recently published details in the *The Montreal Gazette* of a heretofore-secret study reporting death and illness resulting from a cost-containment plan introduced in Quebec in 1997 (Authier and Robinson 1998). This bombshell came in the middle of a provincial election and told of 3,926 extra hospitalizations as well as increased mortality. The plan, which involved a substantial increase in drug costs for 93,950 seniors and 55,333 welfare recipients, gives an indication of the effects of the sudden implementation of a poorly conceived cost-containment program.

Other well known reports include that by Stephen B. Soumerai *et al.* (1994), who described the impact of withholding drugs from schizophrenic patients—increased admissions and increased utilization of medical services. Susan D. Horn *et al.* (1996) have demonstrated that health maintenance organizations (HMOs) that employ rigorous cost-containment measures have more unintended outcomes than HMOs using less rigorous constraint measures. These unintended consequences include more visits to the emergency department, more hospital admissions, and overall increased utilization of health-care resources. Recently J.E. Calfee (1999) has described how pharmaceutical price controls in the United States are causing economic inefficiencies as well as reducing the quality of care available.

These and other papers provide evidence that patients suffer when pharmaceutical cost containment is imposed. There appears to be no evidence in the literature to suggest that patients have improved medical outcomes when attempts are made to reduce spending on drugs.

Summary

Over the past 10 years, there has been a vigorous international effort to increase the protection of intellectual property rights. These efforts culminated in the TRIPS agreement, which is now the standard by which all nations are judged.

Patent protection has been stabilized at 20 years from the date of filing but other constraints have been added to this 20-year minimum. Patent-term restoration has become the norm in Europe, the United States, Japan, and some other countries. Discrimination against foreigners is no longer permitted and procedures such as "early working" and the practice of manufacturing and stockpiling generic products prior to patent expiration are no longer acceptable to the international community.

The protection of data exclusivity is also becoming a focus for more attention. The unfairness of permitting generic manufacturers to gain access to the research data of the original patent holder prior to the expiration of patent expiry is addressed in article 39 of TRIPS. The 134 signatories to the WTO agreement are required to put a stop to such disclosure by January 1, 2000 or face the penalties that can be imposed under the agreement. There is little doubt that complaints regarding this will be filed with the WTO early in 2000; Japan and Canada appear to be two countries that may become the focus of complaint.

Many countries have imposed different types of pharmaceutical cost containment, or price controls. Some of these are benign and do little to effect market access while others are more draconian. While some of these measures are probably subject to appeal under international treaty, no appeal has been launched to date. The probable reason for this is that price controls appear to cause more economic harm to the countries that introduce them than to other countries. Under these circumstances, the industry appears willing to let the countries concerned learn the painful lessons of experience.

An examination of some of the countries of the European Union, the United States, and Japan reveals that they have been quick to capitalize on the new international treaties concerning the manufacture and sale of pharmaceuticals. These countries have passed legislation harmonizing the national law with the TRIPS agreement. As a result, they are now reaping the rewards of increased skilled employment, increased exports of these valuable products, and an escalating industrial investment in this high-technology industry. Another important benefit is increasing investment in R&D, which tends to improve overall industrial R&D.

Apart from the economic impact, there is also an impact upon the health of the citizens of these countries. It is not by chance that some of the best and most sophisticated health care in the world is observed in those countries that have adapted rapidly to the changing international environment in pharmaceutical production. The improved employment, the increase in high-technology R&D, and the rapid availability of the newest and most effective medications are characteristics that complement and contribute to high-quality health care.

These countries also seem to be recognizing the futility of pharmaceutical cost containment. The overwhelming evidence to date is that the most effective method of controlling the price of drugs is to permit the manufacturers to compete on a free and open market for the opportunity to sell their product. There are still attempts being made to control pharmaceutical prices, particularly in the United States, but as more studies reveal the negative effects of this upon both economics and health care, these efforts will probably diminish.

Overall it is clear that countries that seek front-line status in the pharmaceutical industry have huge gains to make, both economically and in terms of improved health outcomes for their citizens. To achieve these goals they must make an irrevocable commitment to:

- establishing long-term goals for the pharmaceutical industry

- introducing legislation to protect intellectual property rights, including patent protection and data exclusivity that conforms with TRIPS

- creating a free, competitive market for pharmaceuticals

- avoiding price controls and other artificial distortions of the market place.

Note

1 OECD data reveal that pharmaceutical employment per capita in Australia, Canada, and New Zealand is less than half that in France, Germany, and the United Kingdom.

References

Authier P, and J. Robinson (1998). Cuts to Drug Plan Killed 120 People, Quebec Study Finds. *The National Post* (November 12).

Butler, Stuart M. (1993). The Fatal Attraction of Price Controls. In Robt. B. Helms (ed.), *Health Policy Reform: Competition and Controls* (Washington, DC: AEI Press).

Calfee, J.E. (1999). Why Pharmaceutical Price Controls Are Bad for Patients. *On The Issues* (March). The American Enterprise Institute.

Horn, Susan D. et al. (1996). Intended and Unintended Consequences of HMO Cost Containment Strategies: Results from the Managed Care Outcomes Project. *Journal of Managed Care* 2, 3 (March): 253–64.

Kettler, H. (1998). *Updating the Cost of a New Chemical Entity*. London: Office of Health Economics. Summary in *OHE News* 7 (Winter 1998/99).

Levy, R.A., and D. Cocks (1996). Component Management Fails to Save Health Care System Costs: The Case of Restrictive Formularies. US National Pharmaceutical Council.

McArthur, W.J. (1997). Pharmaceutical Price Controls: A Canadian Dilemma. Proceedings of the 1997 Pharmac Conference, Toronto, September 22, 1997. Copies available from the Fraser Institute.

Rockoff H. (1984). *Drastic Measures: A History of Wage and Price Controls in the United States*. New York: Cambridge University Press.

Schuettinger, R.L. (1976). *The Illusion of Wage and Price Control in the Historical Record*. Vancouver, BC: The Fraser Institute.

Soumerai, Stephen B., et al. (1994). Effects of Limiting Medicaid Drug Reimbursement Benefits on the Use of Psychotropic Agents and Acute Mental Health Services by Patients with Schizophrenia. *New England Journal of Medicine* 331: 650–55.

Stein, H. (1976). Fiscal policy: Reflections on the Past Decade. *Contemporary Economic Problems*. Washington, DC: American Enterprise Institute.

World Trade Organization [WTO] (1999). *Intellectual Property Page Index*. Digital document: www.wto.org/wto/itellec/intell1.htm.

Verband Forschender Arzneimittelhersteller e.V. (VFA) (www.vfa.de/extern/index_c.html)

Implementing the TRIPS Agreement on Patents
Optimal Legislative Strategies for Developing Countries

Jayashree Watal

The Agreement on the Trade-Related Aspects of Intellectual Property Rights (TRIPS) entered into force on the first day of 1995 with the establishment of the World Trade Organization (WTO). The negotiations on TRIPS were long—they took seven years, from 1986 to 1993—arduous, and sometimes even acrimonious. Despite a formal agreement on the final text of the TRIPS agreement, its eventual implementation has been difficult in many developing countries. While attracting foreign direct investment was perceived positively by a growing number of developing countries even during the negotiations and improvement in intellectual property rights (IPRs) was seen as essential, a smooth transition to higher standards of IPRs was particularly difficult in countries where there were strong domestic vested interests in the pre-existing weak IPR regimes. As a result, even countries that had liberalized their policies towards foreign direct investment before or during the Uruguay Round had to be urged bilaterally, many times with the threat of trade sanctions, to improve their IPR regimes.

Notes will be found on pages 118–22. The views presented here are personal and not attributable to any organization with which the author is associated.

It is in the area of patents,[1] in the particular sectors of pharmaceuticals and agriculture, and the closely related sectors of chemicals and biotechnology, that the resistance to TRIPS standards was the greatest. Developing countries feared that, with the grant of product patents in these sectors, new, innovative and more effective products and technologies would become costly and inaccessible to the vast majority of consumers or users. Further, entrenched domestic interests that were in the business of producing and legitimately profiting from credible equivalents of pharmaceutical and chemical substances patented elsewhere, anticipated reduction in their profits. The interests of these powerful lobbies coincided with those of the consuming public, giving very little margin for maneuverability to governments of the developing country. To make matters worse, developing countries which were meant to get ten years to comply with patent provisions in the most sensitive sectors, viz. pharmaceuticals and agricultural chemicals, in effect did not get even one day's transition for accepting product patent applications for pharmaceuticals and agricultural chemicals, as they had to begin from January 1, 1995.[2] Even developed countries got one full year for the transition and were required to be in compliance with TRIPS only from January 1, 1996.[3] While conceding the difficult context of the negotiations, perhaps more realistic transition periods would have made the ensuing task of ensuring compliance to both the letter and the spirit of TRIPS easier for the *demandeurs*.[4]

Many developing countries have experienced problems in implementing TRIPS obligations on the acceptance product patent applications on pharmaceutical and agricultural chemical inventions by the due date of January 1995. This is particularly true of three countries identified as the strongest opponents to TRIPS in the early phase of the negotiations, viz. Argentina, Brazil, and India.[5] In these and many other cases, the required legislative changes have been made well after this date and, in the case of India, this was done only in March 1999, just before the last date for compliance given under the WTO dispute settlement process. To minimize the perceived disadvantages of such patent protection some developing countries wanted to ensure as great a flexibility as possible in imposing limitations on the rights enjoyed by such patent holders in these sensitive sectors. In the end, TRIPS does allow flexibility in defining the criteria for patentability, in defining and targeting abusive use of patents, and in imposing price controls or other measures necessary to protect public interest.

This chapter shows how developing countries can adopt optimal legislative strategies to be fully in compliance with some of the patent provisions of TRIPS contained in Section 5, while minimizing both the direct and indirect costs of such compliance.[6]

Flexibility in defining the criteria for patentability and exceptions to patentability

The option of using different interpretations of the criteria of patentability, viz. novelty, non-obviousness (or inventive step), and utility (or industrial applicability), clearly exist for developing countries. If higher standards are adopted, patents would be granted only to significant inventions. This is particularly important in the field of biotechnology, where inventions that embody a trivial and obvious manipulation of that which is already pre-existing in nature can be excluded from patent grant as not being novel or non-obvious or even having no clear utility. In addition, TRIPS allows under Article 27.2 specific exemptions of inventions that are contrary to public order and morality, including those whose sale must be prevented in order to protect human, animal, plant life and health or to avoid serious harm to the environment. Article 27.3 (a) further allows the exclusion of inventions relating to the diagnostic, therapeutic, and surgical methods for the treatment of humans or animals. Article 27.3 (b) is crucial as it allows the exclusion of plants and animals and essentially biological processes for their production and obliges the patentability of microorganisms and microbiological and non-biological processes for the production of plants and animals. Plant varieties must, however, at least be protected by an effective *sui generis* law.

On biotechnological inventions, the flexibility given under TRIPS has been used, for instance, by both Brazil and Argentina to formulate fairly broad exceptions in their implementing legislation. In Brazil's Law No. 9.279 of May 1996 to Regulate Rights and Obligations Relating to Industrial Property,[7] Article 10.IX excludes from patentability: "All or part of natural living beings and biological materials found in nature or isolated therefrom, including the genome or the germ plasm of any natural living being, and any natural biological processes."

Similarly Argentina in its new law no. 24.481, Invention Patents and Utility Models Act,[8] in Article 7 (b) excludes from patentability: "All biological and genetical material existing in nature or its replica, in the biological processes implicit in animal, plant and human reproduction, including the genetic processes relating to material capable of conducting its own duplication under normal and free conditions, such as they occur in nature."

Clearly, in these countries genes as found naturally in plants, humans, or animals, cannot be patented even if technical processes were utilized to isolate them. In Europe, however, while ethical concerns led to the clause on exclusion of the human body, at any stage of development, and the "simple" discovery of one of its elements, including partial or full gene sequences in Article 5.1 of the new Biotechnology

Directive,[9] an element isolated from the human body or otherwise produced by means of a technical process, including the sequence or partial sequence of a gene, may constitute a patentable invention, even if the structure of that element is identical to that of a natural element in Article 5.2. This illustrates the difficulties on legislating on the patentability of biotechnological inventions.

If patent claims are interpreted narrowly by patent offices and courts, rival companies could be free to patent 'around' the patented invention. This would reduce the number of "blocking" patents and encourage R&D of an incremental nature, particularly relevant for developing countries. In Japan, patent claims used to be narrower, with patent applicants being limited to one claim per application. This situation has changed dramatically in Japan in recent years, partly under bilateral pressure from the United States and partly due to more liberal court decisions. The American "doctrine of equivalents," which protects patent claims broadly against even other functional equivalents, has also been adopted in Japan.[10] Indeed, some economists view with alarm the trend towards broader and stronger patents arguing that these would hinder rather than stimulate technological and economic progress as they lead to higher barriers to entry for new firms and would have particularly disastrous effects in developing countries.[11] All this would indicate that developing countries must use this flexibility in TRIPS to grant patents sparingly and keep claims narrow.[12]

However, the practical significance of the option of defining the criteria of patentability to suit national interests for countries that do not have skilled examiners or judges appears to be rather limited. Examining of patent applications is a very specialized task performed by highly educated technologists, well-trained in patent law, who can make independent determinations of the patentability of complex, frontline inventions. Developing countries would need to pool their resources to achieve such goals. In this context, the larger issue of harmonized global patent systems[13] and the more specific one of whether every developing country can afford to have individual patent systems or whether they should leave such matters to a regional system operated by the national patent offices of a few qualified countries, becomes important. This is more than just an institutional problem that can be addressed through training and development or the writing and dissemination of detailed manuals for patent examination. Many developing countries are unlikely to have a significant level of local inventive activity in the near future. This is illustrated by American patent statistics where in 1997, of the 95,000 patent applications filed by foreign inventors, only 12 percent were from developing countries. Only a handful of developing countries filed more than 50 patent applications:

Argentina, Brazil, China, Korea, India, Malaysia, Mexico, Singapore, and Taiwan.[14] With the almost universal adherence to TRIPS, the Paris Convention, and its subsidiary agreement, the Patent Cooperation Treaty, there is a case for rationalizing patent decisions and selecting a few centres for patent examination in both developed and developing countries, based on level of inventive activity, education, technological skills, and ability to work in a common international or regional language. Other countries could select the patent office with which they would wish to be affiliated, basing their decision on proximity, language, or similarity of level of development.[15]

Exceptions to rights of patent holders

While TRIPS lays down stringent and virtually harmonized rights for the patent holders of both processes and products, it recognized that there had to be exceptions where the patent could be used without the authorization of the right holder. These exceptions were placed in three categories: first, where the use would be for limited purposes which do not unreasonably prejudice the legitimate interests of the right holder (Article 30); the second, for use authorized to third parties or to government under specified conditions (Article 31); and third, when revocation or forfeiture of the patent could be permitted (Article 32). It is in the text of these exceptions that developing countries wishing to allay the strict requirements of the TRIPS provisions on patents can seek recourse.

Limited exceptions to patentee's exclusive rights

Article 30 could not list out the specific circumstances under which use could be made of patents without the authorization of the right holder due to differences between the approach of the United States and the European Union.[16] It has been rightly recognized by most commentators that the limited exceptions could be those recognized in most patent laws: use for private and non-commercial purposes, prior users' rights, use for research and experimental or teaching purposes, use in the direct preparation of individual medicines by pharmacies or use on ships, aircraft or other vehicles temporarily in foreign jurisdiction.[17] Some would like to add use for obtaining the approval of generic drugs and the international exhaustion of patent rights under this article but this has been contested by others.[18] While the United States allows the exception of generic drug approval under a specific law[19] that simultaneously extends the patent term for pharmaceutical patents by up to five years, the European Union considers such R&D to be directed to a commercial purpose and thus, to infringe the patent. Israel recently faced the wrath of the United States pharmaceutical industry when it allowed this exception despite the simultaneous patent-term extension permitted to pharmaceutical patents.[20] However, the new Argentine patent law, in addition to listing the non-commercial and limited exceptions under Article 36, including parallel importation, ingeniously adds in Article 41 that the National Institute of Industrial Property can establish limited exceptions that do not unjustifiably hamper "the normal working of the patent" or be unjustifiably detrimental to the legitimate interests of third parties. It will be interesting to see the further exceptions established by the National Institute of Industrial Property. In the interests of encouraging early generic competition, developing countries would push the limits of this exception. However, each exception made under this provision of TRIPS will be scrutinized carefully by the *demandeur* countries and there are likely to be disputes on the interpretation of these terms in the WTO.

Compulsory licenses and government use of patents

The rights of the patentee are essentially to prevent third parties from making, using, or selling the patented invention. If these rights are taken away without the authorization of the right holder, as is the case in compulsory licenses and government use, much of the "monopoly" value of patents is lost, even if the right holder obtains "reasonable commercial" payment in return. On the other hand, several studies have found evidence that important patented inventions are generally not licensed voluntarily for financial considerations, except in exchange for patents or technical information of equal importance.[21] Thus, non-voluntary licenses can be an important way for governments in developing countries to make patented inventions available at more competitive prices.

It is, thus, not surprising that one of the most intensely negotiated provisions of TRIPS were those set out in Article 31 on the limitations that could be set by the state on the other use of patents without the authorization of the right holder. All members provided for such limitations either through their competition laws or through their patent laws or both. In addition, the Paris Convention recognizes in Article 5A that Parties could grant compulsory licenses and sets certain conditions where such licenses are granted for correcting abuse of patents, including the failure to work the patent. It is felt by some that this freedom is somewhat restricted by the obligation laid down in Article 27.1 not to discriminate between imported and domestically produced products. This subclause was meant to rule out the forcing of local manufacture or "working" of patents through compulsory licenses.[22]

That "working" should not include importation was a crucial point for many developing countries in the negotiations.[23] It is, however, not clear whether these countries meant to use this condition of local manufacture to help domestic industry to get the necessary licenses and thus force the pace of transfer of technology or to force the use of local labour and materials, thus enabling the manufacturer to offer the patented invention at lower prices. By itself, "working" type of clauses are not likely to encourage the transfer of technology as the right holders are not likely to cooperate in giving the required know-how. Where such cooperation is not required, local licenses can be obtained by making refusal to deal a ground for compulsory licenses without confronting the non-discrimination clause in Article 27.1. Such a ground is not prohibited under Article 31 of TRIPS, even though its use under Article 40 is questionable.

Similarly, if the problem is lower prices, it can also be tackled directly by making the sale of patented inventions on unreasonable terms a ground for compulsory licenses. This is all the more useful since, if "working" were the only ground for compulsory licenses, by working the patent within three years from its grant, and selling the resultant product at unreasonably high prices for the entire patent term, the right holder saves himself from compulsory licensing. In addition, if the ground for compulsory license is not the abusive use of patents but public interest, the conditions and time limits of Article 5A of Paris do not apply.

Some commentators have argued that Article 31 is confined to the grounds laid down in Article 5A(2) of Paris, viz. to prevent abuses of patent rights, and that this is a fundamental requirement even for compulsory licenses granted in public interest.[24] However, a recent decision by the German Federal Supreme Court refutes this contention.[25] Public interest is a ground separate from abuse, as has been explained by a learned commentator of the Paris Convention.[26] Others have rightly pointed out that there are no restrictions whatsoever on the purposes for the grant of compulsory licenses, although there is a reference to some grounds in Articles 7, 8 and 31 of TRIPS.[27]

That the final text of Article 31 places no restrictions on the purposes for which such use could be authorized is quite a significant achievement for developing countries, given that the United States had insisted that there could be only two grounds for such licenses: to remedy an adjudicated violation of competition laws or to address a declared national emergency.[28] This kind of restriction now applies only to semiconductor technology and it is laid down in 31(c) that compulsory licenses can only be granted for a public non-commercial purpose or to remedy an adjudicated violation of competition laws. Such a restriction emphasizes that there are no such restrictions on other fields of technology.[29] Even the European Union had insisted on a governing clause restricting the grant of compulsory licenses to a manner that does not distort trade.[30] No such restriction is found in the final text.

The eleven conditions[31] listed in Article 31 have been called "strict safeguards."[32] However, some of the crucial conditions are entirely dependent on the purposes for which use without authorization of the right holder are granted in the first place. This gives considerable leeway to policy makers in developing countries to construct the grounds such that the conditions do not become restrictions. For example, the ground cited in the law may be, as it is in the case of China, that any qualified entity which fails to obtain an authorization from the patentee on reasonable terms and within a reasonable period of time can apply for, and be granted, a compulsory license.[33] Alternatively, the ground cited could be to supply a market in the country on reasonable terms[34] or even a general condition granting compulsory licenses wherever this is indispensable to the public interest, as is the case in Germany.[35]

Such grounds could be made compatible with each of the conditions of Article 31 and also non-discriminatory in terms of Article 27.1 quite easily. According to the first clause, 31(a), the authorization of such use should be considered on its individual merits. This was meant to terminate the system of automatic licenses of right available, for instance, in the Indian patent law for food and pharmaceuticals.[36] In all the three examples of grounds given above, merits could be considered on an individual basis before authorizing use of the patented invention. In our first example, the merits would be whether the entity is qualified to work the patent and whether the terms are reasonable. Alternatively, it would be to determine whether the market is being supplied and whether the sale price is reasonable or whether a non-voluntary license is indispensable to public interest.

The second clause, 31(b), that the proposed user make efforts to obtain the authorization on reasonable commercial terms over a reasonable period of time, is not unreasonable and can be built into the law as a ground, as in our first example. This clause in TRIPS implicitly acknowledges that unjustifiable refusal to license can be a ground for compulsory licenses, whether or not it can be treated as a violation per se of competition law. As long there is fair and speedy adjudication by domestic authorities of the term "reasonable commercial," both right holders and potential licensees would know their limits and recourse to compulsory licenses may not be required. There is no requirement to judge "reasonableness" by world standards or even those of neighbouring countries.[37] Authorities can take several factors into account, including the ability of the licensee, and eventually of the domestic consumer, to pay. This clause is not applicable when a patent is used, during a national emergency or for a public non-commercial purpose, where a lower standard is used, or to remedy an adjudicated anti-competitive practice (31(k)).

The third clause, 31(c) that the scope and duration of such use should be limited to the purpose for which it was granted, is not as draconian as it appears, as it is linked to the ground for grant. In the first example cited, the scope and duration would be co-terminal with the patent, as the qualified entity is entitled to work the whole patent unless he is granted a voluntary license on reasonable terms earlier. In the second case, it would persist as long as the market is not being supplied and as long as prices remain unreasonably high or, in the third case, as long as public interest is not met. Thus, while theoretically this may seem restrictive, when linked to the grounds for grant this condition may be ineffective.

A similar view could be taken in 31(g): the clause that seeks termination of the license when the circumstances that led to its grant cease to exist is linked to the grounds of grant. To illustrate again, in the first case, this would occur only when a voluntary license is granted on reasonable terms or, in the second case, when prices fall and are unlikely to rise again to unreasonable levels and, in the third case, where public-interest considerations are already met. Moreover, even if such a termination request is made it is TRIPS-compatible to protect the legitimate interests of the compulsory licensee, who may have made a considerable investment or preparation for using the invention. Such considerations need not be restricted to disposal of excess products already produced.[38]

Non-exclusivity of compulsory licenses as required by 31(d) was accepted by all developing countries in the negotiations, although, at one time, it was one of the important causes for the breakdown of the negotiations on the Revision of the Paris Convention between developed and developing countries.[39] Exclusivity of license for compulsory licensees was considered essential to ensure that the right holder does not interfere with the successful operation of the licensees' production of the patented invention. However, it has to be recognized that exclusivity does not guarantee non-interference and that there is no moral justification for depriving the inventor rights over his invention. India is one developing country that will have to amend the patent law on this issue,[40] though even India had accepted this by late 1990.[41]

Non-assignability, except along with the business, as required by 31(e), is only fair as a compulsory license cannot be a tradeable commodity by itself.

The sixth clause, 31(f), that such use shall be predominantly for the supply of the domestic market, does not rule out exports. However, in practical terms, exports will be permissible only to countries that permit parallel imports and, as discussed above, it is unlikely to be an economically significant benefit.[42] Again, this condition does not apply to cases involving adjudicated anti-competitive practices (31(k)).

All compulsory license provisions, even in the law of developing countries during the pre-TRIPS era, provided for remuneration. This provision, 31(h), now speaks of "adequate" remuneration, "taking into account the economic value of such authorization." Significantly, there is no reference a duty to "compensate the right-holder fully" as proposed by the United States or to "an equitable remuneration corresponding to the economic value of the license" as proposed by the European Union.[43] There is also no requirement to pay the right holder his "normal cost," as interpreted by some commentators.[44] Indeed, if this were to be the case, the license would be termed "voluntary." However, it is only fair that the compulsory licensee does not rake in abnormal profits by charging excessively high prices while paying a low remuneration to the right holder. The potential profits of the licensee and, therefore, the economic value of the authorization to him, have to be taken into account. Doubtless, the right holder will make all conceivable arguments for adequate remuneration and the licensee will rebut such claims with counter arguments. Eventually, the interpretation of these terms will be left to the national authorities, subject only to review by a distinct higher authority (31(j)), which can be administrative in nature.[45] No guidelines have been given under TRIPS and none can be imposed in interpretation. Again, this provision does not apply to adjudicated competition cases, where remuneration can be decided on a case-by-case basis (31(k)).

Only the "legal validity" of the decision to authorize the use, and significantly not the grounds for such use, is subject to review by a distinct higher authority, under the ninth clause, 31(i). There is a strong case for instituting a separate administrative authority to deal only with appeals on compulsory licenses, government use, and abuses relating to IPRs, including anti-competitive conditions on contractual licenses, as this would lead to speedy disposal of such cases. Consultation and cooperation with other WTO Members is required under Article 40 only in the latter set of cases.

There is a separate provision on dependent patents, tightening the circumstances for the grant of such compulsory licenses from the generally accepted ground of the second patent being "a substantial contribution to the art" to a more specific requirement that it "involve an important technic.l advance of considerable economic significance." These new terms do not necessarily have to be incorporated *tel quel* into the patent law.[46] Even if this were done, these terms would again have to be interpreted by the national authorities and Courts in the national context.

The above analysis of the clauses of Article 31 demonstrates the flexibility available to policy makers in developing countries in formulating the provisions in their patent laws on compulsory licenses and government use. It is not surprising that the new Argentine patent law follows all these conditions scrupulously.[47] Given the more favorable treatment meted out to use without the authorization of the right holder in cases of public non-commercial use and in cases of adjudicated cases of anti-competition law, these are areas to be examined particularly closely by developing countries.[48] For example, an undertaking in the public or private sector could, in public interest, be authorized by government to manufacture a patented pharmaceutical product for sale to the public through government hospitals or health centers on a no-profit-no-loss basis.

However, there is one note of caution: in cases where secret knowhow, not claimed in the patent application, is required for the use of the patented invention, the cooperation of the right holder has to be ensured and this can be done only through the conclusion of voluntary licenses. It has often been pointed out that the very existence of statutory provisions on compulsory licenses is adequate to encourage the voluntary conclusion of licenses. It is in this spirit that developing countries must incorporate the flexibility available in Article 31 in their patent laws, even while using this instrument sparingly in practice.

Revocation of patents

The provision in Article 32 is entitled "Revocation/Forfeiture" and only calls for the judicial review of decisions to revoke or forfeit patents. An earlier proposal by the United States that a patent may only be revoked if it failed to meet the requirements of patentability[49] and a more specific proposal of the European Union that a patent cannot be revoked on grounds on non-working[50] were both dropped by the end of 1990. Since Article 5A of the Paris Convention already regulated the conditions under which patents could be revoked for non-working, this was accepted as being adequate as this effectively overruled Brazil's proposal in the negotiations to allow revocation as a first remedy for abuse.[51] However, an authentic interpretation of the Paris Convention suggests that the revocation of patents, on grounds other than abuse, in particular in public interest, is not ruled out.[52] For instance, Members may directly revoke patents on grounds not related to abuse of patent, such as public interest or to protect the environment. Indeed some pre-existing laws of developing countries did incorporate such provisions and India had demanded that revocation of patents be allowed if the patent was being used in a manner prejudicial to public interest. India was willing to give an opportunity of hearing to the patent owner and subject the decision on revocation to judicial review.[53] Hence, it can now be construed that this demand was either accepted or was carelessly overlooked by the *demandeurs* in the TRIPS negotiations. On the other hand, given that patents can be revoked on grounds of wrong grant, as per the criteria of patentability and the exceptions laid down in Article 27, it is not clear if any Member that is a developing country would still want to use this loophole. To do so will mean having to face a dispute settlement panel, as it is likely to be contested.[54]

Reversal of burden of proof

Article 34 of TRIPS states that in litigation concerning the infringement of process patents, judicial authorities shall have the authority to order the defendant to prove that the process used to obtain an identical product is different from the patented process. This is a reversal of the burden of proof, as it is normally up to the petitioner to adduce evidence about the infringement of his patent. Members have been given the choice of one of two circumstances under which any identical product produced without the authorization of the patent owner shall, in the absence of proof to the contrary, be deemed to have infringed the patented process: (a) if the product obtained by the patented process is new; or (b) if there is a substantial likelihood that the identical product was made by the patented process and the patent owner has been unable through reasonable efforts to determine the process used.

In the first option, national judicial authorities would, in the absence of proof to the contrary, have to deem the identical product to have been obtained by the patented process if such a product is new. Here the petitioner will only have to adduce evidence that the patented product is new and identical to that put out by the defendant in order to reverse the burden of proof. Some commentators have recommended that developing countries opt for the first option because this is more limited, as it is confined to new products. Some have even suggested that the obligation can be further limited by defining "new" to be the same as in Article 27.1 of TRIPS, i.e. novelty as in state of the art.[55] This is a controversial interpretation and subject to challenge as, in such a case, product patents would allow protection against all processes of manufacture of the product. The first option is said to be detrimental to holders of biotechnological process patents where, in many cases, the substance produced is not new, e.g. insulin. It must be noted that the first option is stricter as it obliges reversal of proof in all cases where the identical product is new. The European Union has adopted this option, considering the extension to known products to be too broad[56] and it played an important role in retaining this option in the text during the TRIPS negotiations. New Zealand has also opted to confine this to "new" products only under section 68 A of its amended patent law in 1994. Among developing countries, Argentina and Korea have chosen the first option.[57]

In the second case, it is clear that the petitioner first has to adduce evidence that there is a "substantial likelihood" that his patented process was used and that he has made "reasonable efforts" to find out the actual process used. It is the national judicial authorities who would then decide if this were indeed the case and then reverse the burden of proof. If the petitioner fails to adduce such evidence or if the defendant convinces the court to the contrary, the burden of proof remains on the petitioner as in any other civil suit.[58] The final judgement on the infringement case would be passed after hearing both sides. Of course, this would apply to all products, whether new or not. The United States favoured this option in its law[59] and insisted on its inclusion in TRIPS. There seems to be an in-built incentive to opt for the second and more general formulation, one that is said to have been chosen by former socialist states in bilateral agreements with the United States.[60] Brazil and China also seem to have chosen the second option as there is no mention of the word "new" in these clauses of their laws, although they do not seem to have taken advantage of the flexibility in Article 34.1(b) of TRIPS.[61] Australia, on the other hand, in Section 121 A of its Patents Act, 1990, has incorporated this flexibility, leaving it to the Court to decide these issues.

Conclusion

This chapter has shown that the TRIPS allows a certain amount of flexibility to developing countries, which can be used while implementing the agreement, to allay the fears of those anticipating high direct and indirect costs, particularly based on its patent provisions. The crucial provision for use without the authorization of the right holder can allay many such fears if implemented imaginatively. The flexibility given in TRIPS in defining the criteria of patentability and the exceptions should be used fully by developing countries. On the burden of proof in process patent infringement, confining this to "new" products does not seem to be more advantageous and it may be advisable to demand some initial evidence of "substantial likelihood" from the petitioner. However, it must be noted that many of these legislative strategies are only optimal for developing countries that are on the defensive about patent protection. On the other hand, some developing countries, where the level of local inventive activity is quite high or is increasing rapidly, may want to use such measures with caution as they may discourage local inventiveness. Last, but certainly not the least, there is a strong case for developing countries to pool their resources and move towards the establishment of regional patent offices.

Acknowledgments

This paper draws heavily upon chapter 4 and chapter 10 of the author's forthcoming book, *Intellectual Property Rights in the World Trade Organization: The Way Forward for Developing Countries* (New Delhi: Oxford University Press, India, 2000). Discussions with John Barton, Nuno Carvalho, and Adrian Otten helped clarify some of the issues. Comments on this paper may be sent to jwatal@iie.com.

Notes

1 Some see the area of computer software as a particular difficulty for several developing countries, particularly in Latin America. However, 14 developing countries agreed, as early as May 1990, in a joint written submission in the TRIPS negotiations (W/71) to protect computer programs under copyright. The current TRIPS obligations do not go much beyond this.
2 Article 65.4 of TRIPS gives developing countries up to January 1, 2005 to extend product patent protection to areas of technology not protected thus far, while Articles 70.8 and 70.9 make the acceptance of product patent applications for pharmaceuticals and agricultural chemicals and the grant of exclusive marketing rights substantively similar to patent rights, applicable from January 1, 1995. Under Article 66, least developed countries have up to 2006 to implement these and other provisions of TRIPS.
3 Article 65.1 of TRIPS.
4 The perception that forcing changes in IPR laws of developing countries prematurely does not necessarily lead to their effective enforcement, appears to be shared by Joseph Papovich, Deputy Assistant Trade Representative for Intellectual Property in the office of the USTR, who at a recent conference on NAFTA cited the example of Mexico (Papovich 1997).
5 See Gadbaw and Richards 1988.
6 For reasons of space, only a summary treatment is accorded to some subjects in this paper. A more detailed analysis is available in Watal 2000.
7 Reproduced in WIPO, Industrial Property and Copyright, November, 1996, [hereinafter the new Brazilian patent law].
8 Reproduced in World Patent Law & Practice, Vol. 2B Rel 75-7/97, (and as translated by Thomas Banzhaf, Esq., Buenos Aires and referred to hereinafter as the new Argentine patent law).
9 Directive of the European Parliament and of the Council on the Legal Protection of Biotechnological Inventions (No. 98/44/EC of 6 July 1998) reproduced in *IIC* 29, 5 (August 1998): 567ff.
10 See Report of the Planning Sub-committee of the Industrial Property Council, To the Better Understanding of Pro-Patent Policy (November 1998), Japanese Patent Office. Digital document: www.jpo.org.
11 See Mazzoleni and Nelson 1998.

12 See Oddi 1996. It is, however, unclear how developing countries can ensure that courts interpret claims in a narrow way, unless this is laid down in detailed guidelines, a stupendous task in itself.

13 See Gervais 1998: 151–52, para 2.136. It is to be seen if the WIPO initiative on patent law harmonization, which since 1995 centres around patent procedures, will close any loopholes in interpretation of this section of TRIPS.

14 Of these countries, Taiwan and Korea filed about 5000, Singapore and Hong Kong more than 200, while Brazil, China, India, and Mexico filed over 100 patent applications. Low patent filing applies to several developed countries as well as economies in transition. See United States Patent and Trademark Office 1997.

15 See Sherwood, Scartezini, and Siemsen 1999; Mossinghoff and Kuo 1998.

16 See Correa and Yusuf 1998: 202–03.

17 Correa and Yusuf 1998: 202–03. Article 43.V of the new Brazilian patent law specifically exempts the non-commercial use of living matter for research or propagation purposes to obtain other products. This shows the special sensitivities on biotechnological inventions.

18 See the report of the World Health Organization's Task Force on Health Economics, *Health Economics: The Uruguay Round and Drugs*, prepared by Carlos. M. Correa, which on page 8 supports this exception citing the law of the United States. On the other hand, Gervais (1998: 159) opines that this exception typically applies to non-commercial research.

19 The Drug Price Competition and Patent Term Restoration Act, 1984, which the American research-based pharmaceutical industry characterizes as decreasing the intellectual property protection for pharmaceutical products. See Report of the Boston Consulting Group, *Sustaining Innovation in US Pharmaceuticals*, January 1996.

20 See Cohen 1998.

21 See, for instance, Taylor and Silberston 1973; Scherer (1997).

22 This interpretation is challenged by some commentators, most notably Correa. See Correa and Yusuf 1998: 203, where it is argued that non-discrimination is meant to be applied only to infringing goods. However, it would be difficult to sustain these arguments in any TRIPS dispute. More importantly, it may not be necessary to do so as there are other ways around this prohibition.

23 Not surprisingly, the implementing legislation of a number of developed and developing countries continue to retain "non-working" or "non-exploitation" of patented inventions as a ground for the grant of compulsory licenses. See, for instance, Article 68 (1).I. of the new Brazilian patent law and Article 43 of the new Argentine patent law. It appears that many countries of the EU also continue with such provisions.

24 See particularly Strauss 1996: 204, footnote 188.

25 An excerpt from the case can be perused (Case no. X ZR 26/92 of December 5 1995) in *IIC* 28, 2, 1997.

26 See Bodenhausen 1968: 70: "member states are therefore free to provide ... compulsory licenses on conditions other than those indicated in paragraph (5A) (4), in other cases where *the public interest is deemed to require such*

measures.(emphasis in original) ... In such cases the rules of paragraph (5A) (3) and (4) ... do not apply, so that the member States have freedom to legislate." Indeed, if this were not the case, even compulsory licenses for dependent patents would be ruled out. Article 31(l) of TRIPS and the patent laws of almost all the countries show that this could not have been the case. See also Reichman 1995 on the public interest exception in TRIPS.

27 See, for instance, Correa 1997. Gervais (1998) rightly notes that negotiators weighed the options of listing the grounds and not doing so and, in the end, opted for the latter.

28 See MTN.GNG/NG11/W/70: Draft Agreement on TRIPS—Communication from United States, May 11, 1990, Article 27.

29 Heinemann 1996: 244 has a similar interpretation.

30 See MTN.GNG/NG11/W/68: Draft Agreement on TRIPS—Communication from the European Communities, March 29, 1990, Article 26.

31 The twelfth clause is restricted to compulsory licenses for dependent patents and is dealt with separately.

32 See Gervais 1998: 65.

33 Now the new Argentine patent law incorporates this ground as well in Article 42, the reasonable time limit being set at 150 calendar days from the date of application for the voluntary license. In addition, Article 44 grants compulsory licenses in adjudicated cases on anti-competitive practices, including excessive pricing and refusal to supply the market at reasonable terms. While refusal to deal may or may not be permissible under anti-competition law, it would be difficult to challenge this ground under Article 31 as this is specifically mentioned in clause (b) of this provision. All compulsory licensing takes away from the exclusive rights granted under Article 27.1, so this cannot be used as an argument to oppose it.

34 For instance, Section 46(2) of New Zealand's amended patent law provides for one ground only for the grant of a compulsory licence, namely where "a market for the patented invention is not being supplied, or is not being supplied on reasonable terms, in New Zealand." Further, Articles 133 to 140 of the Australian Patents Act of 1990, as amended by Part 4 of the Patents (World Trade Organisation Amendments) Act 1994, permit the issuance of compulsory licences on patents within Australia under certain circumstances, notably in cases where a trade or industry in Australia is being unfairly prejudiced, Australian demand for the patented invention is not being met, or the patented invention is not being commercially worked within Australia.

35 In fact the German Supreme Court in case no. X ZR 26/92 of December 5 1995, as cited in *IIC* 28, 2, 1997: 242–50, notes that public interest must take into account the well being of the general public, particularly in the field of general health care. However, in this particular case the ruling was that it was not proved that there was no other substitute for the treatment of the particular disease and hence the demand for compulsory license was rejected. A similar case could be decided in an entirely different manner by the relevant authorities in another country.

36 However, even under the Indian system, actual use is authorized individually after settling the terms of the non-voluntary license (Section 88 of In-

dia's Patents Act, 1970). The license of right system has to be disbanded by India under TRIPS not because of Article 31(a) but because of Article 27.1, which prohibits discrimination amongst fields of technology.

37 See Gervais 1998: 165 where the opposite interpretation is made.

38 See Gervais 1998: 165 where a contrary suggestion is made.

39 See the United States General Accounting Office 1987: 26–27 for a discussion of exclusivity of compulsory licenses and the opposition of the United States Government to this in the context of the Revision of the Paris Convention.

40 Section 93(3) of the Indian Patents Act, 1970 authorized the deprivation of even the patentee or any existing licensee over the patented invention.

41 Sub-section (c) of the Brussels draft of this article reproduced on page 161 of Gervais (1998), like many of the other conditions was not in brackets, showing that it was largely an agreed text by this time.

42 This argument applies also to the use of compulsory licenses to import the patented product; although TRIPS does not prohibit this, it is likely to be an insignificant benefit.

43 See MTN.GNG/NG11W/70 and MTN.GNG/NG11W/68 (cf. notes 28 and 30, above).

44 See Gervais 1998: 166.

45 The advantage of instituting an administrative body to review such decisions as against a court of law are obvious. The United States and the European Union had earlier insisted on a judicial review of compulsory license decisions in MTN.GNG/NG11W/70 and MTN.GNG/NG11W/68 (cf. notes 28 and 30, above).

46 Indeed, there are indications that these terms have not been incorporated in to the laws of many developed countries.

47 See Articles 42 to 50 in 'Invention, Patents and Utility Models Act (No. 24-481)' of Argentina as translated by Matthew Bender & Co., (Rel.75 –7/97 Pub. 622).

48 See 1997 on the use of competition law to curb the abuse of market power.

49 MTN.GNG/NG11/W/70, Article 24(2) (cf. notes 28 and 30, above).

50 MTN.GNG/NG11/W/68, Article 24(3) (cf. notes 28 and 30, above).

51 Brazil was not then a member of the Paris Convention (1967).

52 See Bodenhausen 1968: 70.

53 See MTN.GNG/NG11/W/37: Standards and Principles Concerning the Availability, Scope, and Use of TRIPS—Communication from India, 10 July 1989, page 11-12, paragraph 2.

54 Whether or not such a drastic measure would influence the decision of foreign patentees to patent, and then export, manufacture, or use the patented invention in that country is a moot point and would depend on several factors, including whether or not this provision is likely to be used.

55 See Correa 1994. In Korea, proof of novelty of the product *per se* may be given by submitting a copy of a patent application, even if such an application is not valid for grant of a product patent in Korea. The term "new" here was intended by the *demandeurs* to mean "new in the market" (i.e. not yet introduced in the market) but this was not specified in the text.

56 See Strauss 1996: 210, footnote 208.
57 See new Argentine patent law, Article 88 and the Republic of Korea's patent law, Article 29.
58 See Gervais 1998: 172.
59 Section 295 of USC 35.
60 Gervais 1998: 209–10.
61 See Article 42(2) of the new Brazilian patent law and Article 60 of the Chinese patent law. China is not yet a member of the WTO but its amended patent law was widely seen as being compatible with TRIPS.

References

Bodenhausen, G.H.C. (1968). Guide to the Application of the Paris Convention for the Protection of Industrial Property. Geneva: BIRPI.

Cohen, A. David (1998). Exception to Experimental Use and Limited Patent Term Extension in Israel. *Patent World* 102 (May/June): 24–27.

Correa, C.M. (1994). GATT Agreement: New Standards for Patent Protection. *European Intellectual Property Review* 8: 327–35.

——— (1997). Implementation of the TRIPS Agreement in Latin America and the Caribbean. *European Intellectual Property Review* 8: 435–43.

Correa, Carlos M., and Abdulqawi A. Yusuf (1998). *Intellectual Property and International Trade: The TRIPS Agreement*. London: Kluwer Law International.

Gadbaw, R.M., and T.J. Richards (1988). *Intellectual Property Rights: Global Consensus, Global Conflict*. Boulder, CO: Westview.

Gervais, Daniel(1998). *The TRIPS Agreement: Drafting History and Analysis*. London: Sweet and Maxwell.

Heinemann, Andreas (1996). TRIPs and Antitrust Law. In Friedrich-Karl Beier and Gerhard Schricker, *From GATT to TRIPs – The Agreement on Trade-Related Aspects of Intellectual Property Rights*, IIC Studies 18 (Munich: Max Planck Institute for Foreign and International Patent, Copyright and Competition Law): 239–47.

Mazzoleni, Robert, and Richard R. Nelson (1998). The Benefits and Costs of Strong Patent Protection: A Contribution to the Current Debate. *Research Policy* 27: 273–84.

Mossinghoff, Gerald J., and Vivian S. Kuo (1998). World Patent System circa 20xx A.D. *IDEA: The Journal of Law and Technology* 38: 529–68.

Oddi, S.A.(1996). TRIPS—Natural Rights and a "Polite Form of Economic Imperialism." *Vanderbilt Journal of Transnational Law* 29 (May): 415–70.

Papovich, Joseph (1997). NAFTA's Provisions Regarding Intellectual Property: Are They Working as Intended? A US Perspective. Paper presented at the Canada-US Law Institute Conference: NAFTA Revisited. Proceedings reproduced in the *Canada-US Law Journal* 23: 253–60.

Reichman, J.H. (1995). Universal Minimum Standards of Intellectual Property Protection under the TRIPS Component of the WTO Agreement. *The International Lawyer* 29, 2 (Summer): 345–88.

—— (1997). From Free Riders to Fair Followers: Global Competition Under the TRIPS Agreement. *New York University Journal of International Law and Politics* 29: 101–77.

Scherer, F.M. (1977). *The Economic Effects of Compulsory Licensing.* New York University Graduate School for Business Administration.

Sherwood, Robert M., Vanda Scartezini and Peter Dirk Siemsen (1999): Promotion of Inventiveness in Developing Countries through More Advanced Patent Administration. Unpublished manuscript, available on file with author.

Straus, Joseph (1996). TRIPs and Patent Law. In Friedrich-Karl Beier and Gerhard Schricker, *From GATT to TRIPs – The Agreement on Trade-Related Aspects of Intellectual Property Rights*, IIC Studies 18 (Munich: Max Planck Institute for Foreign and International Patent, Copyright and Competition Law): 160–215.

Taylor, C.T., and Z.A. Silberston (1973). *The Economics of the Patent System: A Study of the British Experience.* Cambridge: Cambridge University Press.

United States General Accounting Office (1987). Report to Selected Congressional Subcommittees on International Trade: Strengthening Worldwide Protection of Intellectual Property Rights (April). Washington, DC: USGAO.

United States Patent and Trademark Office (1997). Number of Utility Patent Applications Filed in the United States, by Country of Origin, Calender Year 1965 to Present. Digital document: www.uspto.gov.

Watal, Jayashree (2000). *Intellectual Property Rights in the World Trade Organization: The Way Forward for Developing Countries.* New Delhi: Oxford University Press (India).

One Trip to the Dentist Is Enough

Reasons to Strengthen Intellectual Property Rights through the Free Trade Area of the Americas Now

OWEN LIPPERT

Negotiating free trade agreements is the political equivalent of a trip to the dentist. Changing intellectual property laws is a trip without anesthetic. It takes a great deal of persuasion for any country to do one, let alone both. Based on my experiences in 1997 and 1998, a stronger case needs to be made for negotiating a high and consistent level of protection for intellectual property rights in the Free Trade Area of the Americas (FTAA).[1]

In 1997 and 1998, I attended the Business Forum sessions that meet just before the annual hemispheric trade ministers' summit to discuss the progress towards FTAA negotiations.[2] The forums were held respectively in Belo Horizonte, Brazil,[3] and San Jose, Costa Rica.[4] I participated in the sessions of the Working Group on Intellectual Property.[5] Watching the discussions would have led anyone to suspect that the intellectual property rights to be negotiated in the FTAA might not advance beyond the current international standard found in the 1994 agreement on Trade Related Aspects of Intellectual Property Rights (TRIPS Agreement)[6] negotiated during the Uruguay Round of trade talks establishing the World Trade Organization (WTO).[7]

Notes will be found on pages 159–65.

I argued as much in an article for the Americas Column of the *Wall Street Journal* under the headline, Pirates Plunder Patents. Will the Rule of Law Prevail? (Lippert 1998). In response to the piece, James Packard Love,[8] who also attended the Business Forum sessions, and I have had several public and private debates. Our debate has mirrored the ongoing North-South discussion on intellectual property rights (IPRs) and trade (Primo Braga 1989). The existence of our debate raises the question that if the benefits of stronger IPRs are so self-evident, why does it take international treaties to prod developing nations into compliance?

The question can be restated in the context of the current effort by 34 nations to negotiate IPRs in the FTAA. Are American trade negotiators acting largely for the benefit of the American pharmaceutical, software, and entertainment industries and are they using the FTAA to advance in a more manageable regional forum those IPR standards that were not secured in TRIPS? Are they seeking an accelerated implementation of TRIPS and possibly a TRIPS Plus in key hemispheric markets? If so, is this a desirable strategy for either or both the United States and the developing Latin American countries?

These questions arise against a background of persistent academic skepticism as to the wisdom of negotiating IPR standards in multilateral trade negotiations at all.[9] Reflective of that analysis is an article by J.H. Reichman (1993), in which he undertakes to refute the following three propositions that, he asserts, underlie the effort of developed nations to strengthen IPR in multilateral negotiations. First, "[s]trong intellectual property rights exert an unreservedly positive influence on developed free-market economies." Second, "[s]trong intellectual property rights benefit all countries regardless of their present stage of development." Last, "[t]he acquisition of non-indigenous technologies by developing countries other than by imports or license usually constitutes an illicit economic loss to the technology exporting countries" (Reichman 1993: 173).

Reichman dismisses the first two propositions as "counter-intuitive and neither historical experience nor the literature support them" (1993: 174). Though he concedes that countries with established IPR regimes are better off with them,[10] Reichman questions whether stronger regimes are necessarily more efficient than weaker ones (1993: 174). He describes the third proposition as "this residual mercantilist attitude [that] conflicts with the underlying competitive ethos from which intellectual property rights derogate and with the territorial nature of these derogations" (1993: 175). Under this view, the negotiation of IPR in the FTAA is just another exercise of raw economic power rather than a principled step towards an optimal regime. As in the Uruguay Round, where trade access to developed nation markets was horse-traded for the developing world's agreement to TRIPS, the FTAA round proposes a similar deal in which the elimination of hemispheric tariffs will be exchanged for a regional TRIPS Plus.

In response to Mr. Love, Professor Reichman, and others, in this chapter I will seek to answer the following three questions.

(1) Should a standard of IPR protection higher than that guaranteed by TRIPS be negotiated in the FTAA?

(2) If yes, what should be the level and scope?

(3) What specific enforcement mechanisms should be negotiated in the FTAA to ensure an effective agreement?

In doing so, I shall propose that the FTAA negotiate a higher and clearer level of intellectual property protection than TRIPS, specifically one that would follow the intellectual property provisions of the North American Free Trade Agreement.

Question I   Should a standard of IPR protection higher than that guaranteed by TRIPS be negotiated in the FTAA?

(A) Strengthening IPR offers long term gains

Strengthening IPR creates only transitional losses for developing countries while providing long-term gains.[11] The economic and social benefits, however, lie as much in strengthening property rights in general as in any specific new investment and transfer of technology. While empirical research can show the balance of economic gains and losses, other benefits, primarily the entrenching of the rule of law, are not so easily proven, though potentially more effective in stimulating sustainable economic growth. The long-term economic and social value of those benefits, not clearly susceptible to empirical measurement, outweigh the losses incurred either by restrictions on copying or by the granting of so-called monopoly privileges.

(1) Empirical debate over the effect of IPR standards

Conventional economic analysis of the effects of patents and other IPRs has tried to compare the social (or total) benefits of increased incentives for innovation against the social cost of the so-called monopoly right. Various efforts have been made to postulate empirical measures with which to validate the respective claims of net social loss or benefit.[12]

The standard "empirical" case against strengthening IPR in developing countries stems from the observation that the short-term losses cannot help but outweigh the long-term gains because such IPR laws would forbid the relatively easy and cheap copying of foreign patented goods.[13] Unable to produce these goods, in particular pharmaceutical drugs, developing countries would face an immediate and insurmountable loss to the welfare of domestic consumers.[14] Further, developing countries would be denied the opportunity to develop their economies through a growth-through-imitation stage such as characterized Japan after World War II.[15] By this view, the immediate costs of stronger IPRs, including higher administrative and enforcement expenses, larger royalty payments, potential price increases in patented products, and the restriction of "pirate" producers, overwhelm any gains from the resulting stronger incentive-to-invent, which, at any rate, would be concentrated in the already developed world (Reichman 1993: 174). This case has been cast as so obviously empirically valid that relatively little research was conducted to verify it.

In the last 20 years, however, numerous studies have sought to measure the effect of changes in IPR standards on such items as economic growth, foreign direct investment (FDI), technology transfer, and consumer welfare (Primo Braga 1990a; Evenson 1990). Special mention must go to the pioneering work of Edwin E. Mansfield of the University of Pennsylvania (Evenson 1990). The literature to 1990 was ably reviewed by Robert E. Evenson and Carlos A. Primo Braga in a World Bank study.[16] It is fair to say that the results up to then were tentative.

Newer studies have, however, begun to demonstrate a consistent positive correlation between stronger IPR and desirable effects in each of these areas.[17] More fine-grained studies have even shown a relationship between the quality of protection for IPRs offered in developing countries and the specific types of investment undertaken by multinational corporations (Sherwood 1997).

Even in the flash-point debate over the cost of stronger patent protection for pharmaceutical drugs, new evidence suggests that earlier concerns may have been somewhat exaggerated. Canada provides an instructive example (Lippert, McArthur, and Ramsay 1998).

In 1993 in preparation for the signing of the North American Free Trade Agreement (NAFTA), Canada upgraded its intellectual property laws. Specifically, the new law, known popularly as Bill C-91, ended the practice of compulsory licensing of patented pharmaceutical drugs developed by foreign drug companies (Patent Act Amendment Act of 1992, S.C., ch. 2, §3 [1993] [Can.]). The fear at the time was that these companies would exploit their "monopoly" position and force up the price of patented drugs.[18] Yet, ever since 1993, the average price of patented drugs has increased below the rate of inflation. For the last two years, prices have dropped by an average annual rate of two percent.[19] In Canada, the difference between the prices of patented and generic drugs is now about 20 percent.[20] Though the claim is made that the Patented Medicine Prices Review Board, set up by Bill C-91 to monitor drug prices and, if necessary, to roll them back, has contributed to price restraint, the actual number and scope of the PMPRB interventions have been modest.[21] Of more importance, one could claim, has been the consistently competitive nature of the pharmaceutical drug market in Canada over which the PMPRB has no mandate to regulate. In 1993, there were 45 drug companies in Canada providing therapeutic-class drugs. The largest held an eight-percent market share; the same is true today.[22] Canada's experience of relatively benign effects of increased patent production on the prices of pharmaceutical drugs is not unique, at least according to a major new study of nine post-IPR reform countries in the developing world by conducted by Richard P. Rozek and Ruth Berkowitz (1998).

Does this mean the empirical argument has been decided in favour of higher IPR? Not yet. On the whole, George Priest's words still ring true, "in the current state of knowledge, economists know almost nothing about the effects on social welfare of the patent system or of other systems of intellectual property" (Priest 1986: 21).

(2) The theoretical debate over stronger IPRs

Beyond the empirical results lies a theoretical debate as to whether weaker IPR benefit developing countries and stronger ones harm them (Oddi 1987). At the core of the debate lies the question of whether IPR are a true individually held property right or a monopoly granted by the state to encourage innovation. If the former, then improvements in IPR protection is presumably desirable, whatever the empirical results as to social costs. If the latter, then any change to IPR protections should be subject to some welfare test.

Much speculation has focused on why implementing stronger IPR protections in developing countries would fail a welfare test. Such reasons include the losses from (1) an inability to copy patented products cheaply and easily (as discussed above), (2) the lack of access to the latest technology and the subsequent dependency of developing countries on developed ones, and, more recently, (3) the creation of market abuses by companies holding monopoly patents. After discussing the core issue of the identity of IPR, I will address these three theories, based on a social welfare analysis, ranged against stronger IPR protection.

(a) Are intellectual property rights subject to the law or are monopoly privileges subject to competition policy?

The debate over the nature of IPRs, and patents in particular, goes back to the very first patent. When the city fathers of Florence granted the patent Number 1 to Filippo Brunelleschi, who had invented a loading crane for ships, their economic self-interest, not any sense of property rights, guided them. The preamble to this first patent bluntly states that "[Brunelleschi] refuses to make such machine available to the public, in order that the fruit of his genius and skill may not be reaped by another without his will and consent; and that, if he enjoyed some prerogative concerning this, he would open up what he is hiding, and would disclose it to all" (Bugbee 1967: 17). From this perspective, patents would appear as a regulatory form of monopoly created to serve the "instrumentalist" end of encouraging inventors to invent.[23]

Yet, if for the rulers of Florence and Venice (and shortly thereafter the German and Dutch trade cities) the granting of a patent was simply a calculation of costs and benefits, for Brunelleschi and inventive individuals who followed him it was a revolution in their economic and legal relationship to both the state and the broader business community. They held a property right, if only temporarily protected, to the relatively exclusive use and control of the physical and practical forms derived from their unique insights into the possibilities of matter. What they owned the state could not seize nor competitors steal. Thus from its beginning the patent embodied, in the words of Michael P. Ryan, "the philosophical tension between natural property rights and public welfare – enhancing incentives for risky investment" (Ryan 1998: 7).

One could, indeed, write the history of patent law as the shifting balance between the relative value of personal property rights and a mere incentive for innovation and investment. Deputies of the National Assembly during the French Revolution asserted that an inventor's property right in his discovery represented one of the "rights of man." They desired in part to restrict the state, and the aristocrats who controlled it, from exploiting productive and innovative members of the bourgeoisie. In contrast, Thomas Jefferson, worried less about aristocrats and more about the social value of proprietary knowledge, wrote Article I, section 8 of the Constitution to establish patents for strictly utilitarian purposes: "to promote the progress of Science and the useful Arts" (Bethell 1998: 262).

One might even conclude that personal interests will forever determine the debate. On the one side, inventors and their lawyers insist that intellectual property rights are about preventing theft. On the other, politicians and economic planners assert that patent "law" concerns the balance between industrial incentives and the diffusion of useful knowledge. Yet, there are three reasons to choose the property rights side in this debate: convention, the evolutionary nature of rights, and capitalism's revealing of the value of IPRs as rights.

(i) Convention Convention, too often, is underrated when compared to supposedly objective analysis. It is convention that gives patent the legal form of a property right and determines its specific length. Economists did not determine that the socially optimal length of a patent should be 20 years; indeed, there are probably too many uncertainties ever to decide such a question. (One could say that patents are not about the duration of an intellectual property right at all, but rather about the length of time the state is willing to defend it on behalf of the inventor.)

A maddening feature of convention is that history provides few straight answers as to why patents evolve from something close to blackmail in Renaissance Florence to a right defined and protected by the common law in the modern Anglo-American tradition. Still, convention, though malleable, deserves respect even if its underlying logic may appear elusive.[24]

There is also the possibility that convention generates its own strong economic efficiency argument for IPR as rights.[25] That argument is the same as the efficiency argument for the common law made by such scholars as Richard Posner, William Landes, and Richard Epstein (Landes and Posner 1987, 1988; Epstein 1995). They contend that, for reasons of historic accident and particular human ingenuity, the English common law developed a set of procedural and substantive principles that over time have generated economically efficient answers to disputes (Landes and Posner 1988: 10, n. 52). Epstein identifies the few "simple rules" that, with the intellectual discipline imposed by the doctrine of *stare decisis*, gave the common law its capacity to lead to efficient results. These are "individual autonomy, first possession property rights, voluntary exchange, control of aggression, limited privileges for cases of necessity, and just compensation for 'takings' of private property" (Epstein 1995: 15, n. 52). These are the same principles that apply, more or less, to intellectual property today in developed countries.

In the end, one can agree that holding a patent differs from owning a shotgun. The distinction between them is that of possessing a thing as opposed to the opportunity to make use of novel and useful idea or insight. Yet, the mutual quality of exclusivity before the eyes of the law binds them together. If it walks like a duck, sounds like a duck, and looks like a duck, it probably is a duck.

One qualification in the context of negotiating IPR in the FTAA is that most Latin American countries have a Civil-Code tradition. As a result, their legal systems do not possess clear counterparts to *stare decisis* and other common law principles.[26] Nevertheless, Civil-Code reasoning itself has changed around the world and the blending of Civil-Code content and common-law reasoning has been a hallmark of this century, particularly as legislation has gradually codified case law (Merryman 1969). Models for further convergence do exist, such as the legal system of the Canadian province of Quebec.[27]

(ii) The evolutionary nature of rights   The power of convention is such that even though IPRs may not have begun as a property rights, they have evolved towards that identity; that is, that their nature as property rights has been discovered gradually over time. This begs the question: what, then, are rights? Simply put, they are protections of behaviour and property that a society decides at some point to place outside of a cost-to-benefit analysis (Mattei 1997: 415).

Critics contend that the defenders of IPRs as rights ultimately base their position on a notion that IPR are natural rights as defined by John Locke (1690/1980). That is, if we have a natural right to own the fruits of our labour, we have no less a right to own the fruits of our ingenuity. What they attack is not the strength of the proposition but rather the somewhat mystical nature of natural rights. It is a reflection of our age that an appeal to the laws of nature falls under immediate suspicion. Nevertheless, what is important about IPRs as rights is not their ultimate source. More significantly, they, as with other property rights, may be seen to represent pre-transactional social values that provide a dividing line between the state and the individual as to the control of material possessions and of physical and mental effort. In contrast, if patents are construed as welfare-based regulations, then they constitute post-transactional distributions of wealth guided by the state towards a variety of social goals (Epstein 1998).

A risk exists in trying too hard to deny the development of IPRs into fully accepted property rights. As Roger E. Meiners and Robert J. Staaf conclude "there is no basis to classify intellectual property as the grant of monopoly rights, unless numerous other rights that involve exclusion, such as home ownership or labour services, are classified as monopoly rights" (1990: 911, 940). The further the state comes to see itself as the creator of value, the greater the temptation to use supposedly neutral utilitarian analysis to further its own, or rather its employees and beneficiaries, self interest.

(iii) The nature of IPRs changes as capitalism changes   Just as the Renaissance created "new facts" as to the nature of capitalism and the nature of man, thus altering profoundly the treatment of innovation, so, too, may contemporary thinking about capitalism and the nature of man re-

shape the value afforded to intellectual-property protections. It may well tip the balance farther towards a property-rights based conception of intellectual property. The impetus—the "new facts"—lies beyond the obvious, an economy increasingly driven by technological advances and thus more heavily dependent upon proprietary knowledge, be it in the new, computers and software, or the traditional, medicine and agriculture. This greater dependence on intellectual property is not changing the nature of modern capitalism but rather allowing it to operate at a *qualitatively* higher level of efficiency.

New communication tools have sped the diffusion of both market information and production, thus speeding up the articulation of consumer preferences and the ability of producers to respond. It is no longer necessary to have either a central market or a central factory. Technology has simplified and automated monitoring and process functions, thus reducing both transaction costs and personnel costs relative to a unit of economic output. Technology has allowed us to become more productive while at the same time subjecting us to fewer hierarchical and personal controls. Just as the innovations of banking and insurance awoke Florence to the possibilities of early capitalism, the greater economic role of intellectual property has brought into clearer focus Friederich Hayek's vision of "extended order" through the "rule of law."

As entrepreneurs flourish and more individuals work for themselves (roughly one in every six North Americans), the concept of productive work in a capitalist economy has embraced new decentralized configurations. Work can be self-directed. High levels of economic activity can be sustained by networks of self-contracting individuals and not just by corporations enjoying economies-of-scale. This emergent free-agent capitalism will, in turn, give greater weight to another insight of Austrian economics: that our "producer surplus" lies less in the hours of our labour and more in our creativity (Postrell 1998: 35).

It would be insufficient to argue circularly that current capitalism's success with "owned" knowledge (patents) proves the case that property law, not policy wishes, guide decision-makers. Just as in the Renaissance, economic opportunity is alone an incomplete force to change attitudes. As in the fifteenth century, the legal recognition of intellectual property arose in response both to a new form of economic organization and to a new sense not just of self but of its abstraction— the individual. If we are not surprised today that the nature of the economy is in flux, neither should we be if our ideas of the individual are shifting. At least, Western history shows individualism to possess an ontology or a story of change (Taylor 1989: 8–14). This cannot help but alter the cultural boundaries within which we cast the nature and treatment of innovation and innovators. After all, it was a champion of the individual, not of economics, Lysander Spooner, the nineteenth-century libertarian, who first coined the potent phrase "intellectual property," recasting unalterably the debate (Bethell 1998: 259, n. 49).

Will our society, in the new millennium, recognize even greater individual autonomy, thus further shielding IPR from state interventions? It should—but wishes are poor predictions. Still, if the hard-edged men of Renaissance Florence could figure out the advantage of patents in the first place, perhaps we can discern the added value of more firmly conceiving of intellectual property as individual property before the law.

(b) The welfare tests for not strengthening IPR

The point here is not to argue against standard normative economic analysis of intellectual property protections. It is just to point out that several of the efforts to do so have been fraught with problems, perhaps less the result of the underlying economic methodology and more that of the researchers' biases in scope, duration and policy. The whole area deserves a thorough intellectual audit (Kuo and Mossinghoff 1998: 537).

(i) The cost of copying A welfare analysis might easily prove governments in developing nations should encourage the free copying of foreign technology in order to jump-start domestic industries at a relatively low cost. There is, however, one good reason to be skeptical that things will work out that way—the behavior of individuals in the market place typically frustrates the best-laid designs of government planners.

The following scenario demonstrates one possible outcome. Suppose a country orders the compulsory licensing of a multinational corporation's patent, then awards the license to a domestic producer. That producer now possesses a "free good." That does not mean, however, that he has withdrawn from the market and all of its familiar dynamics and, thus, that the consumer will benefit from lower prices. First of all, the domestic producer will likely charge a "shadow price," a price that is just below what patent-holders charged, knowing that the market will bear that price (Posner 1992: 16). Though the producer will try to maximize his output with lower prices, he remains committed to increasing his surplus, not the consumer's.[28] In addition, the producer may also wish not to upset the politicians and bureaucrats who control the compulsory licenses.

As a result, the consumer's surplus may be quite small. It is likely to be smaller when the patent holder is forced to retreat from the market and the domestic producer no longer has to worry about competition in future price-setting decisions. More seriously, consumer could face the loss of potential surplus gains from new and improved products as patent holders delay entry into that market.[29] One should not, however, be too much of an alarmist. Patent holders might still sell their products in risky markets, just more cautiously.

One could argue that if compulsory licenses were granted to multiple domestic producers, then this would stimulate the competition necessary to improve the consumer's surplus. Further research is needed to learn the extent to which compulsory licenses have been assigned to single or multiple domestic producers. I suspect that single producer licenses predominate for the reasons given below.

Public-choice theory provides a reason that compulsory licensing might lead to unintended consequences.[30] Compulsory licensing would appear to be a form of "producer capture" by regulatory bodies. That is, domestic producers in developing countries protect their own interests by convincing governments of the need to issue compulsory licenses of the patents of multinational corporations (Griffitts 1996: 283; Shain 1994: 182). After the decision has been made, market tests are concocted to justify the expropriation. The political risk attached to compulsory licensing is initially quite low, as multinational corporations are generally unloved and unappreciated creatures of the United States and Europe (Yelpaala 1985: 246–47). The government officials who dispense these "rent-seeking" licenses do so for reasons ranging from the satisfaction of administering "industrial policy" to the public acclaim of protecting national economic sovereignty to outright bribery.[31]

It is hard to see how the consumers' interest would have a high priority in mutual rent-seeking agreements between domestic producers and government (Dunoff 1996/1997: 772–73). In short, the so-called economic benefits of compulsory licensing may prove to be merely the transfer of income from politically docile consumers to politically potent producers (MacLaughlin, Richards, and Kenny 1988).

The irony here is that domestic producers may not gain as much in the long run as they had expected. Economist Gordon Tullock observed that the profit record of companies protected by tariffs and government regulations did not appear to differ substantially from those not protected. As a result, he postulated that any one company's gains made from government privileges, such as compulsory licenses, will not last (Tullock 1993: 224–35). They will be caught in a transitional-gains trap in which bureaucrats and politicians will seek to capture their own rents from favoured companies through a variety of means.[32] There is also the risk that the government will later cancel IPR privileges, such as compulsory licenses, in order to achieve more desired gains, such as trade access, in multilateral trade agreements.

(ii) Lack of access to technology and dependency   A popular view holds that foreign technology is a necessity *sine qua non* for economic growth in the developing world (Kuo and Mossinghoff 1998). As a result, it is less important how technology is acquired than that it is. Presumably, lower IPR standards best assure access to new technology (Oddi 1987).

The discussion mirrors the error in the post-war development debate that simple capital accumulation could drive economic development (Cao 1997: 551–52). That view is under siege now that the billions spent in development aid are increasingly judged to have produced only marginal benefits for the average citizen in the developing world. To paraphrase the English economists, Peter T. Bauer and Basil S. Yamey, substituting the word "technology" for "capital," "[i]t is often nearer the truth to say that [technology] is created in the process of economic development than that development is a function of [technology] formation" (Waters 1998: 109). Few would deny that new technology plays some role in the economic growth of developing countries. Still, the means by which it was acquired might indicate the quality of pre-transactional property rights, which may help to determine the long-term economic benefits derived.

The focus on foreign technology may also perpetuate the now problematic "dependency" theories of Raul Prebisch, Argentinian social scientist and former director of the United Nations Conference on Trade and Development (UNCTAD).[33] He assumed that technology could only come from the Center, and that dependency of Periphery on the Center is an active cause of under-development.[34] Granted, many Latin American countries have not had the experience of strong IPR and may not fully understand its positive effects on indigenous technology.[35] Still, there is no reason to assume that these countries could not generate as many advances in knowledge on a per-capita basis as any other. The problem lies not in the intelligence and creativity of the citizenry but in the institutional protections afforded the fruits of their labour (Edge 1994: 193–99).

Among the more critical factors is the institutional framework that determines the incentives and transactional costs of contracting. As Douglass C. North asserts, it is institutions and ideology that together shape economic performance. Institutions affect economic performance by determining the costs of transacting and producing. The work of North and others such as Oliver Williamson, referred to as the New Institutional Economics, builds upon the seminal ideas of Ronald Coase in his two now famous articles on the nature of the firm and on transaction costs (see North 1990; Williamson 1987; Coase 1988: 33–35, 174–79).

Briefly stated, one of Coase's fundamental insights is that the sustained economic success of a country does not depend upon any initial or subsequent endowment of capital and technology but rather upon its ability to maintain institutions of formal and informal rules that keep low "the costs of measuring the valuable attributes of what is being exchanged and the costs of protecting rights and policing and enforcing agreements" (North 1990: 27; also Dixit 1996: 37). At the core, reducing transaction costs requires a stable, clear, and enforced system of property rights (Trachtman 1997). As Armen Alchian pointed out over 30 years ago, "[t]he existing system of property rights establishes the system of price determination for the exchange of, or allocation of, scarce resources. Many apparently diverse questions come down to the same element—the structure of property rights over scarce resources. In essence, economics is the study of property rights" (Alchian 1967).

IPRs are part of a legal and institutional framework that, by lowering transaction costs, can create the conditions necessary for economic growth. If strong protections can be created and held in place, contractual efficiency should ensure that not only will new local technology be discovered but, more importantly, domestic and international technology can be fully exploited. Faith in this possibility may explain why both EMBRAPA, the research arm of the Brazilian Ministry of Agriculture, and ABRABI, an association of Brazilian biotechnology companies, have come out in support of their country's upgrading IPR protections.[36] Contractual efficiency should also lower the costs and improve the results of local industries receiving, adapting, and utilizing foreign technology. It is only an assertion, but one worthy of further research, that overall contractual efficiency could also compensate for the costs and inconveniences to second stage innovation caused by researchers having to invent around existing patents (see Merges and Nelson 1990). A society's overall contractual efficiency, however that may be measured, may prove critical to its ability both to adapt and invent new technology.

(iii) IPR and anti-trust law: an uneasy mixture The latest welfare test of IPR has arisen from the application of competition policy or anti-trust law in the American vernacular.[37] The equation of IPR and market "monopolies" has raised the possibility of new constraints on the exercise and scope of IPR.

Whether patents, for instance, should be subject to anti-trust policies is still a fluid question. Kenneth W. Dam argues that the use of the word "monopoly" to describe patents was a political definition of the Depression-era American Supreme Court and the result of the

Depression rather than a product of economic analysis (Dam 1994: 268–70). Still, the United States through case law, and other countries through legislation, have for some time restricted some actions by patent holders if it is determined that their patents create "market power." The American courts have developed the doctrine of "patent abuse,"[38] including the grounds upon which a patent holder may be forced to grant a license.[39] They have also developed prohibitions against patent holders' linking the grant of a license to the purchase of another product.[40]

Linkage is the issue largely at heart in the American Justice Department's current action against the Microsoft Corporation. It is alleged that Microsoft Corporation would not license the Windows Operating System to computer manufacturers unless their Internet Explorer was included.[41]

The risk exists that the use of anti-trust doctrines may unintentionally reduce IPR benefits such as the incentive-to-invent.[42] Potential for misuse grows out of a fundamental misunderstanding of the nature of patents. A patent does not guarantee any position, dominant or otherwise, in a market. It is simply one protection afforded to an individual or company seeking to make an economic rent from a unique innovation. By its definition, a unique innovation creates a unique new market (Gilbert and Shapiro 1996: 249-251). A patent only grants exclusivity to the invention, not to the market served by the invention (Dam 1994: 270). An invention, by its success in a market, may actually stimulate research by others to re-create that success with a new product.

The important questions about the market power of a patented product are whether substitutes exist for a new product—is the market contestable—and whether other individuals have the opportunity to invent new substitutes. If the answer to both is "yes," then there cannot exist a monopoly as understood in economics. In practice, the dominant position of any new bit of intellectual property in the market has not lasted for long and usually not as long as the patent or copyright protection afforded (Brenner 1990). Put another way, Windows™ will eventually face much stiffer competition than it does today, which will arise sooner rather than later. The very ups and downs of the Microsoft case suggest great caution in judging the market effects of patents in an anti-trust legal framework.

To date, international trade agreements have incorporated only a few, relatively ill-defined, anti-trust policies. The TRIPS agreement, however, creates the possibility for the inclusion of further antitrust measures (TRIPS Agreement: art. 2[1]). The issue is a familiar one in which some welfare test rather the procedural protections of property law, might determine the extent of IPR protections.

Indeed, Michael Trebilcock and Robert Howse have argued that countries should be able to use their IPR standards to their competitive advantage. By the same measure, they would also design other forms of regulation, such as environmental and health and safety standards to advance domestic industrial policy (Trebilcock and Howse 1998a, 1998b). They argue further that international trade agreements ought to entrench the flexibility of standards to ensure that such a comparative advantage can be exploited.

One can agree with Trebilcock and Howse that countries should have the scope under any trade negotiation to tailor their regulatory regimes to their advantage within, of course, the bounds of their international commitments. Intellectual Property Rights, however, should be considered part of a country's legal foundation of rights and not of its regulatory regime. As said earlier, IPRs are more properly part of a social pact on pre-transactional values rather than the distribution of post-transactional income. The court of world opinion would rightly condemn a country if it argued that upholding human rights imposed a unfair competitive disadvantage. Property rights are human rights and intellectual property rights are property rights. All deserve respect.

(3) IPR as an integral part of the critical package of rights

In sum, IPRs are just one, perhaps small, part of the complete package of individual rights upon which sustainable economic opportunity and development ultimately depends (Doane 1994: 469). If a country chooses to adopt one set of accepted rights because they are valued and convenient, it cannot then ignore other rights or downgrade them to regulatory options, without weakening rights as a whole. This is consistent with the oft-heard argument that developing countries pursue an immature and short-sighted strategy in solely pursuing property rights while, at the same time, largely ignoring civil and political rights (Gutterman 1993: 122).

The value of adopting stronger IPR protection in developing countries lies in the additional pressure to strengthen their institutional capacity to define, monitor, and enforce property rights as a whole (Stanback 1989: 523). In this light, Edmund Kitch's "prospect theory," which argued that the value of IPR lay in its ability to control the development of breakthrough discoveries deserves a more positive evaluation than it seems to be getting.[43] The short-term costs include the upgrading of judicial, legal, and administrative systems, the training of the legal community, and the bolstering of private managerial competence to contract and license technology (Reichman 1996: 372–79). These are comparatively small costs in dollar terms but much larger in the sense that they depend on conveying a vision of why and how they will benefit a country. The largest cost is the cost of restraining governments from exploiting IPR in order to play industrial favorites for the benefit of some producers, politicians, and bureaucrats (Reichman 1996: 372–79).

In a climate of robust property rights, governments are not unduly restrained. They may choose to expropriate intellectual property as long as due compensation is paid. Consistent with the rule of law, governments can use creative measures such as patent buy-outs to ensure the rapid diffusion of technology and knowledge. This has happened before. In 1839, the French government purchased the patent on the Daguerreotype process and placed it in the public domain.[44] That decision allowed France to lead the world in the creative development of photography during the subsequent century.

(B) If the negotiation of higher IPR standards is an effective lever to advance free trade, then let it be used to greatest effect.

Though often questioned and challenged (Irwin 1996), free trade remains the dominant policy to improve the welfare of individuals in the world. Despite the stunted "import = bad, export = good" mentality of the seven GATT Rounds, they have brought the world closer to realizing the benefits of global free trade. Average global tariffs on manufactured goods have fallen from 40 percent to three percent since the implementation of the Uruguay Round cuts have been implemented (Irwin 1996). Given the importance of trade in the post-war economic growth of developed and developing countries, it is surprising that it took so long to examine the state of domestic IPR regimes, both as source of potential non-tariff barrier to trade and as a bargaining chip in multilateral trade negotiations.

(1) Why did the rise of counterfeiting lead to the linking of IPR and trade?

IPR did not arise as a trade issue out of some theoretical appreciation of the benefits of free trade.[45] The genesis lay in the concluding years of the Tokyo Round when the United States sought a new lever, trade access, to suppress counterfeiting.[46] By raising the matter in the GATT talks, American negotiators sought to bargain wider access to the American market for improved IPR enforcement in other countries. Most nations, unfamiliar with this novel linkage, resisted and nothing initially came of the American initiative. Merits of this particular linkage aside, it made strategic sense to introduce at least some linkages in the GATT talks because of the wider scope for concluding complex agreements when multiple trade-offs are available.[47]

The United States's concern over counterfeiting seemed to some an over-reaction, given both the small percentage of the American economy dependent upon exports (between 10 and 15 percent) and the relatively small amount of lost revenue, which even the most generous of estimates placed at between $15 billion to $20 billion out of an annual foreign trade of $850 billion in 1996 (Aronson et al.: 5). Yet the intensity of the American concern reflected the concentration of those losses in three key industries: computer software, motion pictures, and pharmaceutical drugs (Mossinghoff and Oman 1997: 691–92). These industries, unlike others, purportedly receive roughly 50 percent of their total receipts from overseas markets.

As preparations began for the Uruguay Round, the United States re-thought their way of introducing the counterfeiting issue. As the Americans deliberated, they realized that pursuing counterfeiting alone was the equivalent of looking down the wrong end of the telescope. To achieve any progress in the area of counterfeiting meant addressing the broader issue of intellectual property. Under this view, counterfeiting was just one manifestation of the fragmented and porous IPR regimes that presented American businesses with both the prospect and reality of lost profits due to illegal or legal copying (Mossinghoff and Oman 1997: 691–92).

The American initiative to raise IPR in trade negotiations also reflected a dissatisfaction with the substantive international IPR standards maintained by the World Intellectual Property Organization (WIPO) and the enforcement mechanisms provided by the International Court of Justice (ICJ).[48] To be fair, WIPO and the ICJ were never intended to be the cop and judge of international intellectual property.[49] They were designed as means to help countries look after their own IPR regimes (Trebilcock and Howse 1998a: 258). They faced the challenge of any multilateral organization in setting an international agenda: in order to achieve consensus among the member states, some 129 in the case of WIPO as of 1995, substantial compromises have to be made. In the case of WIPO's model framework law for IPR, exceptions placed the level of protection at the lowest common denominator. As a result, it has continued to lose relevance to the actual contemporary practice of trade in goods and services with significant intellectual property content (Trebilcock and Howse 1998a: 263). The ICJ, suffice it to say, has never actually heard an IPR case and, if it did, it would only serve to clarify what the WIPO model framework law states (Cordray 1994: 131).

The American decision to pursue IPR standards in the Uruguay Round also reflected a need to shore up domestic support for trade liberalization (Schott 1994). The inevitable reaction to any major effort to lower tariffs is fear of new competition in goods and wages. Ross Perot, Patrick Buchanan, and the AFL-CIO all enjoyed substantial amounts of media attention by playing to the "blue-collar" fears of factories packing up in the middle of the night to sneak off to Tiajuana (Schott 1994: 32–33). Allies were needed. What better allies than the industries who stood the most to gain. It is not unfair to say that the pharmaceutical, software, and entertainment industries were maneuvered into fighting some of the American administration's trade battles.[50]

(2) The origins and significance of TRIPS

As a result of the efforts of the American government, the Uruguay Round established a separate set of discussions to reach a minimum set of standards for IPR protection among the GATT signatory nations. These talks ultimately led to the 1994 TRIPS agreement. The content of the discussions has been closely analyzed (Schott 1994: 30). Most agree the nub was a global package deal: in exchange for a agreement on an international standard for IPR, the United States would provide greater access to its market to the agricultural and textile products of the developing world and would pressure the European Community to grant the same (Cordray 1994: 143).

The TRIPS agreement, building on the principles of the Paris and Berne conventions, obliged signatories, first, to adhere to an international baseline for standards of protection for all areas of intellectual property--patents, trademarks, copyrights (TRIPS Agreement: art. 2[1]). Second, TRIPS requires effective enforcement measures, both at the border and internally (TRIPS Agreement: arts. 41–61). Third, the signatories must adhere to the dispute settlement provisions of the World Trade Organization (WTO) (TRIPS Agreement: art. 64).

The prospect of TRIPS helped to motivate American support for the Uruguay Round. Without a strong commitment by the United States Government, the Uruguay Round could have failed to advance the cause of free trade (Schott 1994: 30). It nearly did anyway. Though some developing countries questioned the price of TRIPS in terms of lost economic sovereignty, the gains from increased access for trade proved irresistible, particularly considering the alternative of increased unilateral trade sanctions under the United State's Section 301 and Special or "Super" 301 processes.[51]

The FTAA presents one more opportunity to bring global free trade closer to reality. It would set the example of an entire hemisphere removing tariffs and other barriers—if one takes at face value the declaration of the 34 national leaders at the 1994 Miami Summit of the Americas. The prospect of improved IPR standards may once again persuade the American government to take a strong leadership role.

It would be misleading and counter-productive to suggest that the current negotiations consisted in nothing more than the United States trying to extort concessions from its reluctant neighbors. First, many hemispheric nations are currently upgrading their IPR for purely domestic reasons (Edge 1994: 202–04. Second, and more importantly, after the rebuff of Chile's fast-track request, it remains difficult to assess the United States' will to push forward on hemispheric trade deals (Otero-Lathrop1998: 120). The American administration still has to convince the leaders of influential industries such as agriculture and textiles, which do not have an immediately clear stake in improved IPR, that the prospect of increased competition would be offset by new trade opportunities for all American industries. In a strategic sense, the developing nations of the hemisphere rely on the authority of the President to overcome protectionist lobbies in the Congress (Otero-Lathrop1998: 121–22). A weakened presidency leaves doubt as to the resolve of America's trade leadership (Gantz 1997: 391-405).

(C) TRIPS itself is an evolutionary step towards a yet unknown but implicitly acknowledged international standard

TRIPS is a revolutionary agreement; that no one disputes. It was the first time that an international standard of intellectual property was agreed upon by a majority of nations. Virtually no country has avoided making some commitment to change to its IPR regime. J.H. Reichman and others wisely counsel that realizing practical gains from the textual advances of TRIPS will take far more time and effort than many in the developed world expect (Reichman 1993: 261–63). Yet, TRIPS is not an ideal document. Much is unduly vague and complex.[52] TRIPS' central accomplishment is an acknowledgment that an international standard exists rather than a definitive formulation of such a standard (Dreyfuss and Lowenfeld 1997: 279).

The content of TRIPS itself can be described as defensive. Its articles characterize the existing diversity of IPR regimes, rounding them up rather than down, then apply to this picture a "standstill" provision. The goal of TRIPS for American and European negotiators was more to restrain developing countries from any further erosion of IPR protection and less to revise IPR standards substantially upwards.[53]

TRIPS left issues both of substance and of language unresolved. For instance, the major issues include what restrictions will be imposed on compulsory licensing, the scope of price controls, what to do when patents expire in one country but not another, and how to provide better enforcement at the border (Wolfson 1994: 557–58). In addition, areas such as the treatment of encrypted satellite signals, advanced biotechnology, and commercial data bases were left off the table because of a lack of information or of consensus.[54] It is unclear what is meant by terms such as "significant investment" (TRIPS agreement: 1224) "taking account of the legitimate interests of third parties" (1207), and the limits on remedies (1215). Other terms are sprinkled throughout the text, words such as "substantially" (TRIPS agreement: 1174), "reasonably" (1173, 1183), and "legitimate" (1170, 1197), all of which invite misunderstanding. TRIPS cannot be considered as the final word on an economically efficient and legally coherent global IPR standard.

Both developed and developing countries stand to gain from a prompt outlining of such an optimal global standard. For developing countries, the benefit lies in reducing uncertainty in domestic policy and ameliorating international commercial conflicts created by the constant flux in IPR obligations.[55] The fact that different countries have different capacities to implement such a standard should not deter the effort to define it. It is possible that countries may agree to a IPR standard that they simply do not have the institutional capacity to translate into reality. Yet, they should be able to remove the most offending practices such as discriminatory compulsory licenses.

Non-compliance on the basis of under-developed institutions is in some sense preferable to non-compliance on the basis of unreformed legislation and regulation, though complete compliance should remain the priority. The former is a matter of time, the latter a matter of political determination. By that I mean non-compliance on the basis of institutional capacity is preferable to active non-compliance because it shifts the emphasis to technical issues and away from competing visions of political economy (Edge 1994: 202–04). Opinions differ, however, on how far you should let the cart get ahead of the horse.

It would be a lost opportunity not to employ the FTAA as a means to define further an optimal global standard, notwithstanding the possibility of conflict. Any serious set of negotiations needs some conflict to expose and define the interests at work, ultimately revealing possible compromises. At a bare minimum, the FTAA should ensure no regression towards the notion of two separate IPR standards, one for the developed world and one for the developing world. To do so would impose the model of aboriginal Indian reservations on international IPR law, superficially protective and ultimately debilitating.

(D) The origin of the FTAA in NAFTA suggests a similar or higher standard of IPR protection

More significant than TRIPS to the future of the FTAA negotiations is the IPR chapter of the 1993 North American Free Trade Agreement (NAFTA) treaty among the United States, Canada, and Mexico.[56] The

FTAA came into being as a possible successor to NAFTA. That was the rhetoric, at least, of the 34 leaders who met in Miami, Florida in April 1994 to declare their commitment to eliminating hemispheric tariffs by the year 2005. Since then, the Mexican currency collapsed, President Clinton failed to secure "fast track" approval from the Congress for Chile's entry into a NAFTA-like trade agreement, and strong critics of free trade on both the left and the right have emerged in virtually every country (Bussey 1998b). Still NAFTA remains the model for the FTAA.

Does that then mean that the IPR in the FTAA should resemble the content and structure of NAFTA? The answer is both "Yes" and "No." Yes, in the sense that Canada, the United States, and Mexico would have just cause to deny the complete tariff benefits of an expanded NAFTA to new signatories who tried to "cherry pick" which NAFTA obligations they would adopt. NAFTA was signed as a package deal and was only possible because of its all-or-nothing structure of negotiations (Bussey 1998a). Each country weighed the trade-offs in NAFTA, then signed the agreement because as a whole it promised a net benefit.

Yet every negotiation should have its own dynamic based on an understanding of underlying commonly held principles. What is important is some shared vision as to what IPR protection should produce. Such a vision is not exclusively American, Canadian, or Mexican.

It is also worth noting, as Robert M. Sherwood and Carlos A. Primo Braga have, that a common base for a hemispheric IPR agreement also lies in the intensification of the regional integration accords (RIAs) such as MERCOSUR, the Group of Three Accord and Andean Common Market (ANCOM), through which IPR harmonization is already being addressed (Sherwood and Primo Braga 1996).

(E) If IPRs are going to be strengthened in the western hemisphere, let's go once, not twice, to the dentist, especially with a "Millennium Round" of global trade talks on the horizon

(1) The trouble with the TRIPS deadline

Though good reasons exist to proceed swiftly to the negotiation and implementation of an IPR agreement in the FTAA, strong impediments to prompt action remain. All countries have until 2005 to negotiate the FTAA. Some countries have until 2005 to implement TRIPS fully.[57] Countries—taking the line of least resistance—could argue that, if they have until 2005 to implement TRIPS, there is no reason for them to negotiate a whole new set of IPR obligations in the FTAA. Such a position, however, could jeopardize the current opportunity to put the IPR issue to rest for the foreseeable future.

An unusual feature of TRIPS was the comparatively long deadline set for developing nations to implement the agreement. Developing countries already in transition away from centralized economic control may postpone some of their TRIPS obligations until January 1, 2000. Countries who did not have product patent protection laws for advanced items such as pharmaceuticals at the time of signing, have until 2005 to comply. The very least developed countries have until 2006 to raise their patent protection to the TRIPS standard.[58] In contrast, under NAFTA, Canada and the United States had to give immediate force to the provisions on January 1, 1993.[59] Mexico had a grace period of up to three years on some of its obligations.[60]

Two reasons explain the extended implementation period in TRIPS. It reflects, to a degree, the very uneven state of substantive IPR law and enforcement mechanisms among countries. No one would dispute that developing countries face difficult challenges in bringing the law and the reality of intellectual property up to the level of TRIPS. The possibility exists that the actual commitment to strengthened IPR by some countries was marginal at best.

The long deadlines of TRIPS have likely tempted some current government leaders to avoid dealing with the state of their country's IPR protections. Why bother when the deadlines create the opportunity to pass the problem on to a potential successor, who would be the one to face the political and economic fallout that might accompany any upgrade of domestic IPR standards to the TRIPS level. It is relatively easy to agree to a difficult policy that someone else will have to implement. The deadlines also raise the possibility that succeeding governments, having never signed the original agreement, may not consider themselves bound to it to the same degree as the previous administration.

In Canada, it was a Progressive Conservative government under Brian Mulroney who upgraded the patent laws in 1993 to provide full 20-year protection (Greenspan and McIvoy 1998). Four years later, Alan Rock, the Attorney General of the new Liberal government, was publicly speculating that the term of patent protection could be shortened from 20 years (McArthur 1998).

Long deadlines invite failure and in the absence of sensible deadlines, it is responsible to press for accelerated implementation. If the FTAA negotiations on IPR can be fast-tracked, the nations of the western hemisphere could reach a one-time agreement on IPR standards and move on a single implementation schedule. If there are two overlapping implementation schedules, first TRIPS, then FTAA, it will lead to unnecessary friction. A one-shot implementation schedule is possible given the limited substantive differences between TRIPS and NAFTA's Chapter 17 (see Question II, below).

(2) Millennium Round

The prospect of a "Millennium Round" of WTO talks should give a special impetus to fast-tracked FTAA IPR negotiations with a single short implementation schedule. The FTAA could prove the testing ground for the "Millennium" IPR standard, with the western hemisphere countries pulling ahead of the rest of the world by already having such a standard in place. The President of the European Community, Leon Brittan, has already issued the call for a "Millennium Round" of WTO talks. President Clinton made a similar plea in his 1998 State of the Union Address. Sundry scholars, politicians, and business people have supported this initiative.[61] If a "Millennium Round" begins, say in the year 2000, two things are possible. First, the FTAA talks could be subsumed into it. Second, a TRIPS II could begin.

This is not to suggest that the FTAA could prove to be a waste of time and effort. On the contrary, the FTAA could deliver a NAFTA-level of IPR protection that would serve as a world standard. In addition, with an accelerated implementation schedule, the FTAA nations could, in one shot, reach their TRIPS, FTAA and future TRIPS II obligations. If that is achieved, the issue of IPR could finally be removed from both the international agenda and the domestic agenda of developing nations.

At any rate, even if the Millennium Round absorbs the FTAA, the FTAA will have proven beneficial as a training exercise for both the developing and developed countries of the hemisphere. For developing countries in South America, the FTAA provides an excellent capacity building exercise. They are learning how to handle multilateral trade negotiations of almost incredible complexity more aggressively and effectively.[62] In part, this new-found confidence is the result of the smaller scale and tighter focus of a regional negotiation. The developing countries also have the opportunity to re-affirm among themselves the growing Latin American consensus regarding what stimulates economic growth and the role of government in its achievement.[63]

For the United States, the FTAA provides lessons in both domestic and international trade politics. For one, international trade leadership depends upon first securing domestic support for the basic goals sought. While the FTAA negotiations can and will go ahead in the absence of the "touchstone" of United States approval for "fast track" negotiations with Chile, America's resolve for tariff reduction is being questioned (Scoffield 1998). In the context of the FTAA IPR negotiations, key concessions will not be made until that resolve is clarified.

Whether IPR is addressed in the FTAA or in a TRIPS II during a "Millennium Round," it will be addressed. The nations that have developed the capacity to negotiate the minutiae of IPR will have the best opportunity to assert their various interests.

Question II   If higher than TRIPS protection
should be negotiated in the FTAA,
what should be the level and scope?

NAFTA's Chapter 17 on IPR compels not only the discussion of IPR in the FTAA but also in large part determines its content. That should not prove unduly burdensome because NAFTA's IPR provisions are not so dramatically different from those that TRIPS provides.

Chapter 17 closely follows that of the TRIPS Draft Final Act (Dunkel Draft) brought to the table for negotiations in 1991 by Arthur Dunkel.[64] The compromise text ultimately adopted in TRIPS did not differ substantially in its scope from the Dunkel draft.[65] TRIPS differs from the Dunkel Draft mostly in its continuation of the numerous exception to national treatment obligations contained in the Paris Convention and the Berne Convention (TRIPS Agreement: art. 3(1) & 3(2); Caviedes 1998). In contrast, NAFTA only allows for a few, precisely detailed, exemptions from national-treatment obligations.[66]

The best known national-treatment exemption in NAFTA is for Canada's cultural industries.[67] It is a suspect exemption.[68] Canadian commentators have shown repeatedly that the policy owes little to any nuanced or profound understanding of culture, Canadian or otherwise (Stanbury1998). The absurdity of it all can be seen in the aftermath of the WTO ruling against the Canadian penalties levied on split-run magazines.[69] The government now proposes to restrict Canadian companies from advertising in American magazines sold in Canada although Canadian magazines that are sold in the United States, albeit in small numbers, are actively seeking advertising from American companies (Urquhart 1998: B12). At the time of this writing, a pointless trade war remains a possibility and both countries would lose by any economic or diplomatic yardstick.

NAFTA represents a landmark treaty both in its detailed description of IPR obligations and various mechanisms for dispute resolution. Chapter 17 has four parts. First, it sets forth general provisions on existing IP conventions, national treatment, and anti-competitive practices (arts. 1701–1704). Second, it defines obligations regarding IP standards in the areas of copyrights, patents, trade secrets, and industrial designs across a number of industries (arts. 1705–1713). Third, it introduces obligations regarding enforcement measures, including access to civil courts, judicial review and interim injunctions, and requires that these do not become barriers to legitimate trade (arts.

1714–1718). Fourth, it contains miscellaneous provisions, such as technical cooperation (art. 1719).

As noted, NAFTA, excluding the exceptions to national treatment, closely resembles TRIPS. One commentator notes, "The intellectual property provisions of the NAFTA were designed with the pending TRIPS agreement in mind. In most aspects TRIPS affords roughly the same protection for intellectual property as does the NAFTA" (Schott 1994: 122).[70]

As these issues are generally resolved in NAFTA, the FTAA IPR negotiations should move on to tackle thornier issues. Sherwood and Braga (1996) identify a few key "tough issues" that the FTAA IPR negotiations could address. These issues include compulsory licensing, cultural exemptions, "pipeline" protections, higher life forms, new plant varieties, information network systems, trade secrets, geographical exhaustion of rights, and a hemispheric Intellectual Property Council.[71] If these issues were addressed, the possibility exists of devising not just a TRIPS Plus but a NAFTA Plus agreement that could set the international standard for much of the next century.

Issues most in need of further resolution include the compensation mechanism for compulsory licensing and the definition of cultural exemptions. In the complex area of pharmaceutical and life-sciences patents, there are a number of specific issues to address. one such issues is that of guidelines for determining the trade in goods for which the patents have expired in one country but not another. Another issue, albeit for the more developed countries in the hemisphere, is that of patent term restoration that allows companies to enjoy the full term of their patent protection by adding the time spent securing regulatory approval to the life of the patent.[72] There are issues as to infringement exceptions for regulatory approval and for allowing generic competitors to stockpile products for release the moment the patent expires.[73]

A particularly controversial and important issue is that of data package protection. This refers to the capability of companies to keep the data they submitted in order to receive regulatory approval exclusive for a longer period of time (Coggio and Cerrito 1998: S4, col. 1). Access to data such as the results of human trials gives generic manufacturers a head start on preparing a product for market. Another contentious area is that of "linkage regulations," which allows patent holders to seek court orders to prevent the sale of a drug which appears to violate their patents.[74]

On the assumption that the highest standards of IPR protection could prove the most economically efficient, the FTAA negotiations should seek to achieve a level of IPR consistent with the protections offered in the United States, Canada, Europe, and Japan.

Question III   What specific enforcement mechanisms should the FTAA adopt to ensure effective protection?

The question of the type of enforcement mechanism that should be ne-gotiated into the FTAA has a slight air of unreality given the diversity of legal institutions among the participating countries. A country's ability to enforce IPR standards cannot be separated from its ability to enforce any law. The options are basically three-fold: adopt one of the existing multilateral models such as those in MERCOSUR, NAFTA, or the WTO; start from scratch and build a new enforcement mechanism; or modify elements of existing models to best fit the circumstances (Lopez 1997a: 624). Whatever the choice, countries will also have to give consideration to the interaction between the three identified exist-ing mechanisms and other more specialized mechanisms such as in-vestment protection treaties, including the stalled Multilateral Agreement on Investment (MAI) and the "non-violation complaint al-leging nullification or impairment of benefits" (Burt 1997: 1015; § III, § IV.A.2; discussing MAI).

The first place to start is to suggest what should be the guiding principles. A discussion of guiding principles should address the fol-lowing issues: legality versus informality, exclusively State-to-State ac-tions versus a mixture of state and private rights of action, domestic versus bilateral or multilateral panels, confidentiality versus openness, compensation versus removal of trade benefits, and permanent versus ad hoc enforcement institutions.

(A) Guiding principles for intellectual property protection

(1) Legality versus informality

The NAFTA dispute resolution and enforcement mechanisms are high-ly legalistic, depending upon rules that emerge through carefully de-tailed procedures rather than the "merits of the case" (Lopez 1997b:163, 165, 207). Over time, one expects the procedures laid out in Chapter 20 to become more precise (Lopez 1997b: 208). This trend has a value in promoting transparency and certainty.

Given the diversity of legal institutions and legal cultures within the hemisphere, there is much merit in devising enforcement mecha-nisms that allow numerous opportunities for informal, negotiated so-lutions before disputes reach the stage of a binding panel ruling (Lopez 1997b). This entails recognition of the enforcement mechanisms employed in MERCOSUR, which rely upon informal political negotiations often at a very high level.[75] The downsides are the politicizing of trade disputes in which the scarce time of executives can be wasted on relatively minor issues. Still, it is preferable to have negotiated rather than imposed enforcement. As countries become more accustomed to using international mechanisms, more legalistic forms could evolve.

The question becomes: "Can the model of the NAFTA dispute resolution and enforcement mechanisms be sufficiently modified to allow for opportunities for informality without sacrificing core transparency and certainty?" Company law provides some suggestions. For instance, there could be a defined period during which participants in a dispute could "opt out" of the dispute-resolution process to pursue informal settlement. If an accommodation could not be reached, the more formal rules would be triggered as a default.

The goal is to avoid unnecessary confrontations at times when countries are in a state too chaotic to comply. The example that springs to mind is the WTO rulings against India for its failure to pass complying legislation during a time of political crisis in 1995.[76]

(2) Mixture of state and private actions versus solely state actions

A mixture of state and private rights of action, as exists in NAFTA, provides a greater scope and flexibility for dispute resolution.[77] State-to-state mechanisms tend to be complex and lengthy. They impose costs that may come close to exceeding the value of issue under dispute. Private/state dispute-resolution procedures have the advantage of more closely mirroring the more familiar domestic court processes that allow for negotiated settlements at various points (Shell 1995: 889–90). They also have the benefit of removing a great deal of the politics found in relatively minor disputes.[78]

The most important point here is that alleged violations of IPR almost always involve private companies.[79] To the extent that governments are taking up the cause of these companies, their expenditures represent a subsidy. While clearly governments have a role in protecting the interests of domestic companies in foreign markets, the costs should fall more on companies themselves.

(3) Domestic versus bilateral and multilateral resolution

In an ideal world, disputes about intellectual property would be handled in the country where the alleged violations took place. One can too easily get trapped in the scholastic intricacies of these international dispute settlement mechanisms and forget that the vast majority of IPR disputes are settled within countries themselves, and rightly so.[80] It is the quality of domestic enforcement mechanisms that will best determine the effectiveness of any international IPR standards. Still, the ideal supposes a lot, such as reasonably consistent domestic laws and properly functioning legal institutions.

On this count, the multilateral enforcement provided by TRIPS is problematic.[81] Despite detailed provisions outlining enforcement procedures, TRIPS includes a significant "escape clause." Paragraph 5 of Article 41 states that Part III, laying out the enforcement requirements,

> does not create any obligation to put in place a judicial system for the enforcement of intellectual property rights distinct from that for the enforcement of law in general, nor does it affect the capacity of Members to enforce their law in General. Nothing in this part creates any obligation in respect of the distribution of resources as between the enforcement of intellectual property rights and the enforcement of law in general. (TRIPS Agreement: 1197)

The clause admits that if a country's judicial system does not work very well, intellectual property disputes have no special claim to any better treatment than other disputes similarly caught in the morass of underperforming courts. It would be narrow-minded to suggest that IPR disputes should have better treatment. The better course would be to say that the inevitability of increasing numbers of IPR disputes provides one more reason for nations to upgrade their judicial systems.

Attention to IPR in discussing judicial reform has a number of advantages. Bluntly put, as IPR disputes often involve great amounts of money, they attract attention (Perez 1993: 10). Such attention may be necessary to jump start the hemispheric process of judicial reform. It is time to break out of the mold of hollow and formalistic initiatives that have yet to produce substantive changes. As Rick Messick of the World Bank notes, "[i]n the past five years or so the World Bank and the Inter-American Development Bank have either approved or initiated loans totaling over $300 million for judicial reform projects in some [25] countries."[82]

More importantly, a focus on IPR as property rights can bring to the foreground fundamental rights and "rule of law" issues.[83] The reform of IPR enforcement in domestic judicial systems would contribute to increasing the contractual efficiency identified earlier as a key to economic growth.

(4) Confidentiality versus openness

William Landes and Richard Posner have argued that the courts in supplying judgments create a "public good" (Landes and Posner 1979). The work of mediation and arbitration panels in defining and interpreting the underlying text of trade agreements provides an analogous service. The value of that information, however, is only as good as its dissemination.[84]

Information about court and panel decisions does more than just guide behavior and transactions; it is also a means to hold judges and tribunal members accountable. Jeremy Bentham once wrote:

> In the darkness of secrecy, sinister interest and evil in every shape have full swing. Only in proportion as publicity has place can any of the checks applicable to judicial injustice operate. Where there is no publicity there is no justice. Publicity is the very soul of justice. It is the keenest spur to exertion and sheerest of all guards against improbity. It keeps the judge himself while trying under trial. The security of securities is publicity. (Gall 1995: 51)

The issue of openness has arisen between the United States and Canada involving disputes both in NAFTA and the WTO (Morrison and Alden 1998: 4; Castel and Gastle 1998. Two American companies have recently challenged Canadian policy under NAFTA's Chapter 11 on investments. The hearings were held in strict secrecy. The Canadian Trade Minister, Sergio Marchi, defended the secrecy as necessary to preserve commercial confidentiality.[85] He adopted a similar stance in response to a request from the United States Trade Representative, Charlene Barshefsky to open up to the media the hearings of WTO dispute settlement panel addressing the issue of Canadian dairy exports. As a Toronto Globe and Mail editorial correctly pointed out, "those are our tax dollars at stake and our laws that are on the stand. We have the right to learn the case against us."[86]

(5) Compensation versus removal of trade benefits

The penalties for violations of trade agreements boil down to two elements: (1) compensating the offended company or country or (2) removing the offender's trade benefits in the specific product area or in other areas as well, e.g., cross retaliation. Though both NAFTA and TRIPS have adopted cross-retaliation, this is probably not a healthy trend.[87] Negotiating compensation provides a more economically efficient solution.[88] First, it forces a country to deal squarely with the costs of its discriminatory behavior. Political leaders will have to defend publicly why they are using taxpayers' dollars to defend the commercial advantages of certain industries. Second, it does not weaken the hard-fought advances in free trade. Third, it provides greater scope for variations in domestic policy as long as costs are acknowledged and compensated. At any rate, negotiations on potential compensation should come before the suspension of trade benefits. In the event that countries cannot agree on compensation, there still remains the alternative punishment of canceling trade preferences.

Particularly in the area of IPR, compensation provides an attractive option. The nature of some knowledge-intensive products, such as pharmaceutical drugs, allows for a fairly reliable estimate of lost profits. For instance, if a domestic drug manufacturer violates a multinational corporation's patent by selling copies of a drug, it is reasonably easy to uncover its sales records. In the case of a large number of enterprises copying records and films, though, it is not such a straightforward exercise.

The FTAA negotiators have the opportunity to bring compensation into the forefront of IPR dispute resolution. This could serve the purpose of resolving related disputes such as the scope of cultural exemptions.

(6) Permanent versus ad-hoc enforcement institutions

If the goal is to negotiate most disputes and, to an extent, negotiate enforcement, it is counter-productive to establish expensive permanent tribunals who will inevitably have an incentive to drum up cases and drag them out. NAFTA and the WTO cope well enough with ad-hoc panels.[89] Moreover, as David Lopez suggests in arguing for evolutionary enforcement norms and procedure in the FTAA, a permanent institution is much more prone not to keep up with changing attitudes and capacities.[90]

(B) A modified NAFTA enforcement mechanism should provide the FTAA starting point

Given the diversity of countries in the hemisphere, simply adopting the WTO or NAFTA enforcement procedures would create too legalistic a mechanism to be immediately practical. As a result, expediency gives reason to incorporate some informal negotiation avenues contained in MERCOSUR.[91] The basic framework provided by NAFTA—progressive stages ending in compulsory third-party arbitration both for disputes between states and for disputes between private parties and states, with a final ruling that can require a schedule of compliance—should be used as the starting point. As Boris Kozolchyk writes, "[i]n my opinion, NAFTA's model, and not that of supra-national federalism is more likely to become universally acceptable. In the grand scheme of international cooperative forces, NAFTA is the model most consistent with the nature of the modern nation state and with the limits of man's cooperative impulses" (Lopez 1997a: 600, quoting Kozolchyk 1996: 144).

The starting point should be NAFTA—but with modifications. The modifications should seek to incorporate more openness, more openings for negotiation, and more opportunities for compensation-based remedies. The FTAA should also include a forward-looking statement as to the ultimate goal of resolving the majority of IPR disputes through domestic courts rather than through the ultra-national mechanisms provided for in trade agreements. Trade remedies under the auspices of multilateral agreements should be extraordinary remedies. International trade agreements can only provide a limited substitute for the domestic entrenchment of the "rule of law."

(C) Two complications with the NAFTA model

Though the NAFTA dispute-resolution and enforcement mechanisms could provide a starting point for the FTAA negotiations, they also possess some complex and problematic features, specifically the mechanism for resolving investment disputes (Carter 1998: 19–26) and the non-violation complaint (Hertz 1997: 262).

(1) Investment protections

The FTAA presents the opportunity to make more explicit the connection in NAFTA between IPR and investment obligations.[92] The importance of doing so lies in the fact that the flow of investment among the countries of the hemisphere may already exceed in dollar terms the volume of trade.

A landmark achievement of NAFTA was its Chapter 11 on investment protection (Hertz 1997: 262). Indeed, Allen Z. Hertz writes: "As for NAFTA, none of its multiple personalities is more important than its character as a powerful investment protection instrument" (Hertz 1997: 295). Still, it is little understood that Chapter 11 treats IPR as "intangible property" and, therefore, falling under the definition of "investment" (Hertz 1997: 295). By having IPR covered by Chapter 11, investors are afforded a new avenue of enforcement. According to Hertz, a former Canadian trade negotiator, in the case of a dispute between investor and state over a case of compulsory licensing, NAFTA provides that the merits of dispute would be heard by a Chapter 17 arbitration panel but that the compensation to be paid in the case of a violation might be determined separately by a Chapter 11 arbitration panel.[93]

As with any new wrinkle, NAFTA's linkage of IPR and investment has raised a number of difficult issues. These include: (1) What is the precise interaction between the trade and investment chapters? (2) What definitions should prevail in the case that Most Favored Nation (MFN) status and National Treatment differs between sections? (3) What is the precise scope of the investment chapter's meaning of "expropriation" and, more importantly, "measures tantamount to expropriation"? (4) How do the investment provisions in NAFTA affect other investment and IPR treaties? (5) What effect do the investment provisions have on the possibility of compensation to be paid in trade areas where exemptions have been negotiated, such as Canada's cultural industries? (See Hertz 1997: 295–307.)

If the FTAA process can help to bring some of these very difficult issues closer to resolution, then it will have achieved a great deal. Protection for intellectual property as investments will likely emerge in the next century as the preferred means to enforce rights. And, so it should.

It can be asked what benefit, aside from building negotiating knowledge and skills, would developing nations gain from wading through issues generated by NAFTA and left largely unresolved. For one, success in the FTAA could push the WTO to take over the MAI, a possibility made ever possible by the failure of the Organisation for Economic Cooperation and Development (OECD) to advance talks beyond the short-sighted efforts of the French and Canadian governments to restrict American "cultural" industries.[94] Through the FTAA process, the developing nations of the Americas would prove that negotiating investment agreements does not, and should not, have to remain a rich nation's game. If the MAI is negotiated within the WTO, developing nations will gain a say, rather than face the option of agreeing or not agreeing to a text written by the 29 OECD nations who control 98 percent of international foreign direct investment (FDI).[95] Indeed, the FTAA text could well serve as the basis for the MAI text.

(2) Non-violation complaints

The FTAA negotiations may also address some of the ambiguities of an emerging enforcement mechanism, the non-violation complaint. Allen Z. Hertz has described why this may be necessary, stating "the non-violation complaint alleging nullification or impairment of benefits, first fully elaborated under the General Agreement on Tariffs and Trade (GATT 1947) ... [is] now incorporated in both NAFTA and the WTO Understanding on Rules and Procedures Governing the Settlement of Disputes" (Hertz 1997: 262). There may be no avoiding dealing with the issue.

The non-violation nullification or impairment complaint refers to a right of action in a situation in which no explicit inconsistency or breach of obligations has occurred but the plaintiff party asserts that an action by the defendant has upset the balance of concessions and benefits expected when the original trade agreement was signed. In short, one party complains that even though no rule was broken, they are not receiving the benefits that enticed them to sign the agreement in the first place. As no inconsistency or breach has occurred, the plaintiff cannot request that the defendant remove the offending measure. Instead, through a WTO panel, the plaintiff seeks compensation in order to restore the original trade-off of benefits and concessions (Hertz 1997: 285–86).

The non-violation process presents a powerful tool for both nations and private parties to enforce IPR against the constantly novel ways to circumvent them. It does stress compensation over removal of trade benefits. However, if not properly defined, the non-violation complaint could lead to abuses for which the blame would fall incorrectly on the standard of IPR protection rather than the vagaries of the enforcement mechanism.

NAFTA applies the non-violation complaint to Chapter 17 on intellectual property (Prudhomme 1997: 133). Though there are exceptions, a party could have access to NAFTA's mechanism for settling disputes between states in order to determine whether another party had initiated a novel measure that, while not inconsistent with NAFTA, nullified or impaired a benefit expected under Chapter 17. Potential actions that could trigger a non-violation complaint include new laws on cigarette packaging, domestic content in broadcasting, and reference-based pricing for pharmaceutical drugs (Hertz 1997: 292). Canada agreed to having non-violation complaints apply to IPR out of the belief that it had secured sufficient exemptions, in particular for "cultural industries," to reduce the risk that they would ever be invoked (Hertz 1997: 287). Time and self-interest, of course, prove remarkable inspirations for innovation.

That Canada agreed to have the non-violation complaint in NAFTA surprised observers because it had opposed the American effort to place it in TRIPS and a compromise was found only in the dying days of the TRIPS negotiations, which allowed that non-violation complaints could not be initiated before January 1, 2000. The TRIPS Council is now examining recommendations for using the non-violation complaint that will be sent to the WTO Ministerial Conference, who can either approve its use or order more study. If the WTO ministers cannot reach a consensus, then the non-violation complaint will apply to TRIPS disputes on January 1, 2000 (Hertz 1997: 287–88).

One challenge for the FTAA negotiators is to define what constitutes a "benefit" that a non-violation complaint alleges has been lost (Hertz 1997: 294). If the definition of "benefits" is too narrow, then the non-violation complaint procedure would not be effective. If it is too broad, then the danger exists that any government action could trigger an attempt to secure those benefits through legal means less risky than the vicissitudes of the market. Some definition of "benefit" must exist that allows IPR-holders to use non-violation complaints to protect their market opportunities but does not, at the same time, invite speculative litigation. Finally, there must be some scope for government legislation and regulation that does not trigger trade actions. Without a workable and sensible definition of "benefits," whether by the FTAA, TRIPS, or the WTO, the exercise of the non-violation complaints could provoke an undeserved backlash against high standards of IPR. The accusation would be that such standards had led to an unintended loss of sovereignty. Whether the FTAA can competently deal with the non-violation complaint issue remains a question.

Conclusion

This chapter has sought to answer three questions. The answers to each can be summarized as follows.

- First, the FTAA should negotiate a level of IPR protection higher than that set by TRIPS. Both developed and developing nations will benefit from the resulting further entrenchment of property rights, the expansion of free trade, the shaping of a global optimal standard, and the settling of the intellectual property debate, at least in the short-term.

- Second, the IPR protections in NAFTA provide the starting point for the FTAA IPR negotiations. Negotiators should then go further to address the tough issues including patent-term restoration and data exclusivity. Even though some technologies, such as biotechnology and commercial databases, and some issues, such as compensation for compulsory licensing, may not yield a consensus, the effort to reach one will build knowledge and skills among negotiators and clarify the conflicting interests.

- Lastly, the enforcement mechanism for IPR contained in the FTAA should start with the basic model of NAFTA and should incorporate features from MERCOSUR through the use of "default rules" to provide for more openness, opportunities for negotiation, and the use of compensation rather than removal of trade benefits. The FTAA should proceed to define investment protections and non-violation complaints. More optimistically, the FTAA should provide an impetus to the reform of domestic judicial and administrative institutions to minimize the need to resort to ultra-national procedures.

To the first question, then, one may ask whether the FTAA is being used by American trade negotiators, acting largely for the benefit of the American pharmaceutical, software and entertainment industries, to advance in a more manageable regional forum those IPR standards that they failed to secure in TRIPS and to negotiate an accelerated implementation of TRIPS and possibly a TRIPS Plus in key hemispheric markets? The answer is yes, but developing countries will gain considerable benefits in new trade and investment opportunities.

Though self-interest may drive the American position on IPR, there is no harm if the result increases economic efficiency through the clearer definition and stronger enforcement of property rights. The harms alleged to higher IPR standards are now being shown to be, for the most part, either theoretical or short-term transitional problems. An empirical record is accumulating that shows more clearly the benefits when developing countries adopt higher IPR standards. Ultimately, property rights draw a line between who allocates scarce resources, the state or the individual, in a competitive market. The heavier the line is drawn, the greater the restraint upon state opportunism and favoritism. The more clearly the line is recognized, the greater the ability of individuals to pursue the economic opportunities borne out of their own labour, talent, and invention.

Acknowledgments

An earlier version of this article appeared in *Fordham Intellectual Property, Media and Entertainment Law Journal* 9, 1 (Autumn 1998): 241–300.

Notes

1 The Heads of State of 34 democracies in the western hemisphere at the Summit of the Americas agreed to construct a "Free Trade Area of the Americas" (FTAA) in an effort to eliminate tariff and non-tariff barriers in the region.

2 The resolution to construct the FTAA was a result of the Summit of the Americas' desire to eliminate barriers to trade and investment and advance economic integration and free trade. See Summit of the Americas: Declaration of Principles and Plan of Action, Dec. 11, 1994, 34 I.L.M. 808 (1995).

3 Third Trade Ministerial and Business Forum of the Americas, Belo Horizonte, Brazil, May 13-16, 1998.

4 Fourth Trade Ministerial and Americas Business Forum, San Jose, Costa Rica, March 16-19, 1998.

5 The Working Group on Intellectual Property Rights, one of the 12 FTAA Working Groups established by the Trade Ministers was created at the March 1996 ministerial in Cartagena, Columbia.

6 Agreement on Trade-Related Aspects of Intellectual Property Rights, Apr. 15, 1994, Marrakesh Agreement Establishing the World Trade Organization, Annex 1C, 33 I.L.M. 1197 (1994).

7 The Uruguay Round of Multilateral Trade Negotiations established the WTO. See Final Act Embodying the Results of the Uruguay Round of Multilateral Trade Negotiations ("Uruguay Round"), Apr. 15, 1994, 33 I.L.M. 1125 (1994).

8 James Packard Love is a lawyer working at the Center for Study of Responsive Law (CSRL) in Washington, D.C. The CSRL was created by Ralph Nader in 1968 as an independent research and advocacy organization that advances the interests of consumers and citizens on a wide range of topics. Ralph Nader is a leading consumer advocate and the founder of several organizations, including the CSRL.

9 For articles laying out some of these concerns, see Maskus and Penubarti1995 and Deardoff 1990.

10 See generally Reichman (1993) discussing the benefits afforded countries with established IPR regimes.

11 See Cheng (1998) briefly discussing short-run economic disincentives to intellectual property law enforcement in China; Wilson (1997) explaining that enforcement of intellectual property laws "offer[s] long-term benefits of enhanced employment, economic development, and innovation" (1997: 23).

12 See generally Bale (1997) discussing debate over patent protection.

13 See generally Primo Braga (1990) discussing the effect on developing countries of strengthened IPR protection; also the interesting discussion by Arvind Subramanian (1990).

14 E.g., Chin and Grossman (1990) discussing effects of international trade; Grossman and Helpman (1991)examining international trade; Trebilcock and Howse (1995) discussing regulation of international trade.

15 See a supporting view of the need for growth through imitation in Thurow (1997).

16 Evenson (1990); also Rapp et al. (1990) discussing costs and benefits of intellectual property protection in developing countries); Sherwood (1990)examining the relationship between economic development and intellectual property.

17 For correlations between IPRs and economic growth, see Park and Ginarte (1997); Torstensson (1994); Sachs and Warner (1995). For correlations between IPRs and technology transfer and FDI, see Mansfield (1994, 1995).

18 Debate Rages in Parliament Over Drug-Patent Legislation, BNA Pat., Tr., & Copyr. L. Daily (January 6, 1993): 3; Ip 1994: 39, discussing positive effects of patent, including Canadian pharmaceutical companies increase in research and development of new products and emphasis on export.

19 Patented drug prices decreased by approximately 2 percent in 1995 (McKenna 1997: B4).

20 Bill McArthur, personal communication via e-mail of November 26, 1998.

21 Moore 1994 argues that federal regulation in Canada has held "drug price inflation below the general inflation rate." For the actual listing of interventions, see the PMPRB website at www.pmprb-cepmb.gc.ca for annual reports.

22 IMS Canada Reports New Treatments Push Canadian Pharmaceutical Sales Up 10% Over 1997, Canada Newswire (March 17, 1998); available in WESTLAW, 3/17/98 CANWIRE 20:10:00.

23 See Oddi 1996, discussing the concept of natural rights in patent law.

24 Convention has no more solemn voice than that of the Encyclopedia Brittanica, which states: "[a] patent is recognized as a species of property and has the attributes of personal property. It may be sold (assigned) to others or mortgaged or may pass to the heirs of a deceased inventor" (15th ed. [1994], vol. 9: 194, col. 3).

25 Gordon 1993: 1533, 1573, n. 202: "A plausible argument can be made that intellectual property rights will indeed increase efficiency. The focus of such arguments tends to be the contention that, in the absence of property rights, there will be underproduction due to 'free rider' problems."

26 Merryman 1969, discussing the civil law tradition effect upon judicial systems.

27 Mattei 1997 identifies Quebec as a "mixed system"; Friesen 1996 argues that Quebec combines civil and common-law traditions in its legal system.

28 See Patterson 1997: 89 n. 186, presenting the debate surrounding "consumer surplus" and "product surplus"; also Goldman and Bodrug 1997: 583, revealing another perspective in this debate.

29 For an analysis of the lost consumer surplus from "market chill" due to price controls, see Lippert forthcoming. For an attempt to measure the effect of access to improved drugs in terms of life span and lifetime income, see Lichtenberg 1998.

30 For a general discussion of public-choice theory, see Stephan 1995.

31 See: Finland: Computer Networking Hardware/Software Market, Indus. Sector Analysis (June 29, 1998), available in 1998 WL 11163465.

32 Tulloch states that "[t]he successors to the original beneficiaries will not normally make exceptional profits. Unfortunately, they will usually be injured by any cancellation of the original gift. It would seem, as David Friedman has put it, that 'government cannot even give anything away'" (1993: 476–78).

33 See, e.g., Prebisch 1959, examining commercial policies in underdeveloped countries.

34 Prebisch 1959; see also Bernal 1993: 699, discussing trade arrangements in the Western Hemisphere).

35 See, e.g., Edge 1994: 193–95, examining Mexico's response to software piracy through trade agreements.

36 Personal communication with Robert Sherwood, Attorney and Consultant, in Washington, DC, July 30, 1998.

37 See Reichman 1996: 374–78; generally, Anderson and Gallini (eds.) 1998, discussing intellectual property rights and competition policy.

38 See Grason 1994: 117, n.160. The doctrine of patent abuse reflects one view of the judiciary, which thinks that intellectual property rights could pose a danger to a free marketplace. The modern status of the doctrine of patent abuse is somewhat unclear (Arquit 1991: 740–42). The essence of the doctrine is that where a patent is used to restrain trade unreasonably, it cannot be enforced until a "purge" has been effected (Hoerner 1991: 689–92). The patent abuse doctrine derives from the observation that patents are "an exception to the general rule against monopolies," and thus cannot be unlimited (Precision Instrument Mfg. Co. v. Automotive Maintenance Mach. Co., 324 US 806, 846 [1945]).

39 See, e.g., Dawson Chem. Co. v. Rohm and Haas, 448 US 176 (1980), holding that company conduct did not arise to patent abuse.

40 See United States v. Microsoft Corp., 147 F.3d 935, 937 (D.C. Cir. 1998).

41 United States v. Microsoft Corp., 147 F.3d 935, 937 (D.C. Cir. 1998).

42 For a supporting discussion based on a study of the results of using the "essential facilities doctrine" to order compulsory licenses, see Gilbert and Shapiro 1996: 249–55.

43 For a discussion of Kitch's "prospect theory," see Reichman 1996: 371–72.

44 See Kremer (1997), who claims "such patent buy-outs could eliminate monopoly price distortions and incentives for wasteful reverse engineering, while raising private incentives for original research closer to their social value."

45 For the latest background on this development, see Ryan 1998.

46 The following section owes its insights to conversations with former Canadian trade officials Michael Hart, Carleton University and Sylvia Ostry, University of Toronto; former United States chief negotiator for NAFTA, Julius Katz, Washington, DC, and professors Michael Trebilcock, University of Toronto and J.A. Van Duser, University of Ottawa.

47 For a discussion of the regional and multilateral approaches, see Maskus 1997: 681–94.

48 Based in Geneva, Switzerland, the World Intellectual Property Organization (WIPO) is responsible for administering, among other things, the terms of the Paris and Berne Conventions as amended by periodic diplomatic conferences. The Paris and Berne Conventions allow countries to bring disputes to the International Court of Justice (ICJ). See Paris Convention for the Protection of Industrial Property, Mar. 20, 1883, revised Oct. 31, 1958, art. 2, 828 U.N.T.S. 109, 115, as last revised at Stockholm, July 14, 1967, 21 U.S.T. 1583, 828 U.N.T.S. 305 (Paris Convention); Berne Convention for the Protection of Literary and Artistic Works, Sept. 9, 1886, completed at Paris on May 4, 1896, revised at Berlin on Nov. 13, 1908, completed at Berne on Mar. 20, 1914, revised at Rome on June 2, 1928, at Brussels on June 26, 1948, at Stockholm on July 14, 1967, and at Paris on July 24, 1971, 1161 U.N.T.S. 3 (Berne Convention).

49 Paris and Berne Conventions.

50 See Bale 1997, examining the trial and tribulations of patent protection and pharmaceutical innovation.

51 See 19 U.S.C. §§ 2411-2420 (1994). Section 301 of the 1974 Trade Act gives the President and his delegate, the United States Trade Representative, the ability to investigate government practices in other countries to see if they present an unfair burden to American firms. Special 301 of the 1988 Trade Act specifically covers IPRs protection and the market access for knowledge-intensive American goods. Special 301 authorizes the United States Trade Representative to remove trade benefits such as MFN trade rates if, after a set deadline, the offending government's practices are not modified or removed. The exercise of penalties under Special 301 remains consistent with the United States's WTO commitments as long as WTO dispute-settlement procedures have been tried first.

52 See Harper 1997, evaluating Article 27.2 of the TRIPS Agreement.

53 See Cheng 1998: 2013, n. 30. TRIPS was intended to provide a minimum of intellectual property rights.

54 See Harper 1997, which provides just one example of the subjects left open to argument and interpretation in TRIPS.

55 Hicks and Holbein 1997, discussing intellectual property norms in international trading agreements.

56 North American Free Trade Agreement, Dec. 17, 1992, Can.-Mex.-U.S., 32 I.L.M. 289 and 605 (1993) (entered into force Jan. 1, 1994). See Bussey 1998b: 1F.

57 Agreement on Trade-Related Aspects of Intellectual Property Rights, Including Trade in Counterfeit Goods, 33 I.L.M. 81, 107 (1994).

58 Agreement on Trade-Related Aspects: 107–08.

59 Canada had earlier taken remedial steps in the area of IPR. In preparation for NAFTA and TRIPS (though NAFTA was implemented before TRIPS, the IP section was negotiated after the general thrust of TRIPS was evident), Canada revised its patent law with Bill C-91 in 1993. It extended a full 20 years of protection to all patents, including those held by brand-name pharmaceutical companies, thus ending its 15 year experiment with compulsory licensing.

60 By July 1994, Mexico's patent law was substantially upgraded and the Mexican Industrial Property Institute (MIPI) was created to monitor and enforce the law including, upon request of private parties, the search and seizure of counterfeit goods. See Troy 1998: 146–51.

61 See generally, WTO's Ruggiero Says New Trade Round Possible at Turn of Century, AFX News (May 26, 1998), revealing support for a new trade round.

62 See Scoffield 1998, examining the circumstances that hinder trade agenda.

63 For a brief introduction to this new consensus, see Roberts and Araujo 1997.

64 Draft Final Act Embodying the Results of the Uruguay Round of Multilateral Trade Negotiations (Dunkel Draft), GATT Doc. No. MTN.TNC/W/FA (Dec. 20, 1991).

65 Compare Dunkel Draft with TRIPS Agreement. The most substantial difference in scope between TRIPS and the Dunkel draft deals with performers, phonogram producers, and broadcasters for whom national treatment only applies to rights specified in TRIPS itself.

66 Hertz 1997: 261: "NAFTA ... establishes a sweeping national treatment requirement ... which [is] subject to a few specific exceptions." For example, with respect to secondary use of sound recordings such as broadcasting or other public communication, NAFTA, art. 1703(1) states that a Party may limit the rights of another Party's performers to those rights its nationals are accorded in the territory of such other Party (NAFTA: 671, art. 1703.

67 NAFTA: 702, art.2106. The article refers to annex 2106, which states "Notwithstanding any other provision of this Agreement, as between the United States and Canada, any measure adopted or maintained with respect to cultural industries, except as, specifically provided in Article 302 (Market Access—Tariff Elimination), and any measure of equivalent commercial effect

taken in response, shall be governed exclusively in accordance with the terms of the Canada-United States Free Trade Agreement. The rights and obligations between Canada and any other Party with respect to such measures shall be identical to those applying between Canada and the United States.

68 See generally Larrea 1997, arguing against the cultural industries exemption); Hedley 1995, discussing the effect of Canadian cultural policy on United States copyright industries.

69 Morton 1998: 1, discussing the aftermath of the WTO ruling.

70 Sherwood and Braga (1996: 3–4) provide a detailed list of NAFTA provisions that exceed the protections in TRIPS: "[M]ore precise and comprehensive treaty adherence requirements including UPOV adherence for new plant varieties, a more positive statement of national treatment, highly constrained transition periods, protection of encrypted satellite signals, narrower controls on abusive conditions, enhanced protection for software, databases, and sound recordings, enhanced contractual rights in copyright, tighter language regarding rental rights, extended minimum trademark terms, broader definition of the relevant public in determining whether trademarks are well known, tighter compulsory licensing constraints, disallowance of dependent patents, 'pipeline' protection, and reversal of the burden of proof for process patents. The treatment of patent exhaustion, sometimes called parallel imports, is not entirely clear cut but appears to be constrained."

71 See Lopez1997, examining dispute resolution methods in the free trade area.

72 Waxman/Hatch Act has not "lived up to its promise," PhRMA's Bantham Maintains. The Pink Sheet (March. 3, 1997), available in 1997 WL 16952088.

73 One Year Later, Canadian Patent Laws to Stay about the Same. Biotechnology Newswatch (February 16, 1998), available in 1998 WL 8765022.

74 Canada's Linkage System "Is Unfair." Marketletter (July 6, 1998), available in 1998 WL 11623102 (discussing Canada's linkage system).

75 Taylor 1996-1997: 850, 853, addressing dispute resolution in Section II.

76 See Report of the Appellate Body, India – Patent Protection for Pharmaceutical and Agricultural Chemical Products, WT/DS50/AB/R (Sept. 5, 1997).

77 NAFTA: 682, ch. 19; also Shell1995: 829, 834–39, 887.

78 Shell 1995: 837, noting the desirability of removal of government influence from the realm of international trade); see generally Gal-Or 1998, comparing NAFTA and European Union disciplines.

79 See, e.g., Perez1993. A recent estimate by the United States International Trade Commission indicates that American companies are incurring $40 billion to $60 billion per year due to violations of intellectual property rights.

80 See, e.g., China: Courts Handle More IPR Lawsuits (China Business Information Network, July 17, 1997).

81 Kuo & Mossinghoff 1998: 539. TRIPS did provide the significant advance of placing IPR disputes within the ambit of WTO dispute-settlement procedures. What must be noted here is the improvement of the new WTO procedures over the older GATT procedures. Specifically, the new WTO procedures curtail the ability of defendant WTO members to block the adoption of WTO panel reports and to drag out decisions indefinitely.

82 Messick 1997: 1. Messick continues: "New courts have been created, the number of judges increased, and computers and other modern technologies introduced. The codes controlling civil and criminal procedures have been streamlined, and the judicial sector has been reorganized to make it more independent. But, despite these changes, many systems still perform poorly."

83 Helter 1998: 357, offering a proposal that would deepen the rights nature of IPRs.

84 See Panel Discussion, Transnational Litigation: International Arbitration and Alternatives, Opportunities and Pitfalls, 10 AUT Int'l L. Practicum 74, 84 (1997).

85 NAFTA Secrecy. Toronto Star (Aug. 27, 1998): A27; Why the Secrecy over Investors' Rights? Financial Post (August 29, 1998): sec.1, p. 20.

86 Settle Trade Disputes in the Open. Financial Post (Sept. 11, 1998): sec.1, p.10; Can We Talk. Globe and Mail (Sept. 10, 1998): A24.

87 It must also be noted that with IPR disputes subject to WTO jurisdiction, WIPO dispute settlement mechanisms are left in a weakened position because they have far weaker powers to compel resolution and to impose penalties. This must be interpreted as making moot, in practice, the WIPO's promotion of the Draft Treaty on the Settlement of Disputes between States in the Field of Intellectual Property.

88 For a discussion of efficiency costs of negotiation over legal rules, see Cheffins 1997: 25.

89 See, e.g., Schmertz and Meier 1998, detailing the United States' victory; see also Schmertz and Meier 1997a, 1997b.

90 Lopez 1997b: 208, discussing dispute settlement in trade disputes of environmental and labor agreements.

91 See, e.g., Why All the MERCOSUR Excitement? Mkt. Latin Amer. 9, 4 (Sept. 1, 1996).

92 See, Greater IP Protection Sought within the FTAA, 5 J. Proprietary Rts. 24, 27 (1997).

93 Personal communication with Allen Z. Hertz, former Canadian Trade Negotiator, Ottawa, Ontario, August 10, 1998.

94 See generally, A Survey of MERCOSUR, The Economist (October 12, 1996), available in 1996 WL 11247186 (surveying MERCOSUR).

95 See, Does the WTO Need Special Rules for Foreign Direct Investment? The Economist (October 3, 1998): 10; see also, All Free Traders Now? The Economist (December 7, 1996): 25, available in 1996 WL 11247482.

References

Alchian, Armen A. (1967). *Pricing and Society 6*. Institute of Economic Affairs .

Anderson, Robert D., and Nancy T. Gallini, eds. (1998). *Competition Policy and Intellectual Property Rights in the Knowledge-based Economy*.

Aronson, Jonathan D., et al. (1998). *Protecting Intellectual Property*.

Arquit, Kevin J. (1991). Patent Abuse and the Antitrust Laws. *Antitrust L. J.* 59: 735, 740–42.

Bale, Harvey E., Jr., (1997). Patent Protection and Pharmaceutical Innovation. *N.Y.U. J. Int'l L. & Pol.* 29: 95.

Bernal, Richard (1993). Regional Trade Arrangements in the Western Hemisphere. *Am. U. J. Int. L. & Pol'y* 8: 683, 699.

Bethell, Tom (1998). *The Noblest Triumph: Property and Prosperity through the Ages.* St. Martin's Press.

Brenner, Reuven (1990). Market Power: Innovations and Anti-Trust. In F. Mattheson et al. (eds.), *The Law and Economics of Competition Policy* (The Fraser Institute).

Bugbee, Bruce W. 1967). *Genesis of American Patent and Copyright Law.* Public Affairs Press.

Burt, Eric M. (1997). Developing Countries and the Framework for Negotiations on Foreign Direct Investment in the World Trade Organization. *Am. U.J. Int'l L. & Pol'y* 12: 1015, § III, § IV.A.2.

Bussey, Jane (1998a). Not Willing to Wait, Countries Lay Their Own Fast Tracks. *Miami Herald* (April 13): 1H.

——— (1998b). Optimism Amid Upheaval—Regional Woes Could Impact Talks. *Miami Herald* (August 30): 1F.

Cao, Lena (1997). Law and Economic Development: A New Beginning?. *Tex. Int'l L.J.* 32: 545, 551–52.

Carter, James H. (1998). *Litigating in Foreign Territory: Arbitration Alternatives and Enforcement.* A.B.A. Center for Continuing Legal Education.

Castel, J.-G., Q.C., and C.M. Gastle (1998). Deep Economic Integration between Canada and the United States, the Emergence of Strategic Innovation Policy and the Need for Trade Law Reform. *Minn. J. Global Trade* 7: 1.

Caviedes, Alexander A. (1998). International Copyright Law: Should the European Union Dictate Its Development? *B.U. Int'l L.J.* 16: 165, 192–94.

Cheffins, Brian R. (1997). *Company Law: Theory, Structure and Operation.*

Cheng, Julia (1998). Note, China's Copyright System: Rising to the Spirit of TRIPS Requires an Internal Focus and WTO Membership. *Fordham Int'l. L.J.* 1941, 1982.

Chin, Judith C., and Gene M. Grossman (1990). The Political Economy of International Trade. In R.W. Jones and A.O. Krueger (eds.), *Essays in Honor of Robert Baldwin* (London: Basil Blackwell).

Coase, Ronald H. (1988). *The Firm, the Market and the Law.* University of Chicago Press.

Coggio, Brian D., and Frances D. Cerrito (1998). Immunity for the Drug Approval Process, No Patent Infringement under Certain Circumstances. *N.Y.L.J.* (March 9): col. 1, S4.

Cordray, Monique L. (1994). GATT v. WIPO. *J. Pat & Trademark Off. Soc'y* 76: 121, 131.

Dam, Kenneth W. (1994). The Economic Underpinning of Patent Law. *J. Legal Stud.* 23: 247, 268–70.

Deardoff, Alan V. (1990). Should Patent Protection Be Extended to All Developing Countries. *World Econ.* 13: 497–521.

Dixit, Avinash (1996). The Making of Economic Policy: A Transaction-Cost Politics Perspective. In *Munich Lectures in Economics 37* (MIT Press).

Doane, Michael L. (1994). TRIPS and International Intellectual Property Protection in an Age of Advancing Technology. *Am. U. J. Int'l L. & Pol'y* 9: 465, 469.

Dreyfuss, Rochelle C., and Andreas F. Lowenfeld (1997). Two Achievements of the Uruguay Round: Putting TRIPS and Dispute Settlement Together. *Va. J. Int'l L.* 37: 275, 279.

Dunoff, Jeffrey L. (1996/1997). "Trade and": Recent Developments in Trade and Policy and Scholarship—and Their Surprising Political Implications. *NW. J. Int'l. L. & Bus.* 17: 759, 772–73.

Edge, Amy R. (1994). Preventing Software Piracy through Regional Trade Agreements: The Mexican Example. *N.C. J. Int'l L. & Com. Reg.* 20: 175, 193–95.

Epstein, Richard A. (1995). *Simple Rules for a Complex World.* Harvard University Press.

Epstein, Richard A. (1998). Foreword: Unconstitutional Conditions, State Power, and the Limits of Consent. *Harv. L. Rev.* 102: 4.

Evenson, Robert E. (1990). Survey of Empirical Studies. World Bank Discussion Paper.

Friesen, Jeffrey L. (1996). When Common Law Courts Interpret Civil Codes. *Wis. Int'l L.J.* 15: 1, 2.

Gal-Or, Noemi (1998). Private Party Direct Access: A Comparison of the NAFTA and the EU Disciplines. *B.C. Int'l & Comp. L. Rev.* 21: 1.

Gall, Gerald (1995). *The Canadian Legal System* (4th ed.) Carswell.

Gantz, David A. (1997). The United States and the Expansion of Western Hemisphere Free Trade: Participant or Observer? *Ariz. J. Int'l & Comp. L.* 14: 381, 391–405.

Gilbert, R. J., and C. Shapiro (1996). An Economic Analysis of Unilateral Refusals to License Intellectual Property. *Proc. Natl. Acad. Sci. U.S.* 93: 12749, 12749–55.

Goldman, Calvin S., and John D. Bodrug (1997). The Merger Review Process: The Canadian Experience. *Antitrust L.J.* 65: 573, 583.

Gordon, Wendy J. (1993). A Property Right in Self-Expression: Equality and Individualism in the Natural Law of Intellectual Property. *Yale L.J.* 102: 1533, 1573 n. 202.

Grason, Amy Jacqueline (1994). IBM vs. Comdisco: Are Modified 3090 Computers Counterfeit? *J. Marshall J. Computer & Info. L.* 13: 93, 117 & n.160.

Greenspan, Edward, and Anne McIvoy (1998). Rock Gets Ready to Roll. *The Globe and Mail* (January 19): A1.

Griffitts, Robert C. (1996). Broadening the States' Power to Tax Foreign Multinational Corporations: Barclays Bank vs. Franchise Tax Board. *Cath. U. L. Rev.* 46: 243, 283.

Grossman, Gene, and E. Helpman (1991). *Innovation and Growth in the Global Economy.* Cambridge, MA: MIT Press.

Gutterman, Alan S. (1993). The North-South Debate Regarding the Protection of Intellectual Property Rights. *Wake Forest L. Rev.* 28: 89, 122.

Harper, M. Bruce (1997). TRIPS Article 27.2: An Argument for Caution. *Wm. & Mary Envtl. L. & Pol'y Rev.* 21: 381.

Hedley, Hale E. (1995). Canadian Cultural Policy and the NAFTA: Problems Facing The U.S. Copyright Industries. *Geo. Wash. J. Int'l L. & Econ.* 28: 655.

Helter, Laurence R. (1998). Adjudicating Copyright Claims under the TRIPS Agreement: The Case for a European Human Rights Analogy. *Harv. Int'l L.J.* 39: 357.

Hertz, Allen Z. (1997). Shaping the Trident: Intellectual Property under NAFTA, Investment Protection Agreements and at the World Trade Organization. *Can-U.S. L.J.* 23: 261, 281–82.

Hicks, Laurinda L., and James R. Holbein (1997). Convergence of National Intellectual Property Norms in International Trading Agreements. *Am. U. J. Int'l L. & Pol'y* 12: 769.

Hoerner, Robert J. (1991). Patent Misuse: Portents for the 1990s. Antitrust L. J. 59: 687, 689–92.

Ip, Greg (1994). State Intervention, Canadian-Style: There's a Right Way and Wrong Way to Guide Markets. *The Financial Post* (December 31): 39.

Irwin, Douglas A. (1996). *Against the Tide: An Intellectual History of Free Trade.*

Kozolchyk, Boris (1996). NAFTA in the Grand and Small Scheme of Things. *Ariz. J. Int'l & Competition L.* 13: 135, 144.

Kremer, Michael (1997). Patent Buy-Outs: A Mechanism for Encouraging Innovation Program. National Bureau of Economic Research Working Paper No. 6304.

Kuo, Vivian S. and Gerald J. Mossinghoff (1998). World Patent System circa 20XX, A.D. *IDEA: J.L. & Tech.* 38: 529, 537.

Landes, William M., and Richard A. Posner (1979). Adjudication as a Private Good. *J. Legal Stud.* 8: 235.

——— (1987). *An Economic Analysis of Tort Law* (4th ed.). Harvard University Press.

——— (1988). *An Economic Structure of Tort Law* (3rd ed.). Harvard University Press.

Larrea, Theresa A. (1997). Eliminate the Cultural Industries Exemption from NAFTA. *Santa Clara L. Rev.* 37: 1107.

Lichtenberg, Frank (1998). Pharmaceutical Innovation, Mortality Reduction, and Economic Growth. National Bureau of Economic Research Working Paper No. 6569.

Lippert, Owen (1998). Pirates Plunder Patents. Will the Rule of Law Prevail? *Wall St. J.* (April 17): A15.

Lippert, Owen, Dr. Bill McArthur, and Cynthia Ramsay (1998). A Submission Prepared by The Fraser Institute For the House of Commons Industry Committee Concerning Bill C-91 (A Bill to Amend The Patent Act). Digital document: www.fraserinstitute.ca (Oct. 10, 1998).

Lippert, Owen (forthcoming). Drug Price Controls: Wrong Solution for a Nonexistent Problem. The Fraser Institute.

Locke, John (1690/1980). Second Treatise of Government, § V. (C.B. Macpherson, ed.) Hackett.

Lopez, David (1997a). Dispute Resolution under a Free Trade Area of the Americas: The Shape of Things to Come. *U. Miami Inter-Am. L. Rev.* 28: 597.

Lopez, David (1997b). Dispute Resolution under NAFTA: Lessons from the Early Experience. *Tex. Int'l L.J.* 32: 163, 165, 207.

MacLaughlin, J.H., T.J. Richards, and L.A. Kenny (1988). The Economic Significance of Piracy. In R.M. Gadbaw and T.J. Richards (eds.), *Intellectual Property Rights: Global Consensus, Global Conflict?* (Westview Press).

Mansfield, Edwin E. (1994). Intellectual Property Protection, Foreign Direct Investment, and Technology Transfer. Int'l Fin. Corp. Discussion Papers 19.

Mansfield, Edwin E. (1995). Intellectual Property Protection, Foreign Direct Investment, and Technology Transfer: Germany, Japan and the United States. Int'l Fin. Corp. Discussion Papers 27.

Maskus, Keith E. (1997). Implications of Regional and Multilateral Agreements for Intellectual Property Rights. *The World Economy* 20: 5, 681–94.

Maskus, Keith E., and M. Penubarti (1995). How Trade-Related are Intellectual Property Rights? *J. Int'l. Econ.* 39: 227–48.

Mattei, Ugo (1997). Three Patterns of Law: Toxonomy and Change in the World's Legal Systems. *Am. J. Comp. L.* 45: 5, 26.

McArthur, Bill (1998). Property Rights and The Pharmaceutical Industry. Paper presented at the The Canadian Property Rights Research Institute meeting, Calgary, Alberta, March 21, 1998. Available as digital document at www.canprri.org.

McKenna, Barrie (1997). Ottawa Seeks Prescription for Drug Patent Battle. *Globe and Mail* (February 17): B4.

Meiners, Roger E., and Robert J. Staaf (1990). Patents, Copyrights, and Trademarks: Property or Monopoly? *Harv. J. L. & Pub. Pol'y* 13: 911, 940.

Merges, R.P., and R.R. Nelson (1990). On the Complex Economics of Patent Scope. *Colum. L. Rev.* 90: 839.

Merryman, John H. (1969). *The Civil Law Tradition.*

Messick, Richard (1997). Judicial Reform: A Survey of the Issues. World Bank Internal Working Paper.

Moore, Michael B. (1994). "Open Wide" (Your Pocketbook That Is!)—A Call for the Establishment in the United States of a Prescription Drug Price Regulatory Agency. *Sw. J.L. & Trade AM.* 1: 149, 151.

Morrison, Scott, and Edward Alden (1998). Ottawa Faces Claim over PCB Waste Ban. *Fin. Times (London)* (Sept. 2): 4.

Morton, Peter (1998). Ottawa Loads? Another Round in Magazine Wars. *The Financial Post* (July 25): 1.

Mossinghoff, Gerald J., and Ralph Oman (1997). The World Intellectual Property Organization: A United Nations Success Story. *J. Pat. & Trademark Off. Soc'y* 79: 691, 691–92.

North, Douglass C. (1990). *Institutions, Institutional Change, and Economic Performance.* Cambridge University Press.

Oddi, A. Samuel (1987). The International Patent System and Third World Development: Reality or Myth? *Duke L.J.* 1987: 831.

Oddi, A. Samuel (1996). TRIPS: Natural Rights and a "Polite Form of Economic Imperialism." *Vand. J. Transnat'l L.* 29: 415.

Otero-Lathrop, Miguel (1998). MERCOSUR and NAFTA: The Need for Convergence. *4-SUM NAFTA: L. & Bus. Rev. Am.*: 116, 120.

Park, Walter G., and Juan Carlos Ginarte (1997). Intellectual Property Rights and Economic Growth. *Contemp. Econ. Pol'y* 15: 51–61.

Patterson, Mark R. (1997). Coercion, Deception, and Other Demand-Increasing Practices in Antitrust Law. *Antitrust L.J.* 66: 1, 89 n.186.

Perez, Daniel F. (1993). Exploitation and Enforcement of Intellectual Property Rights. *Computer Lawyer* 10: 10.

Posner, Richard (1992). *Economic Analysis of Law* § 1.2 (4th ed.).

Postrell, Virginia (1998). *The Future and Its Enemies: The Growing Conflict over Creativity, Enterprise, and Progress.* The Free Press.

Prebisch, Raul (1959). Commercial Policy in Underdeveloped Countries, *Am. Econ. Rev.* (May): 251–73.

Priest, George L. (1986). What Economists Can Tell Lawyers about Intellectual Property. In John Palmer (ed.), *Research in Law and Economics 8: The Economics of Patents and Copyrights*: 21

Primo Braga, Carlos A. (1989). The Economics of Intellectual Property Rights and the GATT: A View from the South. *Vand. J. Transnat'l L.* 22: 243.

Primo Braga, Carlos A. (1990). The Developing Country Case for and against Intellectual Property Protection. In Wolfgang Siebeck (ed.), *Strengthening Protection of Intellectual Property in Developing Countries: A Survey of the Literature.*

Primo Braga, Carlos A. (1990). Guidance from Economic Theory. World Bank Discussion Paper.

Prudhomme, Linda E. (1997). The Margarita War: Does the Popular Mixed Drink "Margarita" Qualify as Intellectual Property? *SW. U.J.L. & Trade Am.* 4: 109, 133.

Rapp, Richard T. et al. (1990). Benefits and Costs of Intellectual Property Protection in Developing Countries. *J. World Trade* 24: 75, 77–90.

Reichman, J.H. (1993). The TRIPS Component of the GATT's Uruguay Round: Competitive Prospects for Intellectual Property Owners in an Integrated World Market. *Fordham Intell. Prop. Media & Ent. L.J.* 4: 171, 173 .

Reichman, J.H. (1996). Compliance with the TRIPS Agreement: Introduction to Scholarly Debate. *Vand. J. Transnat'l L.* 29: 363, 374–78.

Roberts, Paul Craig, and Karen LaFollette Araujo (1997). *The Capitalist Revolution in Latin America.* Oxford University Press.

Rozek, Richard P., and Ruth Berkowitz (1998). The Effects of Patent Protection on the Prices of Pharmaceutical Products: Is Intellectual Property Protection Raising the Drug Bill in Developing Countries?. *J. World Intell. Prop.* 1: 2, 179–243.

Ryan, Michael P. (1998). *Knowledge Diplomacy: Global Competition and the Politics of Intellectual Property.* Brookings Institution Press.

Sachs, Jeffrey D., and Andrew M. Warner (1995). Economic Reform and the Process of Global Integration. *Brookings Papers on Econ. Activity* 1: 1–95.

Schmertz, John R., Jr., and Mike Meier (1997a). Before Dispute Settlement Panel of WTO, U.S. Prevails over Canada Regarding Its Imposition of Discriminatory Taxes and Postal Rates on U.S Magazine Imports. *Int'l Law Update* 3, 4 (April).

——— (1997b). WTO Holds in Favor of U.S. in Trade Dispute with India over Intellectual Property Rights. *Int'l Law Update* 3, 10 (October).

——— (1998). U.S. Prevails before WTO Panel in Dispute over Argentina's ad Valorem Import Tax and Duties. Int'l Law Update 4, 1 (January).

Schott, Jeffrey J., assisted by Johanna W. Buurman (1994). *The Uruguay Round: An Assessment.* Institute for International Economics.

Scoffield, Heather (1998). Turmoil Hinders Trade Agenda. *Globe & Mail* (September 21): B1.

Shain, Michael L. (1994). Thailand's Board of Investment: Towards a More Appropriate and Effective Rural Investment Promotion Policy. *Pac. Rim L. & Pol'y J.* 3: 141, 182.

Shell, G. Richard (1995). Trade Legalism and International Relations Theory: An Analysis of the World Trade Organization. *Duke L.J.* 44: 829, 834–39, 887.

Sherwood, Robert M. (1990). Intellectual Property and Economic Development. Westview.

Sherwood, Robert M. (1997). Intellectual Property in the Western Hemisphere. *Inter Am. L. Rev.* 28: 3, 565.

Sherwood, Robert M., and Carlos A. Primo Braga (1996). Intellectual Property, Trade and Economic Development: A Road Map for the FTAA Negotiations. In *The North-South Agenda Paper* 21, §§ 3–4 (North-South Center, University of Miami).

Stanback, Willard Alonzo (1989). International Intellectual Property Protection: An Integrated Solution to the Inadequate Protection Problem. *Va. J. Int'l L.* 29: 517, 523.

Stanbury, William T. (1998). Canadian Content Regulations: The Intrusive State at Work. *The Fraser Institute.*

Stephan, Paul B., III (1995). Barbarians inside the Gate: Public Choice Theory and International Economic Law. *Am. U. J. Int'l L. & Pol'y* 10: 745.

Subramanian, Arvind (1990). TRIPs and the Paradigm of the GATT: A Tropical, Temperate View *World Econ.* 13: 509–21.

Taylor, Charles (1989). *Sources of the Self: The Making of the Modern Identity.* Harvard University Press.

Taylor, Cherie O. (1996/1997). Dispute Resolution as a Catalyst for Economic Integration and an Agent for Deepening Integration: NAFTA and MERCOSUR? *NW. J. Int'l L. & Bus.* 17: 850, 853.

Thurow, Lester C. (1997). Needed: A New System of Intellectual Property Rights. *Harv. Bus. Rev.* 75: 5, 94–103.

Torstensson Johan (1994). Property Rights and Economic Growth: An Empirical Study. *Kyklos* 47: 2, 231–47.

Trachtman, Joel P. (1997). Section IV: A Sketch of the Law and Economics of Property Rights (in chap. 17, Externalities and Extraterritoriality: The Law and Economics of Prescriptive Jurisdiction). In Jagdeep S. Bhandari and Alan O. Sykes (eds.), *Economic Dimensions in International Law: Comparative and Empirical Perspectives* (Cambridge University Press): 658–682.

Trebilcock, Michael and Robert Howse (1995). *The Regulation of International Trade.* Routledge.

——— (1998a). Trade Liberalization and Regulatory Diversity: Reconciling Competitive Markets with Competitive Politics. *Euro. J.L. & Econ.* 6: 5, 5–37.

——— (1998b). Trade-Related Intellectual Property in The Regulation of International Trade (2nd ed.). Routledge.

Troy, Edwin S. Flores (1998). The Development of Modern Frameworks for Patent Protection: Mexico, A Model For Reform. *Tex. Intell. Prop. L.J.* 6: 133, 146–151.

Tullock, Gordon (1993). *The Political Economy of Rent Seeking.* Edward Elgar.

Urquhart, John (1998). Canada Seeks to Protect Its Magazines from Losing Ad Revenue to Foreigners. *Wall St. J.* (July 30): B12.

Waters, Alan Rufus (1998). Economic Growth and the Property Rights Regime. In James A. Dorn et al. (eds.), *The Revolution in Development Economics* (Cato Institute).

Williamson, Oliver E. (1987). *The Economic Institutions of Capitalism.* Free Press.

Wilson, Marie (1997). TRIPS Agreement Implications for ASEAN Protection of Computer Technology. *Ann. Surv. Int'l & Comp. L.* 4: 18, 22–23.

Wolfson, Jeffrey A. (1994). Patent Flooding in the Japanese Patent Office: Methods for Reducing Patent Flooding and Obtaining Effective Patent Protection. *Geo. Wash. J. Int'l L. & Econ.* 27: 531, 557–58.

Yelpaala, Kojo (1985). In Search of Effective Policies for Foreign Direct Investment: Alternatives to Tax Incentive Policies *NW. J. Int'l L. & Bus.* 7: 208, 246–47.

Entering the Jungle
The Exhaustion of Intellectual
Property Rights and Parallel Imports

CARSTEN FINK

The doctrine of exhaustion related to the protection of intellectual property rights (IPRs) is one of the most complicated regulations of international business. It defines the territorial rights of intellectual property owners after the first sale of their protected products. Under a system of *national* exhaustion, a title holder can prevent parallel importation of his product from a foreign country, where it is sold either by the IPR's owner himself or by an authorized dealer. In contrast, if rights exhaust *internationally*, the title-holder loses his exclusive privilege after the first distribution of his product, thus allowing parallel imports from abroad. A hybrid between national and international exhaustion is *regional* exhaustion, whereby parallel trading is allowed within a particular group of countries but parallel imports from countries outside the region are banned.

Parallel trade refers to trade in genuine products outside official channels of distribution; it should not be confused with trade in counterfeit goods, i.e., trade in products that infringe on someone's IPRs. If unrestricted, parallel trading activities can generally take two forms. The most common form is *passive* parallel imports, whereby arbitrageurs buy goods in a foreign country and sell them in the domestic market. The other form, *active* parallel imports, occurs when a foreign

Notes will be found on pages 187–90. The views expressed in this paper are the author's own and should not be attributed to the World Bank, its Executive Board of Directors, its management, or any of its member countries.

licensee (or distributor) of the IPR holder enters the domestic market to compete with the IPR holder himself or his official domestic licensee. Regardless of the form parallel imports take, they are subject to the same border measures as "regular" imports, including tariffs, quantitative restrictions, and technical standards.

The economic significance of the exhaustion doctrine is difficult to evaluate. The size of the market that could be subject to parallel trading activities, if unrestricted, is undoubtedly significant as most tradable goods (besides commodities) and services are protected by at least one form of IPR (e.g. trademarks).[1] There are virtually no statistics available on this so-called gray-market segment of international trade. In addition, if intellectual property owners and their licensees respond to the threat of parallel imports by pricing more uniformly across national markets—thereby eroding opportunities for international arbitrage—trade statistics would give an insufficient indication of the economic impact of international exhaustion.

The significance of the exhaustion doctrine depends also on the extent to which private contractual means can substitute for territorial rights exhaustion in restricting parallel imports. Territorial restraints in licensing agreements can put limits to active parallel imports and restrictive purchasing contracts can do so to passive parallel imports, even though IPRs may exhaust internationally. The extent to which such private contractual means can be used depends, in turn, on whether or not they are considered to be anti-competitive.

Current exhaustion regimes differ widely among countries and across the different forms of IPRs. Although most developed countries maintain significant restrictions on parallel imports, recent initiatives by policy-makers in several OECD countries have been favourable to international exhaustion. It would be premature, however, to interpret these initiatives as a fundamental shift in the regulations governing parallel imports. Nonetheless, there has been mounting interest in the economic implications of parallel trade—reinforced by the possibility that the exhaustion issue may be revisited within the multilateral trading system.

The effects of national or international exhaustion are highly complex and have been subject to extensive debate among economists, lawyers, lobbyists, and policy-makers. This chapter offers an introduction into this "jungle" of intellectual property exhaustion, focusing on the economic aspects of the debate. It starts by outlining the current state of national and international regulations that govern parallel imports. The subsequent two sections discuss the pros and cons of national and international exhaustion and review the (limited) empirical evidence. The chapter concludes by pointing to some issues that may be of relevance in the context of multilateral negotiations on the exhaustion of intellectual property rights.

The current legal framework

Unless bound by an international agreement, countries are free to adopt their preferred exhaustion regime for each form of IPR. So far, no international convention or multilateral agreement on IPRs has mandated a particular regime. The only provision in the various multilateral and plurilateral agreements of the World Trade Organization (WTO) that explicitly addresses exhaustion is Article 6 of the Agreement on Trade Related Intellectual Property Rights (TRIPS), which states: "For the purposes of dispute settlement under this Agreement, subject to the provisions of Articles 3 and 4 above nothing in this Agreement shall be used to address the issue of the exhaustion of intellectual property rights."[2] Article 6 of TRIPS is widely interpreted as an "agreement to disagree," giving WTO members the freedom to opt for national, regional, or international exhaustion.[3] It reflects the negotiating history of the TRIPS Agreement, in which the exhaustion issue was raised, but member countries could not form consensus on a multilateral statute.

At regional level, the European Union (EU) applies a system of regional exhaustion that denies parallel imports from outside the EU territories but does not restrict parallel trading within those territories. This system has emerged from jurisprudence by the European Court of Justice (ECJ), which, in the early 1970s, ruled that national exhaustion would be inconsistent with the Treaty of Rome, which aims at "[uniting] national markets into a single market."[4] The regional exhaustion regime applies to all forms of intellectual property. At the time of writing, however, the European Commission was considering the revision of the EU trademark directive, so as to free parallel imports from outside the EU.[5]

Other regional trade agreements largely remain silent on the exhaustion issue. The North American Free Trade Agreement (NAFTA), for example, has no explicit provision on the exhaustion question and the substantive provisions of NAFTA's Chapter 17 on IPRs can be interpreted as giving member countries freedom on their preferred exhaustion regime. The Treaty of Asunción, establishing the Southern Cone Common Market (MERCOSUR) among Argentina, Brazil, Paraguay, and Uruguay, also does not address the question of parallel imports.[6]

At national level, the United States applies (with few exceptions) a system of national exhaustion for all forms of IPRs.[7] The exhaustion regimes of other OECD countries also lean toward national exhaustion, although there are important cases where IPRs exhaust internationally. In Japan, for example, a recent decision by the Supreme Court confirmed the lawfulness of parallel imports of patented products unless restrictions are clearly displayed on the products.[8] In 1998, New Zealand became the first OECD country to adopt a system of international exhaustion with respect to copyright.[9] Following the removal of parallel

import restrictions on CDs in 1998, the Australian government is currently considering to expand the international exhaustion rule in the
area of copyright to books and computer software (*Financial Times*,
March 4, 1999).

In non-OECD countries, regulations regarding parallel imports differ widely. According to a recent survey on parallel import protection in
the area of copyright, for example, 25 non-OECD country were classified
as providing such protection and 21 non-OECD countries were classified
as allowing parallel imports (the regime was unclear in 33 non-OECD
countries).[10] The exhaustion regimes of Argentina and Chile generally
seem to follow many other Latin American countries in not imposing restrictions on parallel imports. The new Argentine patent law, for example, explicitly establishes a rule of international exhaustion.[11]

The recent decisions by New Zealand and Australia to open their
markets for parallel imports of products protected by copyright as well
as the current initiative on reforming the EU's trademark directive on
this issue have brought increased attention to the parallel-import
question. The exhaustion issue may also be revisited within the multilateral trading system. Article 71 of TRIPS mandates a review of the
Agreement in the year 2000 and proposals for a multilateral statute on
the exhaustion of IPRs have been brought forward in the context of
the Millennium Round of trade negotiations that may be launched in
late 1999.[12]

The pros and cons of national and international exhaustion of international property rights

Before turning to the various arguments and counter-arguments that
have been brought forward to defend either exhaustion regime, it is
useful to recall the economic justification for granting intellectual
property rights.[13] One can broadly classify the various forms of IPRs
into two categories: (1) IPRs that stimulate inventive and creative activities (patents, utility models, industrial designs, copyright, plant
breeders' rights, and layout designs for integrated circuits); (2) IPRs
that resolve information asymmetries (trademarks and geographical
indications).[14] IPRs in both categories seek to address certain failures
of private markets to provide for an efficient allocation of resources.

IPRs in the first category can be seen as a solution to the problems
created by the public-good characteristic of knowledge and information. If creators of intellectual works cannot protect themselves against
imitation and copying, they may not have an incentive to engage in inventive or creative activities, as they may be unable to recoup any expenditures incurred in the process of creating new knowledge or
information. Societies have, therefore, granted exclusive commercial

rights to intellectual works—most prominently patents to foster industrial innovation and copyright to promote literary and artistic expression as well as, from the late 1980s, the development of computer software and digital information. IPRs in the second category resolve inefficiencies that result from asymmetries of information between buyers and sellers on certain attributes of goods and services. Thus, trademarks identify a product with its producer and his reputation for quality; they assure consumers that they are purchasing what they intend to purchase.

There is an important difference between these two basic groups of intellectual property. IPRs that stimulate inventive and creative activities explicitly confer market power in the supply of the protected good to the title holder, who can thereby reap monopolistic profits that finance knowledge and information-generating investments. From a welfare perspective, the market power entailed in patents and copyright poses a cost to society, which, however, is outweighed by the benefits that the creation of new knowledge and information brings to society. IPRs that resolve information asymmetries, in contrast, are not designed to confer any direct market power. Trademarks do not restrict imitation or copying of protected goods as long as they are sold under a different brand name. This difference is reflected in the attribute that protection of IPRs in the first category is limited to a fixed time period (e.g., 20 years for patents) in order to minimize the costs of a distorted market structure, whereas IPRs in the second category can endure virtually indefinitely provided they remain in use. At the same time, it should be noted that trademark owners typically differentiate their products (e.g. through promotional activities) and are thus also able to create market power.

The remainder of this section will present and discuss the main arguments that have been made for or against a particular exhaustion regime. Although these arguments are not necessarily independent of each other, it is for analytical purposes useful to consider them separately.

The classic free-trade argument

The most general argument in favour of international exhaustion has been that a system of territorial market segmentation is at odds with the principle of free trade (Abbott 1998). For a long time, economists have been arguing the case for free trade. Through the international exchange of goods and services, countries have the possibility of specializing in what they can do best, leading to mutual gains for all trading partners. A dismantling of trade barriers causes a reallocation of production based on comparative advantage, which expands countries' production possibility frontiers. As illustrated in the previous section, the free-trade argument has been at the core of the European Union's adoption of a regional exhaustion regime.

Undoubtedly, a system of national exhaustion poses a non-tariff barrier to trade. Yet, can the classic free-trade argument be applied in an ad-hoc manner to parallel trade? To put it differently, do the assumptions on which economists base their case for free trade fit into the environment in which parallel trade takes place? The standard trade theory of comparative advantage—which has arguably provided the most significant intellectual thrust toward the worldwide liberalization of international trade—assumes that trade occurs under the conditions of free entry and perfect competition. In perfectly competitive markets, however, competition between different producers forces firms to set their prices equal to marginal costs in all free-trading countries, thereby eroding the basis for parallel imports. Parallel trading opportunities can only arise in an environment of imperfect competition, where firms have pricing power and therefore the ability to set different prices in different markets. Thus, parallel imports do not seem to fit into the standard framework in which economists make their case for free trade based on comparative advantage.[15] An ad-hoc application of the classic free trade argument to parallel trade seems therefore problematic.

Abusive price discrimination or welfare-enhancing price differentiation?

A system of national exhaustion allows firms to charge different prices in different markets for the same goods and services. Some observers generally consider price discrimination as the result of anticompetitive behaviour and have stressed the policing function parallel imports exercise in restraining abusive business practices (Abbott 1998). The potential for anticompetitive behaviour in the presence of the ownership of IPRs is well known, as firms may attempt to exploit their exclusive rights beyond the established limits.[16] The policing function of parallel imports may be especially important for small developing countries, where competition from substitute goods may be limited and competition policies are often absent or undeveloped (Hoekman and Holmes 1999).

Nevertheless, while price discrimination can indeed be related to anticompetitive practices, it can also take a benign form and is then sometimes labeled with the more neutral term "price differentiation." Such welfare-enhancing price discrimination *may* occur when firms charge different prices to different consumer groups with heterogeneous demand structures (so-called third degree price discrimination). In the context of international price discrimination, it may be illustrated by the following example. Suppose there are two countries—one rich, one poor—and a firm would serve only the consumers in the rich country if parallel trade between the two countries were allowed and the firm could thus not engage in price discrimination. In contrast, it would charge the same price to consumers in the rich country but also serve the consumers of the poor country at a lower price if parallel trade were prohibited. In the latter scenario, both the firm and consumers in the poor country would be better off while consumers in the rich country would not be worse off.[17]

Malueg and Schwartz (1994) develop a formal partial equilibrium model and find that uniform pricing by a monopolist can yield lower global welfare than discriminatory pricing if the dispersion of demand across countries is sufficiently large. Moreover, they show that global welfare can be maximized if one places countries into designated groups and allows discriminatory pricing among those groups but uniform pricing within groups.

Can this theoretical result give useful guidance about welfare-maximizing exhaustion regimes? It should first be pointed out that national regulations that would maximize global welfare may not necessarily maximize national welfare: consumers in countries that would have lower prices under international price discrimination than under uniform pricing would benefit from restrictions on parallel trade whereas consumers in countries that would have higher prices under price discrimination would be worse off from such restrictions. Yet, it would be the country with high prices that would decide whether or not to curb parallel trade (ignoring voluntary restraints on parallel exports by low-price countries). This may partly explain why countries such as Australia and New Zealand, which are not significant producers of intellectual property, have begun to lift restrictions on parallel imports.

Second, holders of IPRs hardly operate as full monopolists. They typically compete with substitute goods in national and international markets and are thus limited in their pricing power and their ability to practise price discrimination. Third, it is difficult to generalize in which countries market demand is relatively more elastic for a given product and would thus imply a lower price. Although demand elasticities typically vary with per-capita incomes, prices in developing countries are not always lower than in developed countries. One example would be that suppliers target their products in poorer countries to richer income classes where demand is less elastic than in the mass consumer market of developed countries. Observed price differentials between countries may be a misleading indicator of differences in demand structures. Aside from transportation, distribution and marketing costs, duties and other taxes, price differentials can be the result of differences in market structure or other supply characteristics.

The possibility of welfare-enhancing price discrimination is likely to be higher for goods covered by IPRs that stimulate inventive or creative activities rather than the other category of IPRs, because the exclusive rights of patents and copyright put explicit limits to the degree to which a protected product may be substituted by competing products. Examples of goods where the possibility of benign price discrimination has been pointed out include pharmaceuticals and educational and scientific publications, which are often priced at substantial discounts in developing countries.

Assuming that there are cases where price discrimination is indeed welfare-enhancing, it would nonetheless be difficult to translate this into explicit proposals for countries' exhaustion regimes. A system of territorial exhaustion would extend to all goods covered by a particular IPR although price discrimination may only be desirable for a selected range of products. In addition, the concept of national exhaustion has its origin in the territorial character of IPRs in general. However, it seems unlikely that "optimum exhaustion areas" as proposed by Malueg and Schwartz would coincide with national boundaries. The formation of regional exhaustion areas, in turn, would face many practical and political difficulties.[18] Notwithstanding these difficulties, the proposition that price discrimination may open otherwise unserved markets could be of importance with respect to certain developing (especially least developed) countries.

National exhaustion as a reinforcement of IPRs

Restrictions on parallel trade give holders of IPRs the ability to fix a profit-maximizing price in each national market and therefore tend to raise their overall profitability. Consequently, firms may boost their investments in knowledge and information-generating activities and this may lead to an accelerated pace of industrial innovation and increased production of new literary and artistic works. Obviously, this argument applies only to IPRs that stimulate inventive and creative activities, not to trademarks and geographical indications. Simply stated, it means that a system of national exhaustion increases the strength of intellectual property protection.[19] This explains, for example, why the United States—as the world's largest producer of intellectual property—generally favours national exhaustion of patent rights and copyright both at home and abroad.

The optimal scope of the protection of IPRs and the desirability of stronger IPRs have been subject to extensive debate, yet there is only limited empirical evidence available to policy-makers. As such, it remains inherently difficult to evaluate the desirability of a national exhaustion regime in this context. It could be argued, however, that for the sake of policy coherence it would be better (if possible) to adjust the strength of the protection of IPRs through other regulations—notably the length of protection—given the various other implications of parallel import protection.

The special case of government intervention

So far, it has implicitly been assumed that prices are the outcome of competitive market forces. This is not always the case, however. In some industries, governments intervene in private markets by controlling prices or regulating companies' rates of return. Some observers have argued that parallel trade in goods covered by an IPR and subject to "artificially" low prices due to government intervention would represent "unfair" competition in intervention-free countries. This has been repeatedly pointed out in the pharmaceutical industry, where government price controls are common in both developed and developing countries. A system of national exhaustion would deny parallel imports from countries where the holder of the IPRs or his licensee are subject to government intervention.

Obviously, this argument applies only to industries and countries where governments intervene in private markets. In addition, it is only relevant for those government interventions that target domestic consumption and would thus lead to a different treatment of parallel exports vis-à-vis regular exports. In the particular case of pharmaceutical price controls—leaving aside their desirability and effectiveness—one could argue that parallel import restrictions are appropriate, as the commonly stated goal of price controls is to make medicines affordable to domestic low-income consumers and there would be little justification of extending such a national policy to foreign consumers.[20] At the same time, it could be reasoned that consumers in a particular country would benefit from low-priced parallel imports regardless of the cause of low prices.[21] However, if significant "leakage" from price-controlled countries would lead to markedly lower worldwide profits for holders of IPRs, they may decide to stop serving price-controlled markets altogether.

National exhaustion as an extension of vertical control

Some observers have advocated national exhaustion on the ground that such a system extends the control of the holders of IPRs over the international distribution of their goods and services. Several benefits of territorial market segmentation have been brought forward in this context. First, segmented distribution systems may protect investments in marketing as well as services that may be associated with the sale of certain goods before and after sales. Parallel imports from different sales territories that do not provide these services—or where such activities are substantially cheaper—would have a "free ride" on the investments made by official licensees and distributors. Territorial sales restraints are therefore in the interest of consumers because the threat of parallel imports would lead firms to relinquish any marketing and sales-support activities. At the same time, it should be mentioned that this argument is only valid insofar sales support services (e.g., warranty or product maintenance) cannot be extended beyond territories.

Second, parallel imports from different territories may be of a different quality from goods sold through official distribution channels and this may lead to the deception of consumers. It has even been suggested that, in some cases, parallel imports may undermine the enforcement of technical, health, and safety standards in the importing country.[22] The potential magnitude of consumer deception is hard to generalize, however. Moreover, with the provision of adequate information, parallel imports of different quality can actually increase the choice of consumers and thus be beneficial. Third, holders of IPRs may be reluctant to license proprietary technology to a different market unless they are assured that the licensee will not compete with the holder of the IPRs in his home market or in a third market. This may slow down the pace of technology diffusion and thus be harmful to subsequent innovation and productivity growth.[23]

Although vertical restraints can indeed be beneficial, there is no presumption that this is always the case. They also carry costs—most significantly, in the form of reduced "intra-brand" competition. In fact, there is no consensus among economists and competition lawyers when vertical restrictions are procompetitive and when they are detrimental. An IPR holder may even seek to encourage parallel trade between different territories in order to avoid collusive behaviour among his various dealers. A uniform system of national exhaustion—i.e., a system applied to every good covered by a particular IPR—seems, therefore, an unapt regulation in reaping the potential benefits of vertical restraints. Moreover, such a system would be quite inflexible as it may be desirable to have complete denial of parallel imports for some goods, restrictions on active but not on passive parallel imports for others, and no limits at all on parallel trading for others.

Statutory exhaustion of intellectual property rights or private contractual arrangements?

One fundamental argument that has been brought against national exhaustion is that restrictions on parallel imports—if they are desirable—are better created through private contractual arrangements, which can be scrutinized by competition policies (Gallini and Hollis 1996). This seems appealing for several reasons. First, it would allow a tailor-made approach that could directly address the specific environment of different sectors and products. Second, private restrictions on parallel imports may not necessarily be bound to national territories, which may be especially important for small countries. Third, governments would be able to address country-specific concerns in national competition policies.

Indeed, this approach is followed domestically in the United States and on a regional basis in the European Union with regard to active parallel trading. With few exceptions, American antitrust law and European competition law permit territorial restraints in connection with the licensing of an IPR (Abbott 1998). Vertical restrictions in international licensing agreements are also common practice in many sectors.

Could private contractual means also be used in regulating passive parallel imports? In fact, this occurs under the common-law approach to intellectual property rights exhaustion. In common-law countries, exhaustion remains at the discretion of the holder of the IPR, who can deny parallel imports by including an appropriate notice of restriction in licensing and purchasing agreements (e.g. by attaching a label on a product indicating "Not for sale in countries X, Y, and Z"). It is not clear, however, whether such a system could work effectively on a world-wide level, as holders of IPRs would have to give proper notice— most likely in several languages—to all re-sellers involved (Heath 1997). It would also depend on the degree to which restrictions on passive parallel imports are deemed desirable. Policy-makers in both the United States and the European Union deliberately decided to leave the internal market open to passive parallel trade. However, if restrictions on passive parallel imports are deemed to be welfare-enhancing on a wider scale and uniformly across all goods covered by a particular type of IPR, a statutory regime of national or regional exhaustion may overall be less cumbersome.

Opponents of a system of private contractual arrangements advance that such a system is unrealistic in light of undeveloped competition policies and inadequate enforceability of private contracts in many developing countries. In addition, some observers argue that such a system could not work effectively before a harmonization of national competition policies has taken place at the international level. It is unclear, however, how much harmonization is necessary and to what degree private restraints on parallel imports can effectively be regulated by national competition policies. Undoubtedly, the development of competition institutions in developing countries and increased international harmonization of competition policies would facilitate the functioning of private contractual regulations on parallel imports and thus ease the need for national exhaustion systems.

The (limited) empirical evidence

As mentioned in the introduction, there are virtually no statistics available on the parallel segment of international trade. Available data on parallel trade comes from a few business surveys in developed countries and is mostly confined to goods where producers are particularly sensitive to parallel trade, such as well-known consumer brands, CDs, or pharmaceuticals. Accordingly, it is difficult to develop a picture of the overall direction and magnitude of parallel trade flows. In addition, available evidence on the impact of parallel trade typically concentrates on prices in the importing countries and profits of intellectual property owners; no evidence exists with regard to the price effects in exporting countries. Notwithstanding these caveats, the fragmented evidence that is available gives some indications as to the causes and consequences of parallel trade.

Parallel imports became a cause of concern for American policymakers in the mid-1980s, where they were estimated at 2 to 3 percent of total imports to the United States.[24] They were concentrated in goods with well-known brands that typically involved heavy investments in marketing and promotion, suggesting the free-riding explanation of parallel trade discussed above. At the same time, parallel imports surged in line with the marked appreciation of the US dollar up to the mid-1980s and fell sharply thereafter. This points to incomplete exchange rate pass-through as the cause of parallel trade (i.e. firms adjusted prices in the United States or abroad by a smaller percentage than the dollar's relative appreciation).[25] Incomplete exchange rate pass-through could be due to firms' behaviour to adjust their prices to the new demand conditions created by the movement of the exchange rate (Dornbusch 1987). This would suggest a pattern of international price discrimination, although one could not conclude that pricing to market was necessarily welfare-enhancing. It is likely that parallel imports to the United States during the 1980s were caused both by free riding and by price discrimination and the relevance of these two factors is confirmed by several court cases during this time period (Gallini and Hollis 1996).

Some recent empirical evidence on parallel imports comes from a study that was commissioned by the European Commission as part of its initiative to reform the European Union's trademark directive (National Economic Research Associates 1999). The study focuses on ten consumer-goods sectors in which trademarks are important and where the scope of parallel trade is significant.[26] It is first interesting to note that despite the absence of restrictions on parallel trade within the European Union, there generally remain substantial price differentials among member states. Some of these differentials may reflect factors such as transportation and distribution costs, transitory exchange rate movements and tax differences but it appears that parallel imports do not prevent trademark holders from price discrimination across national markets. The significance of parallel trade varies among the ten sectors, from below 5 percent of sales for footwear and leather goods, domestic appliances and alcoholic drinks to around 13 percent of sales for premium cosmetics and perfumes and up to 20 percent for some releases of musical recordings.

The study then considers the potential impact of opening the market in the European Union to parallel imports from other countries, notably Japan and the United States. The scope of parallel trade in the ten sectors analyzed seems large as there are significant differences between retail prices in the European Union, Japan, and the United States. With some exceptions, it appears that retail prices are generally lower in the United States, and higher in Japan, than in the European Union. When estimating the effect of freeing parallel imports on retail prices and trademark holders' profits in the European Union, the study finds only small or moderate decreases in prices (on average, less than 5 percent), but marked falls in profits—by as much as 35 percent in the consumer electronics sector.

These estimates depend on various assumptions about market structure and demand and it is hard to evaluate how realistic the reported figures are. Anecdotal evidence from Australia, for example, is more optimistic about price reductions that resulted from the removal of parallel import restrictions on CDs in October 1998. Some retailers reduced the price of selected top-selling CDs by nearly one-third (*Financial Times*, March 4, 1999).

Conclusion

The question of whether or not businesses should be allowed to control parallel imports of goods and services from foreign countries on the basis of local ownership of IPRs has been subject to controversy. The foregoing discussion makes it clear that the welfare implications of a particular exhaustion regime are theoretically ambiguous, are likely to differ among the various forms of IPRs, and involve considerations specific to various industries and products. A better case can probably be made for international exhaustion of IPRs that resolve information asymmetries than of IPRs that stimulate inventive and creative activities. In the latter group of IPRs, imperfectly competitive market structures are inherently related to IPRs and the possibilities of benign international price discrimination may thus be higher. At any rate, the empirical evidence on the causes and consequences of parallel imports is still too scattered to make a case for a particular exhaustion regime for one or more forms of IPRs.

A question that is fundamentally related to the exhaustion of IPRs is whether or not it would be more desirable to regulate parallel imports through private contracts scrutinized by competition policy. Such an approach seems attractive because it would offer flexibility in addressing the specific environment of each industry and in accounting for concerns specific to a country. It is not clear, however, whether such a system can be practically implemented on a global basis and to what degree it would presuppose harmonized competition policies.

The exhaustion issue may be revisited within the multilateral trading system—either in the context of the mandatory review of the TRIPS Agreement in the year 2000 or in the framework of a new Millennium Round of trade negotiations. In principle, multilateral negotiations on the exhaustion of IPRs seem warranted, as a country's choice of exhaustion regime imposes an externality on its trading partners in the form of either uniform or discriminatory international pricing strategies. Hence, the exchange of concessions on the exhaustion issue with concessions in other areas that are being negotiated could theoretically be a mutually beneficial affair. For many countries, it is far from obvious, however, whether a particular obligation on exhaustion would mean they would give or receive a concession.

The United States, as the world's single largest producer of intellectual property, is likely to favour a statute of national exhaustion (maybe with the exception of trademarks). The position of other developed countries is less clear. Depending on the economic and political weight of intellectual property producers in these countries on the one hand and the potential benefits countries see in allowing parallel imports on the other, they may be more or less open to a rule of international exhaustion. The stance of developing countries is also uncertain. When the exhaustion issue was raised during the Uruguay Round (1986–1994), many developing countries supported a system of international exhaustion (Watal 1998). They were motivated by the expectation that parallel imports would lead to increased competition and could thus restrain monopolistic prices and potentially abusive behaviour of IPR holders (especially against the background of stronger intellectual property rights standards as mandated by the TRIPS Agreement). Many developing countries also saw the removal of restrictions on parallel imports as opening export opportunities. But there is also a potentially significant downside for developing countries of freeing parallel imports. If the threat of parallel imports would lead holders of IPRs and their licensees to price their goods more uniformly across countries, prices in developing countries may well rise and there may be only limited scope for parallel exports. Moreover, parallel exports are unlikely to be a reliable source of foreign exchange as they are highly sensitive to movements of exchange rates.

Various other considerations besides price discrimination, however, are relevant in setting a regulatory framework for parallel trade. A multilateral agreement on the exhaustion question may also depend on progress in establishing harmonized rules for competition policies. In this regard, it is not clear, whether a "market access-driven" multilateral agreement on competition disciplines, as proposed by some WTO members (Hoekman and Holmes 1999), would make a significant difference in this context. In sum, it remains difficult to assess whether WTO members will be able to agree on a multilateral statute on the exhaustion of IPRs (if the issue is raised) and whether or not a possible agreement would be "globally" beneficial.

Acknowledgments

This paper was prepared for the two conferences *Competitive Strategies for Intellectual Property Protection* organized by the Fraser Institute in Santiago, Chile, April 19, 1999 and Buenos Aires, Argentina, April 22, 1999. Helpful comments by Octavio Espinosa and Jayashree Watal are gratefully acknowledged.

Notes

1 Arguably, the scope for parallel trade in services is smaller than that for parallel trade in goods. Most services are closely related to the person supplying the service, thus confining parallel trade to active parallel imports. In addition, differences in national standards or languages limit the substitutability of foreign and domestic services even though they may be supplied under the same service mark.

2 Articles 3 and 4 of TRIPS require national treatment and most-favoured-nation treatment of intellectual property owners. Hence, exhaustion regimes that discriminate between foreign and national holders of IPRs or among foreign holders of IPRs can be challenged in the WTO's dispute settlement proceedings (Bronckers 1998). The full text of the TRIPS Agreement is available on the website of the World Trade Organization at www.wto.org.

3 Notwithstanding Article 6, some observers have argued that other provisions of the TRIPS Agreement, notably Article 28 expounding the exclusive rights of patent owners (Barfield and Groombridge 1999) or obligations under the General Agreement on Trade and Tariffs (GATT) 1994 (Cottier 1998) mandate the adoption of a particular exhaustion regime. However, Bronckers (1998) convincingly argues that the TRIPS Agreement, as a lex specialis, is the relevant WTO agreement that establishes multilateral disciplines on the protection of IPRs (including exhaustion of IPRs) and it is quite clear that Article 6 is the overriding provision of TRIPS that removes

exhaustion from WTO dispute settlement. This view is supported by the fact that, to date, no case related to the exhaustion question has been brought to the WTO's dispute settlement system.

4 The quotation is from the ECJ's seminal ruling on the case of Deutsche Grammophon vs. Metro of 1971, whereby Deutsche Grammophon invoked its copyright in order to block parallel imports. The regional exhaustion doctrine was subsequently applied by the ECJ to other forms of intellectual property (see Yusuf and von Hase 1992). In 1998, the ECJ underscored this doctrine by ruling that the EU trademark directive precludes individual member states from applying a rule of international exhaustion with respect to trademarks (*Silhouette International vs. Hartlauer*, Case C-355/96, July 16, 1998).

5 See *Financial Times*, February 24, 1999: 7 and *The Economist*, February 27, 1999: 72–73.

6 In 1995, the MERCOSUR countries concluded a Protocol on the Harmonization of Provisions on Marks, Indications of Source and Appellations of Origin (MERCOSUR/CMC/Decision N° 8/95), of which Article 13 could be interpreted as sustaining a rule of international exhaustion. This Protocol has not yet been ratified by the MERCOSUR member states, however.

7 One exception is the "common control exception" in the field of trademarks, which allows parallel imports if the domestic and foreign trademark holder are the same, affiliated companies, or otherwise subject to common ownership or control (see Gallini and Hollis 1996). In addition, a recent ruling by the United States Supreme Court found that a copyright holder cannot block parallel importation if the copyrighted work was lawfully manufactured under the United States copyright title and subsequently exported abroad (Quality King Distributors vs. L'anza Reseach International, 96-470, March 1998).

8 See *BBS vs. Rasimex* cited in Heath 1997.

9 New Zealand's move prompted severe protests from the United States Trade Representative, since it was feared that parallel imports could harm American car, pharmaceutical, and CD manufactures. See *Financial Times*, May 20, 1998.

10 See International Intellectual Property Alliance 1998. It should be noted that the survey excluded sub-Saharan African countries except South Africa.

11 This information is based on informal correspondence with lawyers acquainted with the Argentinean and Chilean IPRs systems. In several cases, intellectual property laws in Chile and Argentina do not contain provisions on exhaustion and it is unclear to what extent other provisions can be applied to deny parallel importation.

12 An entirely different development that has raised new questions about parallel trade has been the rapid growth of electronic commerce. If goods protected by an IPR are delivered through computer-mediated networks, it becomes close to impossible to enforce a system of national exhaustion, as goods no longer cross borders in the traditional sense. In this regard, it is worth mentioning that the two new treaties that were concluded in 1996 to address copyright questions posed by the convergence of information

and communication technologies—the WIPO Copyright Treaty and the WIPO Performance and Phonograms Treaty—contain provisions similar to Article 6 of TRIPS, giving member countries freedom on the exhaustion question.

13 For a more comprehensive review of the economic principles of intellectual property protection, see Primo Braga and Fink 1997 and Primo Braga, Fink, and Sepulveda forthcoming.

14 Trade secrets, which are also part of IPRs systems, could be either classified as an IPR that stimulates inventive and creative activity or put in a separate category. They are not relevant for the present discussion, however, as they do not grant an exclusive right and are thus not subject to exhaustion.

15 It is worth noting that the so-called new trade theory introduces imperfectly competitive market structures into models of international trade (see, for example, Helpman and Krugman 1985). However, I am not aware of any formal general equilibrium trade model that has incorporated the possibility of price discrimination across national markets under free trade.

16 Article 40 of the TRIPS Agreement recognizes " that some licensing practices or conditions pertaining to intellectual property rights which restrain competition may have adverse effects on trade and may impede the transfer and dissemination of technology." The Agreement gives its signatories the freedom to adopt measures to prevent and control such abusive practices (Primo Braga, Fink and Sepulveda forthcoming).

17 See Hausman and MacKie-Mason 1988 for a formal exposition of this example. They also show that price discrimination can have a further beneficial effect if it allows firms to achieve scale and learning economies.

18 The adoption of regional exhaustion systems based on existing regional trade agreements (RTAs) would be one conceivable possibility. Many RTAs, however, are formed among countries at different stages of development. Malueg and Schwartz conjecture that the European Union may not even constitute an optimum exhaustion area—to the detriment of low income countries such as Greece, Ireland, or Portugal that may experience sharply curtailed sales due to uniform EU-wide pricing. It is interesting to note in this context that regional exhaustion does not violate the non-discrimination requirement of TRIPS Article 6, since non-discrimination is only required with respect to the IPRs holder, not with respect to the origin of parallel imports.

19 Note, however, that the classic IPRs trade-off between innovation incentives and static welfare losses would not hold if price discrimination enhances static welfare—by opening, for example, new markets (see the discussion above). See also Hausman and MacKie-Mason 1988.

20 It should be noted that parallel exports in this case may already violate certain regulations that apply in connection with the price-control regime: regulations, for example, designed to avoid domestic shortages in the supply of drugs.

21 To the extent that price controls lead to lower profitability for the holders of IPRs and thus weaken the innovation incentive, parallel exports would further undermine IPRs by extending price controls to foreign consumers.

22 This argument does not appear convincing, however. As explained in the introduction, parallel imports are subject to the same border measures on technical standards as regular imports. For example, parallel imports of pharmaceutical products into Germany from other members of the European Union are packaged and sold according to German health and safety requirements.

23 A fourth argument that is sometimes made is that the absence of barriers to parallel imports may increase the occurrence of counterfeit imports. This has been pointed out in the musical recording industry, where genuine and counterfeit CDs have been mixed in a single shipment. However, it generally does not seem appropriate to attack an illegal activity by curbing a legitimate activity.

24 The evidence presented on parallel imports to the United States is based on Malueg and Schwartz 1994.

25 It also needs to be pointed out that in 1984 the United States Supreme Court abolished the "authorized use exception," which prevented trademark holders from blocking parallel imports of goods manufactured by (uncontrolled) foreign licensees (Yusuf and von Hase 1992). It remains open to what extent this decision may have contributed to the fall of parallel imports in the second half of the 1980s.

26 The ten sectors are footwear and leather goods, musical recordings, motorcars, consumer electronics, domestic appliances, cosmetics and perfumes, clothing, soft drinks, confectionery, and alcoholic drinks.

References

Abbott, F.M. (1998). First Report (Final) to the Committee on International Trade Law of the International Law Association on the Subject of Parallel Importation. *Journal of International Economic Law* 1: 607–36.

Barfield, C.E., and M.A. Groombridge (1999). Parallel Trade in Pharmaceuticals: Implications for Innovation, Economic Development and Health Policy. Unpublished manuscript. Washington, DC: American Enterprise Institute.

Bronckers, M.C.E.J. (1998). The Exhaustion of Patent Rights under World Trade Organization Law. *Journal of World Trade* 32, 5: 137–159.

Cottier, T. (1998). The WTO System and Exhaustion of Rights. Paper presented at the Conference on *Exhaustion of Intellectual Property Rights and Parallel Importation in World Trade*, Committee on International Trade Law of the International Law Association (November 6–7), Geneva.

Dornbusch, R. (1987). Exchange Rates and Prices. *American Economic Review* 77, 1: 93–106.

Gallini, N.T., and A. Hollis (1996). A Contractual Approach to the Gray Market. Working Paper No. UT-ECIPA-GALLINI-96-01. Department of Economics, University of Toronto.

Hausman, J.A., and J. MacKie-Mason (1988). Price Discrimination and Patent Policy. *RAND Journal of Economics* 19, 2: 253–65.

Heath, C. (1997). Parallel Imports and International Trade. *International Review of Industrial Property and Copyright Law* 28, 5: 623–32.

Helpman, E., and P.R. Krugman (1985). Market Structure and Foreign Trade. Cambridge, MA: MIT Press.

Hoekman, B., and P. Holmes, P. (1999). International Rules for Competition Policies? Unpublished manuscript.

International Intellectual Property Alliance (1998). Parallel Import Protection in 107 Selected Countries. Paper presented at the Conference on *Exhaustion of Intellectual Property Rights and Parallel Importation in World Trade*, Committee on International Trade Law of the International Law Association (November 6-7), Geneva.

Malueg, D.A., and M. Schwartz (1994). Parallel Imports, Demand Dispersion, and International Price Discrimination. *Journal of International Economics* 37: 167–95.

National Economic Research Associates (1999). The Economic Consequences of the Choice of a Regime of Exhaustion in the Area of Trademarks. Final Report prepared for DGXV of the European Commission.

Primo Braga, C.A., and C. Fink (1997). The Economic Justification for the Grant of Intellectual Property Rights: Patterns of Convergence and Conflict. In F.M. Abbott and D.J. Gerber (eds), *Public Policy and Global Technological Integration* (The Netherlands: Kluwer Academic Publishers): 99–121.

Primo Braga, C.A., C. Fink, and C.P. Sepulveda (forthcoming). Intellectual Property Rights and Economic Development. *World Bank Discussion Paper*.

Watal, J. (1998). The TRIPS Agreement and Developing Countries: Strong, Weak, or Balanced Protection? *Journal of World Intellectual Property Protection* 1, 2 (March): 281–307.

Yusuf, A.A., and A.M von Hase (1992). Intellectual Property Protection and International Trade: Exhaustion of Rights Revisited. *World Competition: Law and Economics Review* 16, 1: 115–31.

Intellectual Property Protection in the World Trade Organization
Major Issues in the Millennium Round

Sylvia Ostry

Trade-related aspects of intellectual property rights (TRIPS) and the Uruguay Round

The negotiation to launch the Uruguay Round negotiation took almost as long as the entire Tokyo Round negotiations of the 1970s. The Americans had been trying to launch a new round since the early 1980s because of dissatisfaction with the results of the Tokyo Round and rising protectionist fury in Congress (mainly because of the over-valued dollar). After a number of near failures, the Uruguay Round was launched in Punta del Este in September 1986 and formally concluded in Marrakesh, Morocco in April 1994, several years later than the target completion date originally announced. The extraordinary difficulty in both initiating and completing the Round stemmed essentially from two fundamental factors: the nearly insuperable problem of finishing the unfinished business of past negotiations, most of all business about agriculture, and the equally contentious issue of introducing quite new agenda items, notably trade in services and intellectual property and, though in a more limited way, investment. The Europeans blocked the opening of negotiations to avoid coming to grips with the Common

---

Notes will be found on page 204.

Agricultural Policy (CAP) and a number of developing countries, led by Brazil and India, were bitterly opposed to including these so-called new issues. In the end, the final trade-off involved a deal across the old and new issues, a deal that transformed the world trading system.

Although the new issues are *not* identical—obviously negotiations on telecommunications or financial services differ from intellectual property rights—they do have one common characteristic: they involve not the border barriers of the original GATT but domestic policies embedded in the institutional infrastructure of the economy. The barriers to access for service providers stem from laws, administrative actions, or regulations that impede cross-border trade and investment. Further, since these laws and administrative actions are for the most part invisible, a key element in any negotiation is *transparency*—i.e. the publication of all relevant laws, regulations, and administrative procedures. These principles are now embodied in the General Agreement on Trade in Services or GATS, an integral part of the new world trading system housed in the WTO.

While GATS was hailed as a major breakthrough, especially since the United States had been trying since the 1970s to include trade in services in GATT negotiations, the inclusion of intellectual property rights in the world trading system was arguably an even more radical transformation of the traditional concept of a trading system. In the case of intellectual property, the negotiations covered not only comprehensive *standards* for domestic laws but, perhaps more importantly, detailed provisions for *enforcement procedures*. And, transparency was highlighted by the establishment of a separate council to which notification of all regulations and administrative arrangements must be made and this council is mandated to monitor compliance.

Perhaps most significantly, the preamble to the TRIPS Agreement states that intellectual property rights are "private rights" that must be enforced by member countries. If such rights are not enforced, the WTO dispute settlement procedures—"the most ambitious worldwide system for the settlement of disputes among more than 130 states ever adopted in the history of international law" (Petersmann 1998: 183)—provides the ultimate guarantee of protection. It is important to note that a major reason business lobbies wanted intellectual property in the Uruguay Round (see below) was that the United Nations agency, World Intellectual Property Organization (WIPO), had no enforcement mechanism.

The inclusion of the new issues in the Uruguay Round was entirely an American initiative and the policy was largely driven by the American multinational enterprises (MNEs). Indeed, without a fundamental rebalancing of the GATT, it seems highly improbable that the American business community or politicians would have continued to support the multilateral system for much longer (Ostry 1990: 23). On the intellectual property issue, the main impetus came from the pharmaceutical, software, and entertainment industries with the CEO of Pfizer playing a lead role as Chairman of the Intellectual Property Rights Committee (IPC). At the Punta del Este meeting in September 1986, many delegates were somewhat surprised to learn that the top priority of President Reagan for the Uruguay Round was to stop piracy since, unlike the services issue, the position of the United States on intellectual property had only been formalized a few months earlier.[1] But, by May 1988 the IPC, which had created an international business coalition including European and Japanese business organizations, presented a proposal that went well beyond eliminating piracy and included "minimum standards, enforcement mechanisms, and dispute settlement" (Ostry 1990: 24). This became the official American position and was supported by the European Union and Japan, who had been lukewarm or even hostile to including Intellectual Property Rights (IPRs) in a "trade" negotiation until prodded by their corporations.

While business lobbying was a major force in securing the TRIPS agreement, the role of the American government cannot be overlooked. Given the divide between North and South at the outset, the United States launched a multi-track policy. The NAFTA, completed two years prior to the conclusion of the Uruguay Round, helped the ratification of TRIPS not only by "locking-in" high standards but also by undermining Latin American cohesion in opposition. Equally effective was the use of unilateralism in the form of a new Special 301 of the 1988 Trade and Competitiveness Act targeted at developing countries with inadequate standards and enforcement procedures for the protection of intellectual property. Given a choice between American sanctions or a negotiated multilateral arrangement, the TRIPS agreement began to look better.

While TRIPS delivered the basic elements of the Intellectual Property Rights Committee (IPC) agenda, because all complex negotiations involve trade-offs—and the Uruguay Round was the most complex and ambitious in history—some key issues were left unsettled. These will be tackled in new negotiations, both regional and multilateral. What I want to deal with in the remainder of this paper are those that, in my judgement, are the most significant for the WTO's Millennium Round.

Intellectual property and the Millennium Round

The TRIPS Agreement rested on a trade-off between the North and the South that gave improved access to OECD markets for Southern agricultural and industrial products in exchange for a restructuring of the trading system in line with OECD countries' comparative advantage.

The new agenda will include some of the unfinished business of the Uruguay Round: cross-cutting issues such as parallel imports; the role of competition policy; the monitoring and enforcement and perhaps upgrading of standards. But, in the overall negotiations, these and, indeed, all other issues in the new intellectual-property negotiations will be profoundly shaped by the ongoing revolution in biotechnology and information technology, especially the former because of linkage with other key items in the agenda.

Biotechnology and environmental concerns

The TRIPS Agreement allows members to exclude from patentability certain plant and animal inventions. Article 27.3(b) provided for a review of these provisions in 1999 as part of the so-called built-in agenda. However, there have been such major changes in biotechnology in the 1990s that it is highly unlikely that the TRIPS Council can grapple with the issue. It will have to await a new round of negotiations.

As we have seen, the American pharmaceutical industry played a leading role in establishing TRIPS as a key part of the new trading system. The industry began undergoing a fundamental change in the 1990s as a consequence of what is called the molecular revolution, launched over 40 years ago by the discovery of DNA. Major advances in basic biological research, new experimental techniques such as X-ray crystallography and nuclear magnetic resonance, and vastly increased computing power have combined to transform the structure of the pharmaceutical industry. The large pharmaceutical companies have utilized scientific advances in genetics and molecular biology to "design" and manufacture synthetic drugs. At the same time, small-scale new entrants—often university spin-offs—are exploiting the techniques of genetic engineering, which involves the manufacture of proteins for treatment of disease. Collaborative arrangements such as research and development contracts, joint ventures, and venture capital investment are proliferating. The result of all this is a resurgent industry that has established a dominant position in world markets. As is shown by patent data in the 1990s, the United States has vastly outstripped Europe and Japan in biotechnology (Kortum and Lerner 1997). In the early 1990s, American companies held patents for 92 of the 100 most prescribed drugs.[2]

As described earlier, the American pharmaceutical companies led the international business coalition that forged the TRIPS Agreement and, since the stakes are even higher today, they are likely to play a similar role in the new negotiations. But the deal between North and South that underlay the Uruguay agreement is no longer feasible because of the prominence of environmental issues as a feature of trade negotiations.

The issues linking biotechnology and environment are complex. At the same time as the pharmaceutical industry was transformed by the technological revolution in biotechnology, another revolution in information and communication technology (ICT) was transforming the policy environment. The International Non-Governmental Organizations (INGOs) have existed for decades or longer but are far more active in the policy process today because ICT permits rapid and inexpensive global networking. And, they are very skilled in dealing with the media, especially television. The most prominent INGOs are the greens and they were already evident during the final stages of the TRIPS negotiations, covering Swiss highway bridges with graffiti admonishing "GATT: no patents on life!" and draping GATT headquarters building with a huge banner carrying the same message (Croome 1995: 255). Shortly after, Geneva was plastered with Gattzilla posters in response to a 1991 panel ruling that the United States violated its GATT obligations by banning Mexican tuna caught by a process that killed dolphins. But, their power today is far greater than in the early 1990s: marching in cyberspace is much cheaper and more effective than covering bridges with graffiti and buildings with posters. Moreover, the greens have mobilized impressive support among a wide range of other advocacy groups who, although for different reasons, see the WTO as an institution captured by, and serving only corporate interests. The green message seems to be the most effective rallying point because it is attractive to a large proportion of the populations, especially the younger generation searching for a worthy cause.

By way of a brief digression to illustrate this point, it is worth describing the successful campaign by the INGOs to defeat the OECD negotiations for a Multilateral Agreement on Investment (MAI) since it vividly illustrates the power of these new transnational actors. In October 1997, 47 NGOs from 23 countries and 5 continents met in Paris at OECD headquarters. The consultation had been arranged at the request of the World Wildlife Fund and some national representatives who had been lobbied by domestic advocacy organizations. The INGOs argued that the MAI would undermine sustainable development and national sovereignty. The most powerful case for this argument concerned the MAI's investor-protection mechanism. This replicated the investment provisions in NAFTA, which included procedures for resolving disputes by which private parties as well as governments could take action and adopted a very broad definition of investment expropriation, so broad it could lead to investor claims against government regulation in, say, environmental or health areas that negatively affect the value of investment. In Canada, American corporations had launched several cases against the government that aroused a storm of opposition led by a coalition of NGOs. These same NGOs were among the most prominent in Paris in October 1997.

After the consultation, the groups at the meeting organized an anti-MAI coalition and launched an international campaign to stop the negotiations. A World Wide MAI Website List[3] displays 55 sites mainly from OECD countries and covering a wide range of interests; environmental and legal groups together accounted for more than half the total. Groups in Canada and the United States provided a constant flow of information to coordinate the campaign. By October 1998, the negotiations had been suspended and in December, after the official withdrawal of the French government at the request of the red-green members of the coalition, they were officially terminated. (The action of the French government is not without significance. While North American greens have chosen an advocacy route to contest the market for policy ideas, the European environmentalists have formed political parties and greens are now members of government coalitions in four countries in the European Union—Germany, France, Italy, and Finland—as well as increasingly prominent in the European parliament.)

Of course, there were a number of reasons why the MAI failed but there seems little doubt that the INGOs played a key role. At the press conference announcing the suspension of the negotiations, the two key problems cited were "countries' sovereignty with respect to regulation without being charged with expropriation and without being sued for compensation" and "the issue of protecting labour and the environment" (OECD Nations Forego MAI Decision, Agree to Examine Possible Changes 1998).

The example of opposition to the MAI illustrates the new contestability of the market for ideas shaping the policy process. And, whereas the ideas for TRIPS came mainly from the business community, the INGOs now are major players in the policy domain covering trade and the environment. While a full exploration of the trade and the environment agenda go well beyond the subject of this conference, the issue of IPRs is of central importance in the ongoing debate about how the WTO will handle environmental issues.

The WTO's Committee on Trade and Environment (CTE) was established at the Marrakesh meeting that concluded the Uruguay Round in April 1994 and its mandate was renewed in Singapore in December 1996. To date, however, it has accomplished little in achieving consensus on contentious issues such as patents for "genetically modified organisms" (GMOs) as well as the impact of inventions on the environment. In a recent review of the CTE's discussions prepared for a WTO Symposium on Trade and Environment in Geneva on March 15/16, 1999, the serious North-South conflicts are discreetly mentioned:

The Relevant Provisions of the Agreement on Trade-Related Aspects of Intellectual Property Rights (TRIPS) (Item 8 of the Work Programme)

The objective of the TRIPS Agreement is to promote effective and adequate protection of intellectual property rights (IPRs). IPRs serve various functions, including the encouragement of innovation and the disclosure of information on inventions, including environmentally sound technology. In the context of trade and environment, the TRIPS Agreement has assumed increasing significance.

With respect to technology transfer, patents are perceived by some as increasing the difficulty and costs of obtaining new technologies which are required either due to changes agreed under certain MEAs (such as the Montreal Protocol) or in order to meet environmental requirements, both generally and in certain export markets. Also, there has been an increasing concern for the conservation and sustainable use of biological diversity. The rapid progress in the area of biotechnology has meant that greater importance is attached to easy access to genetic resources. Developing countries (many of which are the main suppliers of such genetic resources and biological diversity) have emphasized a *quid pro quo* in this context, involving easier transfer of technologies in return for them providing access to their genetic resources, and for undertaking policies aimed at conservation and sustainable use of biological diversity.

This has proven to be a particularly sensitive element of the CTE's work programme, particularly for India (who has proposed that exceptions be made in the TRIPS Agreement on environmental grounds for the transfer of technology mandated for use in an MEA), and for the United States (who defend IPRs as a necessary precondition for the transfer of technology). The links between TRIPS and the environment are complex and many of the issues involved are contentious.

The CTE has recommended that further work be undertaken on several issues. The issues which it raised include: the transfer of environmentally friendly technology, the protection of traditional rights and knowledge, controlling adverse environmental effects of technologies such as biotechnology, the WTO-consistency of certain provisions of the Convention on Biological Diversity (an MEA), and the agreement that would prevail if there was to be a conflict between the TRIPS Agreement and the Convention on Biological Diversity.

(World Trade Organization 1999: Annex 1, [7])

What is hinted at in this summary was much more explicit in the debate at the Symposium, which included government officials, representatives from intergovernmental institutions, and a large number of INGOs from both OECD and developing countries: a different kind of deal involving the transfer of funds and technology in exchange for access to the South's genetic resources between North and South would be needed to achieve consensus on IPRs in biotechnology . The idea of some sort of "distributional deal" aimed at achieving global environmental objectives had already been raised at the 1994 United Nations Conference on Environment and Development—the Rio Earth Summit— but there was no policy follow-up. And, the issue of IPRs adds another layer of complexity to the distributional matrix.

At the risk of great oversimplification, the basics of the game that will have to be played out involve two players: the OECD (mainly the United States), which generates the technology and know-how for the innovation process, and the less developed countries, which own 90 percent of the world's genetic resources that provide the major input for the innovation process. The legal system that will define rights to genetic resources will also help determine the allocation of the gains of innovation. Added to this dichotomy between North and South is the question of preserving biodiversity, the main concern of the Northern INGOs. Thus, while Northern and Southern INGOs often disagree, they were able to form a coalition on this subject—a good example of their skill in issue and venue shifting as required.

And, of course, it is not only the pharmaceutical industry with stakes in the outcome. As the 1999 Conference on Biosafety so vividly illustrated, the agriculture industries are also major stakeholders and, in this sector, countries like Mexico and Argentina, which are exporters, joined forces with the United States and Canada to foil the completion of an agreement. So, even the LDC alliance has some cracks in it. On the other hand, the profound differences now apparent between the attitudes of European and American consumers with respect to food made from genetically modified plants (what some British groups call "Frankenstein food") or hormone-treated beef demonstrate that all is not quiet on the Western front either.

So what does all this augur for IPR negotiations in the Millennium Round? Those without a reliable crystal ball would be wise to say it's impossible to forecast at this stage. It is reasonably clear, however, that while arguments can be made for the potential benefits to developing countries from the biotechnology revolution—for example, improving agricultural productivity with new plant varieties customized for specific climates, developing new drugs against disease prevalent in the developing world, using genetically modified micro organisms for environmental clean-up—the *quid pro quo* issue will remain and the final bargain will include a distributional element, not necessarily confined to IPRs but perhaps covering the negotiations as a whole.

Although biotechnology patents will be at the forefront of the new negotiations, because of the revolution in ICT a number of copyright issues will also have to be re-visited. These will be contentious but there is no clear divide between North and South. Rather, within the OECD countries themselves there are deep divisions among different interest groups (content producers, on-line service providers, hardware producers, and, of course, users or consumers). Thus the spillover from the copyright discussions to the rest of the negotiating agenda is likely to be constrained. The WTO has established a work program on electronic commerce as requested by the May 1998 Ministerial Meeting and this program includes an examination by the TRIPS Council of the implications for copyrights and other related issues. The results of this new program are unlikely to be conclusive but should provide a useful background to the new negotiations.

Finally, the built-in agenda of TRIPS also includes a number of important cross-cutting or generic issues left open at the end of the Uruguay Round. Of these, the most difficult is likely to be parallel imports or "exhaustion" in legal parlance. But it is also useful to review briefly competition policy and the basic issue of monitoring and enforcement.

TRIPS built-in agenda: generic issues

A key, but unsettled, issue in the TRIPS agreement concerns the question of where and when the property rights are "exhausted." Since IPRs are granted in a given country, they ensure that the owner can prevent others from producing and distributing the good or service in that country. But what about the same goods imported from other countries on the basis of local ownership of IPRs? Different countries have different rules about such "parallel imports": the European Union permits parallel trade internally but forbids it externally and the United States has a total ban on parallel imports. TRIPS negotiators failed to reach an agreement on the subject and thus Article (6) in effect permits each WTO member to treat parallel imports in the manner it considers best-suited to its own interests: "For the purpose of dispute settlement under this Agreement ... nothing in this Agreement shall be used to address the issue of exhaustion of intellectual property rights." Related to this question of parallel imports is the interrelationships of IPRs and competition policy since, in effect, restriction of parallel imports amounts to government permission for vertical restraints in a specified territory. The TRIPS agreement does not spell out what practices should be treated as illegal but provides some illustrative examples that could be treated as abuses; i.e. the Agreement is permissive rather than mandatory.

The ongoing debate among IPR experts and economists about the pros and cons has been well presented in a number of legal and economic journals; indeed a cottage industry has now emerged in preparation for the Millennium Round (Special Issue [JIEL] 1998; Barfield and Groombridge 1999). One version of the argument in favour of restriction of parallel imports is that the positive dynamic benefits that would accrue from the MNE's ability to customize production (and prices) for different markets would outweigh the static efficiency losses from restricting trade. Further, along this line of thought, if there is a competition policy problem in any given market, it is likely to arise from lack of horizontal (*inter*-brand) rather than vertical (*intra*-brand) competition and should be handled by anti-trust and not intellectual property policy.

The arguments against restriction—supported most strongly by the LDCs—usually begin by noting the irony or paradox of a WTO based on liberalizing trade but supporting protectionism. Of course this gambit gives way quickly to the more sophisticated arguments: *viz.* the impact of exhaustion must be assessed on a case-by-case basis since it will vary by type of IPR; type of technology; type of economy. This issue of the impact on LDCs of a global ban on parallel imports (likely to be the American position in the new negotiations) must also be examined by detailed empirical studies. Do IPRs increase foreign direct investment, enhance technology transfer, and improve trade? In other words, are the static efficiency losses outweighed by dynamic efficiency gains? Just by way of a footnote, it may be that American antitrust policy and innovation is undergoing a sea-change, at least with respect to network industries, as the cases against Microsoft and Intel seem to suggest. But this seems unlikely to affect the American position, which would be to amend Article (6) to ban parallel imports, or change the push by some LDCs for a global exhaustion rule.

Another issue likely to be re-visited in the new negotiations concerns standards. As noted earlier, the inclusion of standards was not proposed at the outset of the Uruguay Round but emerged a couple of years later as a result of the international business coalition led by the Americans. The standards incorporated in the TRIPS Agreement represented a consensus among the OECD countries. They cannot be described as minimal but even so there is likely to be a push for higher standards in some areas and, perhaps more importantly, for more harmonization among countries. In both instances it is important to note that significant differences exist among major OECD countries.

Before explicitly moving to harmonization, there is still an important question that remains unsettled with respect to the existing standards in TRIPS: how much "wiggle room" remains for diversity in domestic laws, a diversity likely to be exploited mainly by LDCs (Special Issue [JIEL] 1998: 591). The answer will depend on the dispute settlement system, and thus far only one significant case (the United States versus India) involving a developing country has reached the Appellate Board. The result is instructive, though obviously one cannot generalize on the basis of a single case. There will be many more, however, when the LDCs have to implement the TRIPS standards in 2000 (see below).

The case concerned the so-called mailbox for filing patent applications for pharmaceutical and agricultural chemical products which India had failed to establish at the outset of the TRIPS Agreement (Articles 70.8 and 70.9). While the Appellate Board upheld the panel's decision that India had violated its commitments, it adopted a much more cautious stance on several other aspects of the Panel report, sending a strong signal of deference to domestic law (Special Issue [JIEL] 1998: 595). This concept of a deferential standard of review means that when several interpretations of a particular article are possible, the Appellate Board should accept that of the national administrative body— as the United States insisted in the case of WTO anti-dumping provisions (Dreyfuss and Lowenfeld 1997: 321).

As a final point on the issue of standards, the TRIPS Agreement involved, as I have noted, a more radical transformation of the concept of the global "trading" system than the other new issue (e.g. trade in services) because it involved protection of individual property rights. By incorporating standards and due process for one factor of production—capital—the door was opened to claims for similar treatment for the two other factors, i.e. labour and land (read "the environment"). Thus many INGOs are now presenting proposals for basic labour rights and environmental standards to be incorporated into the WTO. While these issues are not directly related to the new negotiations on TRIPS, because of the complex dynamics of the multilateral negotiations, it would be prudent not to rule out the possibility of some linkage in the final deal.

The last generic issue I want to mention concerns enforcement. The cost of establishing the institutional infrastructure for enforcing IPRs is likely to be very high not only for the poorest countries but for many middle-income or emerging market economies with inadequate monitoring capabilities and weak civil-justice systems. The extent and nature of the gaps in enforcement will become evident as the TRIPS Council begins its own monitoring process in 2000. Although Article 67 of the TRIPS Agreement recognizes the need for technical assistance, the language is vague and involves no real commitment on the part of the developed countries. Since the WTO has very limited resources for training or technical assistance, the task has been undertaken by WIPO, a very rich institution. Cooperation between the WTO and WIPO is essential and a joint initiative in technical assistance was launched in July 1998 (Special Issue [JIEL] 1998: 529–30). A matter for consideration, as part of this cooperative effort, should be a time-limited "peace accord" which would exempt LDCs from the dispute settlement process contingent on their sustained improvement in enforcement capabilities. There is a danger that as the monitoring process beginning in 2000 reveals more gaps in implementation, a flurry of disputes could overburden the WTO dispute body and poison the atmosphere for the new negotiations.

Conclusions

A central theme of this paper is that the TRIPS Agreement exemplifies the transition from the traditional GATT focus on border barriers to the new agenda of deeper integration in a more radical fashion than was the case in services. The TRIPS Agreement was conceived and facilitated mainly by American MNEs and the deal reflected a North-South trade-off between traditional GATT issues and a radical "new issue." For a variety of reasons explained in the discussion—including technological change and new policy actors—the TRIPS negotiations in the Millennial Round will be far more complex and contentious. However, despite the importance of the MNEs and the INGOs, it is governments who will sit at the bargaining table. And, as in the past, it will be government leadership that will determine the final outcome. All things considered, the demands on leadership in the next round will be far greater than at any time in the past 50 years. Given the current state of transatlantic trade tensions, the absence of American fast track, and so on, the next round of WTO Ministerial negotiations should be very interesting—in the Chinese sense of that word!

Notes

1   Preeg 1995: 65; the American statement on piracy was not "official" but informal and derived from my own recollections.
2   Barfield and Groombridge 1999: 22. This paper provides an excellent analysis of the impact of technological change on the structure of the pharmaceutical industry.
3   MAI Websites—World Wide: An Annotated listing. Prepared by Janet M. Eaton (jeaton@fox.nstn.ca) for the Nova Scotia Network for Creative Change Website (www.chebucto.ns.ca/CommunitySupport/NCC/MAI4 www.html) and for the general use of Citizens and Groups everywhere (November 10, 1999).

References

Barfield, Claude E., and Mark A. Groombridge (1999). Parallel Trade in Pharmaceuticals: Economic Development and Health Policy. Unpublished draft no. 1 (February 4). Washington, DC: American Enterprise Institute.
Croome, John (1995). *Reshaping the World Trading System.* Geneva: World Trade Organization.
Dreyfuss, Rochelle Cooper, and Andreas F. Lowenfeld (1997). Two Achievements of the Uruguay Round: Putting Trips and Dispute Settlement Together. *Virgina Journal of International Law* 37, 2 (Winter): 275–333.
Kortum, Samuel, and Josh Lerner (1997). *Stronger Protection or Technological Revolution: What is Behind the Recent Surge in Patenting?* NBER Working Paper Series, No. 6204 (September). Cambridge, MA: National Bureau of Economic Research.
OECD Nations Forego MAI Decision, Agree to Examine Possible Changes (1998). *Inside US Trade* (October 23).
Ostry, Sylvia (1990). *Governments and Corporations in a Shrinking World* New York: Council on Foreign Relations.
Petersmann, Ernst-Ulrich (1998). From the Hobbesian International Law of Coexistence to Modern Integration Law: The WTO Dispute Settlement System. *Journal of International Economic Law* 1, 2 (June): 175–198.
Preeg, Ernest H. (1995). *Traders in a Brave New World.* Chicago: University of Chicago Press.
Special Issue: Trade-Related Aspects of Intellectual Property Rights [JIEL] (1998). *Journal of International Economic Law* 1, 4 (December): 497–698.
World Trade Organization (1999). World Trade Organization Informal Briefing Note for WTO Symposium, High Level Doc, Annex 1, (7).